Lust

Lust

LIVING UNDER SEVERE TORMENT

The Guide to Beating Addiction

Lance McCormack

ISBN: 0692826777
ISBN 13: 9780692826775
Library of Congress Control Number: 2016921428
LIFE FORCE INDEPENDENT PUBLISHING, WARWICK, RHODE ISLAND

List of Illustrations

I dedicate this book to Connie; my wife, my muse, and the love of my life! With this book, my hopes are to change the world, or at very least, effect change in every reader.

—Lance C. McCormack

Contents

Introduction

A man walks into a Batterers Anonymous group and reports happily, "It's been forty-three days since I've beaten my wife," and then on the next breath says, "One day at a time!"

What was that? What does that actually mean? Based on what this man just said, do you feel the least bit convinced that his battering days are over? I don't. But that's what we say or what we hear other people say every day, and it's supposed to mean something, and it does—nothing! It means *absolutely nothing* in regards to a person's desire to change a behavior, and it screams volumes about that person's desire to remain the same. It's that simple. We have to stop playing games. We aren't playing games with ourselves when we say these things, because we know what we mean; it's everyone else that we're playing games with, because they don't know what we mean. Who are these people? These people are the duped masses who love and care about us and choose not to read between the lines but instead choose to continue to just accept things naively based on their memories of us in the past. They clearly look the other way when all the evidence points to us, because they can't bring themselves to believe what we're doing.

A forty-year-old woman shared a story with me just the other day about how her mom just won't see her for who she is. She said, "No matter what I tell my mom about what has happened, or about what I've done, she always sees me as the victim. She says, 'Don't hang around with this person or that person, because they'll corrupt you and make you do all kinds of bad things.' Then I'll say how I actually corrupted them and not the other way around, but she won't listen. She just wants to see me as her sweet little girl who can do no wrong." Well, parents, I hope you are listening now. Most of the time we don't hear the truth verbally communicated as blatantly as this, but close. Usually the signs are staring us right in the face, but we're just not willing to accept what we see.

Usually we see the blatant signs and behaviors and just choose to ignore them. It's time to wake up, because we're not doing anyone any favors by sticking our heads in the sand.

"I just want to be 'normal' and be able to drink like everyone else, without having a problem. Everybody drinks, but I just drink too much!" *Normal* is an interesting word by definition because it means so many things, most of which we say we don't want to be. It means "standard, basic, common, garden variety, a dime a dozen, unremarkable," just to list a few. Who sets out with a desire to become someone who's a dime a dozen? No one that I've ever met! Yet, when it comes to talking about using alcohol and other drugs; including caffeine, nicotine and food to excess or participating exceedingly in a host of activities like sex, gambling, shopping, etc., things start to get confusing. We claim we do *these* things to "fit in" and to be or feel "normal"—that is, unremarkable—but on the other hand, we say we want to be unique and one of a kind. Which is it? Clearly we can't be both; unremarkable and unique! Who knows? Maybe we do these things for an entirely different reason.

Getting back to the word *normal*, do you think it sounds normal to put something called ethanol into your body, when it's the same chemical used in the gas that you pump into your car? How can ethanol be good for your car's engine and also be good for your body's engine? Ethanol is a neurotoxin, a nervous system poison, a deadly substance that terrorizes our brains, spinal cords, peripheral nerves, and every cell of our bodies. Ethanol is a highly volatile, flammable substance capable of burning down skyscrapers! Do you think it sounds "normal" to want to ingest this neurotoxic flamethrower just because "normal" people are doing it? Or it is acceptable to consume this neurotoxin because it's legal to consume at age twenty-one? Here's an interesting question: Is it legal to die from consuming something that's legal? I guess the answer is yes, but the question is, do you want to? I remember my mom's response to me when I was a boy and told her I wanted to do something because the other kids were doing it: "If the other kids were jumping off a cliff, does that mean you should too?" The point is, why strive to be normal when you can be exceptional? Followers are a dime a dozen; leaders, however, are exceptional.

Welcome to *Lust: Living Under Severe Torment*, the book that shatters the way we've seen and spoken about obsessions and compulsions for centuries. My title

Lust, was designed as an acronym for how I've interpreted the lives of the people I've met struggling to be *normal.* Countless books have already been written about alcohol and other drug use and compulsions to food, sex, gambling, and whatever else, but *Lust* is different in several critical ways. *Lust* not only highlights the merits of what's been said but also discredits theories and practices that deserve little merit. *Lust* takes this controversial subject to a new level, one not based on a discussion of gene pool selections or scientific breakthroughs, but to a much simpler level, one based on common sense and everyday observations. *Lust* contains the psychological extraction of actual accounts from people struggling with compulsions of all types. Well, that in itself isn't necessarily new. What is new however, is the careful interpretation of these observations that have led to these simple but game-changing unique facts and strategies regarding this woefully misunderstood subject. Yes, I did say "facts" and not "theories."

For more than a decade, I have worked with and closely observed people struggling with addictions of all kinds. Between my experiences as a degreed, licensed counselor, a certified hypnotherapist, and a certified specialist in fitness nutrition, I have been taught what it takes to become free from addiction. Based on these experiences with thousands of people, I have compiled the facts about obsessions and compulsions—that is, addictions—into this book called *Lust,* and in this book, I offer anyone interested in knowing the truth, the opportunity to change their lives forever. I understand there is no one way that will work for everyone, so I have listed many ways, each of which works. To be successful, however, I do know that two critical questions must be answered: How will I handle my life's challenges once I stop drinking, drugging, and so on, and what will I do for pleasure once I stop? Think about your answers as you read each page. Now, within these pages it is up to you to find and apply the way that will work best for you. Also within these pages, you will find many of my original sayings that I have coined "Lanceisms" and these reflect my personal views, experiences and predictions regarding this very challenging field of addiction. Hopefully, these sayings will provide additional insights and motivation to consider new ways to address old, unrelenting problems.

This book is about recovery, and true recovery is about adopting a new desire and a new expectation. Therefore, *Lust* is not just for those directly struggling, but for all those confused caregivers also struggling. I hope this book brings you peace, for if it does, it has served its purpose. Caution: Once you've read this book, you will never, ever be the same!

SECTION I

Addiction

What it is isn't nearly as important as what we believe it is.
—A LANCEISM

A supernatural wonderland or an endless hole of despair? *Lust* will help you decide which world is which and which world you'll choose. This section is devoted to a single chapter describing how I see addiction, who are the addicted and how the addicted got addicted.

CHAPTER 1

Welcome to the Rathole!

No one saves us but ourselves. No one can and no
one may. We ourselves must walk the path.
—BUDDHA

It's another Friday night in the Big Apple. Somebody's at Radio City Music Hall, and somebody else is watching those high-kicking legs of the Rockettes. It's not me in either case. I'm at the Hudson River at 125th Street in Harlem...fishing. Even though it's dark out, there's a full moon lighting up everything. My fishing buddies didn't show up tonight, but I'm not alone. I'm never alone at the river. The scent of my bait awakens the night as squeaks, squeals, and shrill screams fill the air with every cast of my line toward the water. Out from holes in the ground emerge frantic bodies balanced on frantic feet, darting all around me up and down the cement and the wooden planks of the dock. Grab and go, grab and go, grab and go—that's the plan.

The newbies occasionally share, but the ones old to the game...no way, they want it all for themselves. "Mine, mine...it's all mine" is what they're saying as they run back into their filthy little holes with their prizes. Some of these holes run pretty deep and cover a lot of ground; the size of these holes gives us a rough idea of how long the players have been playing the game and how deeply entrenched they are. Peeking and sneaking, slipping and sliding, running and dodging, all night long, for days at a time. They can't be that hungry—they've already taken in more than their body weight—but that doesn't seem to matter. They know that whatever they can't use now, they'll hide away for later. They know they'll always want more later. It's like they're possessed...something keeps them coming: grab and go, grab and go, grab and go.

They're even unaware that I'm standing right here, because they're in a frenzy. They only care about one thing right now: getting more and more until their bodies can't take any more. I can't stop them, not now, so if I've got any sense at all, I'd better get out of the way, or I'll be the next thing they're feeding on.

Does this scene sound familiar? Does it remind you of anyone you know? Is someone you know feeling caught in a deep, dirty hole and fighting to get out? If so, you're in the right place, reading the right thing. Read on.

Whether you're reading this to help yourself or someone else stop using alcohol or other drugs, eradicate the compulsion to eat destructively, end using sex corrosively, forgo gambling down to your last pair of shorts, or cease smoking cigarettes while you're on oxygen, this book is for you, because make no mistake, all these behaviors share the same common elements, and they all can kill you.

Whoever the person is, is in a world of hurt right now, feeling confused, rattled, sick, scared and alone, and hopefully downright stupid! Yeah, feeling stupid is good; not feeling that what you're doing is stupid is not so good. Because you were designed from greatness, from the same elements that exist in the glorious stars in the universe. To compromise for anything less than greatness is a betrayal of what you are and who you are. It's like what the Lion King said to his son: "Simba, you have forsaken me; you have forsaken who you are, and so forsaken me. Look around you, Simba. You are more than what you have become. Take your place in the circle of life. Remember who you are. You are my son and the one true king. Remember who you are!"

In this book we will be discussing the filthy, slimy, sickening, isolating facades of the existences we have allowed to replace our life's true intention. The world of wet brain, cancer, cirrhosis, pancreatitis, Hep C, HIV, HPV, AIDS, TB, type II diabetes, domestic violence, sexual assault, child abuse, death, suicide, and murder. Please feel free to add to this list as you see fit. Surely, this list is by no means comprehensive of the diseases, disorders, maladies, or crimes that may result from underappreciating and undervaluing our lives.

Does any of this sound like fun yet? Admit it, you've dug yourself a deep, nasty hole and then thrown yourself into it, but the good news is, as soon as you start looking up and stop digging yourself any deeper, you can still climb out! I know this because this has been my life's work for more than a decade, helping thousands of individuals dig out of the wreckage they've created. Helping those struggling to understand why they keep screwing things up.

"Why can't I just stop drinking or using other drugs?" "I know I should stop—for my family, my job, my health—but I just keep on relapsing. I'm getting older, and I just don't have it in me anymore to keep using." Do any of these lines sound familiar?

This is the rathole, claiming to want to stay away, but going in and out of that dirty hole over and over again because, as crazy as it sounds, it's become home. They say "familiarity breeds contempt," but in this case, it breeds lust. If you've ever seen experiments with rats being offered cocaine, it's downright ugly, with every single rat chasing the drug from its first use until it's dead from cardiac arrest, 100 percent of the time. How many of us will have to die in search of this unforgiving illusion of a worthwhile pleasure? Will our uniquely human ability of self-awareness be strong enough to deter our path of self-destruction? Or will a power infinitely greater than ours be needed to exert an influence beyond all others and return the willing among us to a life without endless craving?

This is the world of endless craving—that is, chemical and/or psychological obsession and withdrawal and it's like nothing else, because it involves so many painfully contradictory facets of our human nature. The chemicals involved are not just the ones derived from external sources but include the ones we've brought to life in our own chemistry due to our thoughts and behaviors. Whether it's physical, psychological, or both, this obsession has been the ruin of millions and will continue to be, as millions continue to credit this world of obsession with much more power and allure than it rightfully deserves.

Notice that I haven't used the word *addiction* since the title of this section. It wasn't an oversight; there's a deliberate reason why I didn't use it. This word has been so often used inappropriately, and jokingly, that many of us are left not knowing what the hell it really means. Even the *Diagnostic and Statistical Manual*—that is, the book responsible for providing diagnostic criteria for assessing a wide range of psychiatric conditions—doesn't list the word *addiction*. It's that tricky! To be safe, the manual uses the terms *substance abuse* and *substance dependence* under the heading "Substance-Related Disorders." We, however, will delve very deeply into the word *addiction*, and as a result, you will have a new, much deeper appreciation for the word. I promise.

If you must have all the clinical terms for the rathole, just consult the DSM or other clinical sources. I won't be getting into those here because since you are here, you already qualify. You don't need someone to assess whether you have a problem when you already know that you do. Plus, we don't have the time to go through the list of criteria, because for us every minute counts. It's kind of like when a refrigerator falls on your foot and visibly smashes it. You don't need someone to assess whether it's broken. You already know that—you just want it fixed!

Who Are We?

We are your mothers, fathers, sons, daughters, sisters, brothers, aunts, uncles, nieces, nephews, cousins, friends, and everyone else I may have missed. We are general practitioners, specialists, teachers, nurses, social workers, lawyers, therapists, builders, painters, roofers, technicians, farmers, managers, administrators, assistants, lobbyists, salespeople, politicians, and again, everyone else I've missed.

We are poor, middle class, rich, illiterate, high school–, college-, and Ivy League–educated, and with below-average, average, high, or genius-level intelligence. This is not about social class, money, or intellect. We come from the North, the South, the East, and the West, and everywhere in between. We look like anyone you've ever seen—every color, every shape, every age—and we come from every socioeconomic background. Here in the rathole, the filthy rich rub elbows and everything else with the downright filthy, and the only differences between them lie within their opportunities to get high.

I've always believed that the human being is opportunistic by nature, always seeking opportunities for self-satisfaction through food, water, shelter, money, power, love, and pleasure. We are always seeking opportunities for gratification, and we will not stop until we find it. It may take months or even years, but we will do whatever it takes to derive the pleasures we seek. And that nature is very apparent here in the rathole, the ultimate status equalizer, wherein if the rich lose all their wealth, they succumb equally to all the same low-down, scumbag, pleasure-seeking activities as do their poor counterparts. Sadly, the one place where we are all equal is in the nondiscriminatory rathole!

How Did We Get Here?

My mother was an alcoholic, and my father shot heroin. I always told myself I would never use because I grew up seeing all the terrible things alcohol and other drugs caused, but here I am.

I came from a good family, and my parents gave me virtually everything. It wasn't that I didn't have a good upbringing, because I did. Neither of my parents were addicts—they drank a little, but nothing to excess—but here I am.

There were ten of us in our family, and everybody was either using or on a program, so I guess I never thought much about it either way. I guess I expected it would happen to me sooner or later; I guess it's in my blood.

I grew up in a time when drugs were pretty common and it was kinda the thing to do, especially if you were cool, so here I am.

My neighborhood was pretty bad, with drugs being sold everywhere: in my building, in the playground, in school, everywhere. One day a friend of mine said, "Do you want to get high?" and I said, "Why not?"

I'm not the usual person that gets hooked on drugs. I'm a professional with a family and a house and a nice car and all those things people work hard to get. I was injured in an accident some time ago, and I was in a lot of pain. I went to my doctor and was prescribed some pain meds, and before long she wouldn't continue to refill my scrip, but I was still in pain. I told her that I was still in pain, and she replied that she could no longer help me and suggested that I seek natural pain remedies like yoga and mindfulness exercises. Are you kidding me? So that's why I'm here.

I just wanted to lose some weight that had been creeping up on me ever since having my second child. I tried regular exercise and eating better, but the weight just wasn't coming off fast enough. I found some over-the-counter weight loss pills, and they started to work. I was losing weight and losing it fast. I was looking better and feeling better, but I was feeling anxious all the time, maybe just due to life in general, with being a single parent and all, so I saw my doctor for something to relieve my anxiety. She prescribed me something that would relieve my anxiety, and it did, as long as I used it every day.

Before long it wasn't working anymore, so I knew I needed more, or something stronger. Well, one thing led to another, and before long I was hooked on benzos and using crack to keep my weight down! Imagine me using crack, a soccer mom and all, running all over town looking for doctors for scrips for something to calm me down. I can't believe this all happened so fast.

I remember I was seventeen and the only boy in my family, and we were all out on the porch one day, me, my mom, and my two sisters with their kids. We were goofing on this old man across the street that was always working, either on his old beaten-up car or on their old beaten-up house. Every morning early, he would come out of the house in his blue coveralls and pop open his hood and check the oil or add oil or something, and then he'd go to work. Every evening he'd come home dirty, pop the hood again and do whatever, and then go into the house. Soon he'd come back out and work on the yard or on the house for an hour or so. We always laughed at him for being such a sucker! Working, working, always working and having little to show for it. What a sucker!

Here my mom was getting a check, and my sisters were getting checks for doing absolutely nothing. This day my mom said to me that I'd better start bringing in some money if I wanted to stay living there. I asked her how can I do that when I can't get pregnant like my sisters. She said you can pretend you have a mental disability, and then you'd qualify for a disability check.

I went to a local psych hospital and talked to someone there about having some problems with my mind and about not being able to focus for a long time on anything and about my moods going from happy to sad all the time for no reason and not being able to sleep and how I needed help bad. Within an hour or so, I was told I had ADHD, bipolar disorder, and was suffering from anxiety and was given some scrips for medicine. When I got home, my mom said I'd better take the medication so it's in my blood when the hospital checks next time. I did.

Over the next ten years, I took the six medications I was given, in addition to some other things that I took just to feel normal. Now, I feel like an old man with some very real problems, seizures, neuropathy, liver problems, sexual problems, and I walk with a cane, and I'm only twenty-seven. I'd like to stop taking my meds, but I know I can't. I've really made a mess of my life.

Everybody has a story as to how or why they started doing whatever they do, and everybody still struggling with relapse has an excuse as to why they can't stop. With the aid of this book, you will finally make a definitive decision about your behaviors, one way or the other. I remember a line my old company commander in the navy used to say to us when we gave him a story about why we didn't do what we were supposed to do: "Excuses are like assholes: we all have them, and they all stink." I've always found that line amusing, but now I realize it's true!

SECTION II

What "They" Say about Addiction

Say what you say and think what you think;
the truth remains unchanged.
—A Lanceism

The ways we view addiction are all different, depending on who we ask and according to what that person's relationship or motivation is in regards to the person who is addicted. Maybe dependency is viewed as a moral failing, maybe as a disease due to a genetic vulnerability, maybe as twisted behaviors based on childhood influences and environmental impacts, or maybe some combination of those factors.

Over several short chapters, three popular perspectives will be briefly discussed, and then readers will be asked to vote for the one or ones that make most sense to them. Keep in mind your original selections may change as you read *Lust*. You may even uncover new possible perspectives.

CHAPTER 2

Reckless Spirits

Life has a way of catching up to the impulsive.
—A LANCEISM

With a chapter title like this, I guess you'd have to call this model the "moral model," the model that identifies people overindulging in alcohol and other drugs as morally reckless and reprehensible. Their actions are seen as disgraceful, inexcusable, and blameworthy. We see alcoholics and other drug addicts falling down and languishing in the streets and filling up ambulances and hospitals quicker than rooms can be made available for them. Daily we're bombarded with unbelievable stories about caregivers recklessly driving children around in their vehicles while under the influence of alcohol or other drugs. Videos display people laid out on the ground or on the floors of retail stores while their toddlers hysterically attempt to revive them. We read about the opioid epidemic that's sweeping our country and overwhelming our healthcare system. We see mothers and fathers, blue collar and white collar alike, spending their last dime on alcohol and other drugs, and we want to just tell them to stop it and get a grip!

This moral model presupposes that these people using alcohol and other drugs deliberately choose and decide wantonly to consume these substances and have no moral boundaries in place to deter them. The idea that someone would drink and drug to such excess as to jeopardize their own welfare and that of others is just unconscionable. To suggest even remotely that these users are in some way "victims" of their use is just inconceivable. For anyone to imply that these users have "no choice" in the matter and that they have "lost control" is unimaginable to the supporters of the moral model. The idea that one person can drink in a controlled fashion and another cannot is preposterous. The notion that a person will continue to imbibe and indulge in other drug activity to the detriment of themselves, their families, and everyone else around them is seen as simply sinful. The thought that these sinners among us deserve our kind care and empathic consideration is almost uproarious.

To the believer of the moral model, the solution to this problem of addressing these lawbreakers and home wreckers is simple: fines, punishment, community service, and stern, public condemnation. Why should people just be allowed to do as they please and then hide behind a label like "a disease" and get away with murder, literally, in many cases? Why should a person who deliberately chooses to break the law be treated like they're above the law? Why should a lawbreaker be classified as a member of a protected class and be extended more leniency and opportunities to screw up than your average, hardworking, conscientious individual? Why should users be applauded and congratulated every time they decide to stop terrorizing the masses around them, while the average Joe and Josephine receive no accolades or awards for getting up each day and doing the right things? After all, it's not like someone grabbed them and stuck a needle in their arms, or a crack pipe in their mouths or poured alcohol down their throats. In most cases, they were willing participants.

To the moral model devotee, it appears that the emphasis in our society in regards to drug abuse is on coddling and enabling the defiant, headstrong, stubborn nonconformists among us under the guise of humanitarianism. Some even believe that sinister, monetary motives may exist to promote this idea of "powerlessness" in order to sustain an industry of medicines and treatments. The supporter of the moral model sees no reason for medical interventions or recovery modalities, as they believe the only treatment for what ails these overindulgent individuals is the cessation of their amoral behaviors and the adoption of moral behaviors while steadfastly adhering to the rule of law. They believe that once these individuals are taught to see the errors in their ways, through any means necessary, they will correct their deficiencies and reestablish their lives. And once they are no longer morally and spiritually bankrupt, they will be able to live among us as respectable, reliable, and accepted human beings.

CHAPTER 3

Genetic Deviants

You are what you say you are, until you say you aren't.
—A LANCEISM

Genetically predisposed, genetically vulnerable, diseased mutants are running rampant across our nation, and their numbers are steadily growing! Once, these freaks among us were believed to grow only in poor, ethnic, urban cesspools, but now they're found everywhere, thriving in even our finest of settings. These deviants roam our planet boldly these days in broad daylight and wantonly under the cloak of darkness, while they are comfortably protected under the veil of being "diseased" and incurable and as victims of a cruel, biological hoax.

Born to Be Wild

As you may have guessed, this model of addiction is affectionately known as the "disease model." Actually, there are quite a few disease models, each with its own unique nuances. Honestly, I'm not sure whether they should be called models in their own right or rather subdivisions of the disease model. Nonetheless, for our purposes, allow me to focus on the more well-known disease models or perspectives just to keep things simple. My goal is to provide an overview of what most Americans think about the disease of addiction so we have a better frame of reference when we make our determination as to what it is. It is terrifying to think that as I'm writing these words, beautiful babies are being born with this so-called incurable disease called addiction, that they will be told will exist, until the day they die. This notion alone is enough to scare the bejesus out of anyone! Here we have girls and boys, men and women, drinking and drugging copious amounts of substances, only to *be told* that they're drinking and drugging like that because they've "lost control" due to their disease. The argument is they didn't drink one hundred drinks and become alcoholics; they drank one hundred drinks because they are alcoholics.

There are several key players in the disease model: the medical/scientific industry, the recovery/clinical industry, and the alcohol and pharmaceutical industries. Sure, these players aren't processing any raw materials or producing any finished products per se like traditional industries, but they all definitely qualify as being big businesses, and big businesses mean big money. Although each of these industries has a different take on the disease model, they all emphatically consider addiction to be a disease.

Science Knows Best

The medical industry takes the scientific approach and discusses all the genetic ways addiction is passed from generation to generation. Practitioners in this industry espouse the concept of heredity that assumes the penchant for alcohol or other drugs is passed along at conception or in utero from the parents or hosts to the unfortunate babies or recipients, and this penchant then remains dormant in them until activated. It's like being issued a new credit card that's not activated until you call the special number and input the required data. The difference is that once you activate your addiction, you'll be paying back your debt in blood. On second thought, maybe it's not that different from a credit card after all. OK, let's be serious: science and its findings are nothing to sneeze at. The earth was once considered to be flat until science concluded that it wasn't, although that debate has been raised once again by some conspiracy theorists. Science is known to be at the forefront of evolution and is used as the benchmark by which we understand our natural world. Therefore, it would only be reasonable to think that science would have the answers to why some people become addicted while others don't and would know how to cure the ones that do. Unfortunately, science really has no empirical data that supports the *why* of addiction and purports that addiction is incurable, at least for the time being.

Endorphins, dopamine, neurotransmitters, and serotonin—these are just a few of the terms commonly used in the medical industry. Doctors and scientists talk about brain chemistry and how psychoactive drugs affect the central nervous system and peripheral nerves and about the ways drugs inhibit reuptake of certain chemicals and all that stuff. They theorize about addiction and its genetic probabilities. They purport that those prone to addiction are just unfortunate heirs to the disease due to no fault of their own. They speculate that those predisposed to addiction and not yet in active addiction are like "ticking time bombs" just waiting for the opportunity to explode! Once these so-called bombs explode, these unfortunate heirs will be told, "It's not your fault. We knew it would happen; we just didn't know when. You have an 'addictive' personality. A personality derived from a caustic concoction of cockeyed chromosomes and confused chemicals, cruelly converging within your chaste core." Yeah, that sounds about right!

Unlike in the moral model, compassionate care and nonjudgmental understanding is the expected response to this "disease" under the medical model. The idea is that addiction is not something that anyone would want if given a choice, so we should view those addicted under the same lens as anyone else with a disease. After all, wouldn't you consider alcohol and crack addiction to be similar in nature to diseases like Alzheimer's and breast cancer? Who wouldn't? That's a no-brainer! This medical view of addiction supports and legitimizes the actions of the users and characterizes their use as merely symptomatic of their disease. As a result, users are encouraged to feel vindicated and accepting of their use and more at ease and less stigmatized in their using environments. In this model, we've taken any responsibility and accountability comfortably off of the shoulders of those addicted and placed it squarely on their defective biology.

On the business side, these medical/scientific viewpoints regarding addiction have clearly led to the need for more available medical interventions and to the growing expectation that even more of these interventions will be necessary in the foreseeable future. As, according to this view, addiction is a disease for life and for which there is no present cure, the only alternative is to wait patiently for scientific breakthroughs. This medical view also presupposes that everyone with the disease of addiction will need medical intervention. Therefore, under this assumption, no unfortunate recipients of addiction will be able to stop their use on their own. Not only can they expect to never be able to stop their addiction on their own, they can expect to never be free from it.

Thankfully, however, despite science's belief that no cure for addiction exists, scientists have thankfully produced other medications to combat the appeal of psychoactive drugs: namely other psychoactive drugs such as methadone and Suboxone. To be fair, scientists have also produced nonnarcotic drugs like naltrexone, Vivitrol, Antabuse, Campral, and others, all designed to combat addiction as long as they're taken as prescribed. Addicts just tend to have a problem with that "as prescribed" part. Here's the rub: if the drug is psychoactive, then the addict will likely take more than is prescribed, and if the drug is not psychoactive and presents some unpleasant reaction if a psychoactive drug is taken, then the addict will not likely take the prescription for long.

Sweet Recovery

Whether it's at an AA or NA meeting or at a methadone or Suboxone clinic, you hear the word *disease* a lot in regards to addiction. Not all of the members or all the patients of these organizations necessarily believe they have a disease, but they are told repeatedly that they do. I guess it simplifies things. How can you speak about the lunacy of addiction without elevating its status to something beyond one's control? Also, how do you get funding for something communicated as an "illness" or a "bad habit"? The idea in these recovery environments is that addicts never fully recover because addiction is a disease from which they can never recover. Therefore, the state of being in recovery is always ongoing and is something that requires sustained effort to maintain, and recovery is seen as something always available to anyone who makes the decision to stop using.

In this recovery industry, we have two main factions. There are the recovery groups like AA and NA, and then there's the clinical side, consisting of recovery treatment centers and clinics, many of which support, promote, and integrate the AA/NA philosophy. I understand, however, that some differences exist between the two; for example, AA/NA group members may not consider the use of replacement medications used in recovery centers and clinics as acceptable. Methadone and Suboxone patients appear to be regarded in some cases as less serious about recovery because they are seen as not being "clean" and still using something. AA/NA groups believe that once their members "Trust God, Clean House and Help Others," they will be rewarded with recovery and medications will not be necessary. Nonetheless, despite the differences between recovery groups and recovery centers, they both share many things in common.

Tolerance, titration, stabilization, withdrawal, relapse—these are just a few of the terms commonly used in the recovery industry. Either addicts are no longer feeling the same effects they used to feel from their drugs, despite using the same amount as they used to, or they're jonesing because the drugs' effects have just plain worn off, and they're crashing and scheming how to get their next fix. This is the life of an addict and these are the terms of that life.

Whether addicts are precontemplative, contemplative, preparing, acting, or maintaining their actions, they are in a process of being where they believe they should be at all times.

Between AA/NA and recovery centers, addicts often hear that relapse is a natural part of recovery, so I ask you, why then would they ever want to do anything unnatural like not relapse, if they really want to recover? Now that makes sense! Nonetheless, I do believe that both AA/NA groups and treatment centers honestly want to help motivate addicts to stop using and become more productive, healthy, and happy human beings. They just happen to be misguided.

For the most part, AA/NA group members believe that they were born with this disease of addiction—or at the very least, the predisposition for it—and accept that they will unfortunately die with this disease. It's difficult to imagine how an infant's soul or spirit can be already corrupted at birth. It's downright depressing to think that their corrupt little spirits will one day erupt into full-blown, hell-bent alcoholics and drug addicts, but they say it's just inevitable!

This recovery community advocates that the addict's spirit is "sick" and in dire need of repair. Therefore, they purport that addicts must undergo a "spiritual awakening" to become free from their sickness. In order to accomplish this freedom, addicts are told that they must admit their "powerlessness" to their drugs and surrender their will over to the care of a God of their understanding. Next, they are asked to be honest with themselves and with another trusted human being to convey the nature of their wrongdoings and misdeeds and then to humbly ask their God to remove their defects of character. Once this is completed, participants are asked to make sincere amends to those harmed by their transgressions, whenever possible, and then ask those harmed for their forgiveness.

Through this detailed process known as "the twelve steps," participants are said to experience a spiritual awakening and as a result have all their defects of character removed and their obsessions lifted. And in deep gratitude for this having been done, all participants are asked to help others or "pay it forward" to others still struggling with addiction. The book affectionately known as the "Big Book" is akin to being the bible of AA/NA and is said to be the official guide to all those seeking recovery from addiction. It asserts that the book and their twelve-step program will work for everyone "except for those few unfortunates who are constitutionally incapable of being honest with themselves." The book also stresses the benefits of regular prayer and meditation to remain forever thankful and humble in one's dealings with others and as a means to maintain calm and serenity within.

On the clinical side, recovery treatment centers and clinics see the use of replacement medications as helpful tools for people considering an alternative to illicit substances. Although treatment centers also see addiction as a disease, they tend to primarily view addiction through a medical lens, and one with biological components more so than spiritual ones. They state that medications can restore balance to the lives of those addicted to drugs and allow patients to lead full and productive existences since they no longer need be in the ongoing hot pursuit of drugs just to feel normal.

However, these centers recognize that addiction is a multifaceted problem with many elements to be addressed, and they welcome AA/NA as partners in fighting this battle. They acknowledge how both AA/NA's philosophies and medically assisted treatments can work collaboratively to achieve the results both entities desire.

Counseling is another service offered in many recovery treatment centers to allow patients an opportunity to discuss their treatment plans as well as reconcile their personal feelings and conflicts. Coming from an "addiction as disease" mentality, these counselors are taught to extol the benefits of medicines in recovery and the need for patients to learn coping skills and relapse-prevention strategies. Through individual and group counseling sessions, these counselors utilize assessment tools that focus on biopsychosocial factors—the influences of biology, human behaviors and emotions, environment, and socialization—in addition to the medications, as a comprehensive strategy to combat addiction.

These treatment centers are known to employ many well-intentioned individuals—doctors, nurses, clinicians, and a multitude of support staff—who are intimately aware of the struggle of addiction, many of whom are in recovery themselves and trying their very best to remain abstinent "one day at a time." As a result, these centers and their people have vested interests in their programs and sincerely want to provide a service that will lead to success. Nonetheless, despite their best intentions, like any business, the business side of treatment can on steady occasion rear its ugly head and stand in the way of better judgment and progress!

It's All on You

They say that addiction is a disease that only a small fraction of the population has, and if you have it, you shouldn't use their products. They say if you know you have this disease, then stay away from their products. They say that the problem is "you" and not them. It's that simple! Who are "they"? They are the third faction of the disease model, the alcohol and pharmaceutical industries. They say that alcohol and other drugs are not inherently bad, evil, or even harmful as we claim, if consumed responsibly and as directed. They say that the problems arise when people overindulge and act irresponsibly. They argue that no one is forcing anyone to buy or use their products, and that any side effects of their products are either readily disclosed or easily made available for public knowledge. They state that they cannot control the desires of people, and that people must control themselves. They express sympathy for those who have used their products and succumbed to unfortunate outcomes, but nonetheless they express no culpability for any individual's decision to consume their products to excess or to the point of committing destructive behaviors.

The alcohol and pharmaceutical industries see no correlation between the sales of their products and the sales of tobacco products and deftly decline making comments regarding tobacco manufacturers changing their claims throughout the years in regards to the addictive nature of their products. They reiterate emphatically that they believe addiction is a disease that's initiated within the individual and not by anything external, thereby exonerating all products, namely their products, as the cause for any addiction. Therefore, they assert that no connection exists between their products and any addiction or disease and thereby deny any responsibility or culpability. Finally, they advocate for those individuals living with the disease of addiction to immediately cease and desist the use of their products and seek professional help. Now, wasn't this the response you'd expected? You have to really appreciate that kind of accountability.

CHAPTER 4

Twisted by Nurture

> She did it, he did it, they did it, I did it. Who cares
> now who did it? The damage has already been
> done. The question is, are you willing to fix it?
> —A LANCEISM

t must have been my parents and the way they raised me. They used drugs all their lives and thought nothing of it. I lived in the projects, and drugs were everywhere. My friends all drank and used drugs, and no one ever told me drugs were bad until I was already hooked. I needed something to escape my situation, and alcohol was my ticket. I never expected I could be anybody anyway, so why not use drugs? I thought everyone drank and used drugs as a way of having fun and dealing with being alive. After all, the world is a cold and callous place and no place for a sober mind.

It's called the "maladaptive behavior model," one that extracts input from a lot of different behavioral factors. It theorizes about the effects of one's parents and siblings, one's living environment, one's nutritional habits, one's friends, and one's educational training, among other factors, on one's worldview, one's perception of oneself within the world, and ultimately on one's behaviors. The idea is that all these factors not only play a crucial role in the developing mind of a child, but they could actually predispose children and adults to engage in risky behaviors through no fault of their own.

Interestingly, this model also speculates that the way people adapt to events may even be more important than the events themselves, and that the reason for any maladaptation to any event should be the real concern, rather than all the contributing factors necessarily. So it begs the question as to why some people from bad situations can move on successfully with their lives, while others become stuck as prisoners of their past.

Resilience is one of the hallmarks of adaptation. To have the ability to rebound after adversity is truly a highly prized trait. This characteristic is one counselors routinely seek to develop within their clients so as to dissuade them from placing inordinate emphasis on traumatic events.

Anna's story clearly demonstrates the need for resilience. Anna said she grew up in a tough town, surrounded by tough people:

I never learned how to trust anyone because no one I knew could be trusted. That's why I'm the way I am, doing my own thing and just worrying about me. From a little girl, people took advantage of me, they took my toys, they took my clothes, and before I was ten, my uncle took my virginity. My mother knew it too; she knew what her brother was doing to me and never stopped him. Later, when I was about fourteen, I told her what her brother was still doing to me, just to see what she'd say, and she slapped my face so hard I can still feel it. She called me a lying bitch and said I'd better never spread lies like that again. That was almost thirty years ago, but it seems like yesterday because people are still taking advantage of me, taking my money, taking my things, and doing whatever they want to me. I've been in one program or another since I was fifteen, after my mother kicked me out when she found her boyfriend sneaking out of my bedroom one day. I've been on my own ever since, living wherever and doing whatever. Drinking alcohol, shooting drugs, and prostituting; anything to make it through the day. My psych doctor says I'm all screwed up from what happened to me when I was young and that I should learn to forgive and forget for my own sake. It's easy for her to say that because she hasn't been through what I've been through; maybe if she had, she wouldn't be so quick to tell me to just forgive and forget and move on. How can I move on now that I'm almost forty-four years old with nothing but bad memories? How can I learn to trust people now after all that has happened? It doesn't seem realistic to believe that I can ever be normal or live a normal life.

Sara was a mule, transporting heroin, cocaine, and other drugs in her body all across the United States and she was damn good at it. Whether she was swallowing condoms full of drugs or having them strategically placed in other orifices, she was highly successful at not being caught. She was cheerfully welcomed wherever she went and regularly received bonuses and even special gifts for her greatly admired work. No one ever suspected her, and Sara always delivered. She was the perfect courier; Sara was six. At that tender age, Sara adored her parents and readily did what her drug-addicted biological parents told her to do, just to make them happy.

One day on the way to a routine delivery, some condoms burst in Sara's stomach and blew her tiny colon into pieces. In a cold sweat, Sara clutched at her stomach in pain as her parents frantically shuffled to calculate how much blow had been ruined, so as to have an explanation for their suppliers and their buyers. At the same time, her parents realized Sara's days as a mule had probably come to an end. So like any loving parents would do, Sara was kicked out of the car like a trash bag as they sped along the highway. Why hold on to a sick liability? Luckily for Sara, a trucker saw her body exit the car and abruptly pulled over to help. The trucker quickly lifted Sara into his cab and secured her safely with a seatbelt. Immediately he called 911 and told them what had happened and that he was headed to the nearest hospital. By the time they arrived, Sara had passed out, and her lifeless little body was carefully lifted onto a gurney. Doctors say she was one lucky little girl. They say that sepsis had set in and that Sara should have already been dead. Despite the dire diagnosis, Sara rallied back after surgery and quickly became the hospital's darling dynamo. Despite Sara's new attachment, her colostomy bag, she was a cheerful little thing, quick to smile and laugh. Within the week, Sara's parents had been apprehended by police and charged with multiple counts, ranging from child neglect to attempted murder. Somehow, even with all the evidence implicating her parents, their attorneys were able to make a case that Sara had accidentally opened her door and fallen out. Before long, all charges were dropped, and Sara's parents were free to go.

Toward the end of Sara's hospital stay, her parents started coming around. As soon as Sara saw them, her face lit up like a Christmas tree. Sara couldn't wait to be back with the parents she loved. After Sara was discharged from the hospital, but before she was fully recovered from her injuries, Sara was being offered sexually to drug dealers in exchange for crack and other drugs. Word quickly got around, and before long Sara was recovered by family services and Sara's parents finally arrested. Some things you just don't do, even in the world of scumbags!

A few years passed in state care before Sara was finally adopted by loving parents. Sara was their only child, and by the ripe old age of ten, she was treated like a queen and shown genuine love every day. Sara on occasion asked about her biological parents, but never appeared to linger too long in reverie. She excelled in middle school and was even elected class valedictorian in high school. Sara had a curious mind and never appeared bored. College came easy to Sara, with her exemplary study habits and her uncanny drive to succeed. It was in a well-known hospital that I met Sara some years later; she was my physician's assistant.

Making lemonade out of lemons, that's what we're capable of doing. Subscribers to the maladaptive behavior model believe that with the help of cognitive behavioral therapy (CBT), dialectical behavioral therapy (DBT), and mindfulness training, people can successfully overcome the greatest of obstacles. They believe that, through a process of thinking critically about our feelings and our behaviors, in addition to developing new skills and strategies to address life's challenges while maintaining a genuine sense of acceptance and attention to our responses, we can heal. They do not pass moral judgment on those addicted or view addiction as a disease, but rather see addiction as a "learned" behavior comprising a myriad of misperceptions, misinterpretations, and inadequate training, a behavior that once cognitively redefined and restructured, can readjust and become something new, different and better, and something that no longer includes drugs.

Where Do We Go from Here?

In this section, I briefly outlined what "they" say about addiction. "They" being the moral majority: the people who see addiction as a disease and the ones who view addiction as a behavioral maladjustment. Next, you will read what addicts themselves say about addiction. This should help you develop your own informed opinion about the true nature of addiction.

In the following six sections, I will outline the "six elements of addiction" by chronicling the behaviors and activities that create, sustain, and maintain the mayhem of addiction. In the accompanying diagram, I have illustrated these six elements for greater clarity and visualization. Throughout these six sections and through the use of personal anecdotes, second- and even third-hand accounts, illustrations, and diagrams you will be able to feel what it's like to be addicted and also learn how to break free from addiction.

The Six Elements of Addiction

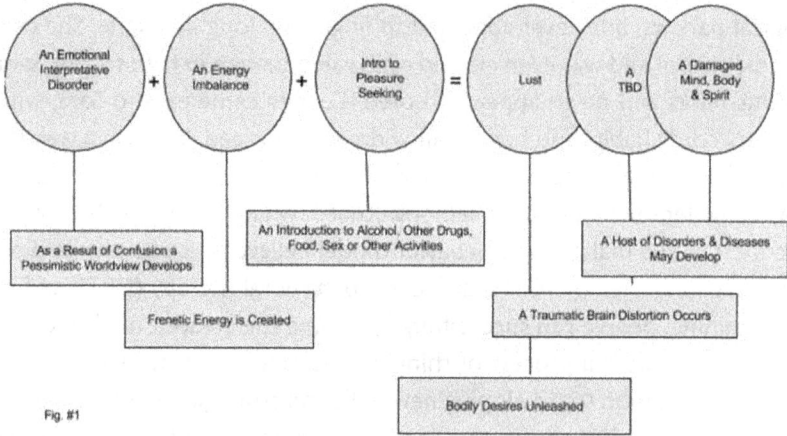

An Emotional Interpretative Disorder + An Energy Imbalance + Intro to Pleasure Seeking = Lust · A TBD · A Damaged Mind, Body & Spirit

As a Result of Confusion a Pessimistic Worldview Develops

Frenetic Energy is Created

An Introduction to Alcohol, Other Drugs, Food, Sex or Other Activities

A Host of Disorders & Diseases May Develop

A Traumatic Brain Distortion Occurs

Bodily Desires Unleashed

Fig. #1

COPYRIGHT © 2015 LANCE C. MCCORMACK

SECTION III

The First Element of Addiction:
An Emotional Interpretative Disorder

When you change the way you look at things,
the things you look at change.
—ANONYMOUS

t's no secret, we all know we have emotions, and we all know our emotions can wreak havoc on our lives if we don't control them. In order to control them, however, we must first understand them. Emotions are feelings, but not necessarily something felt just in response to having been physically touched, as emotions can also be felt, perhaps even more deeply, as a result of having not been physically touched. Emotions can represent intense visceral reactions to how we're mentally and physiologically responding to specific events and to our world in general, through our perceptions and interpretations of them. Several chapters including diagrams will be devoted to how perceptions and interpretations influence emotions and to how runaway interpretations can kick off a roller coaster of emotions leading to disordered perceptions of who we are and what we need. This section explores the first of the six elements of addiction.

CHAPTER 5

I'll Do It My Way

You don't drown by falling in the water.
You drown by staying there.
—EDWIN LOUIS COLE

"Who knows me better than me? Everyone seems to want to tell me what to do and how to do it, when maybe they should just worry about themselves." Maybe you've heard these lines from someone you love, or maybe you've even said them yourself. It appears that no matter how hard we try to "save" someone from experiencing the bad things we've already experienced, it just doesn't work. Strangely enough, many times our efforts seem to have the exact opposite effect and actually create an overwhelming desire in that person to do exactly what we'd hoped they wouldn't do.

I remember reading about Milton Erickson, a famous hypnotherapist back in the 1950s who was stricken with polio as a child and confined to a wheelchair. In his chair he happened to observe many behaviors, especially those of animals since he had lived with his parents on a farm. He had spoken of incidents where his father routinely struggled to pull the cows into the barn after a long day at pasture. One day while watching his father struggle once again with a cow, little Milton decided to pull the cow's tail, and surprisingly the cow ran eagerly into the barn. Even animals demonstrate reluctance to do what you want them to do if they're not inclined to do it; it's not just human nature.

In humans, I call this reluctance to do what's suggested a feature of the 50/20 rule. Picture a fifty-year-old mother talking with her twenty-year-old daughter and saying, "I see you starting to head down the road I did when I was your age, and

I know that road only brings heartache." Then her daughter responds, "Thanks, Mom. I know you love me and want only the best for me, but I have to learn these things myself in order to grow and be an adult. I realize I may fall down at times and even scrape my knees, but I'll just have to get myself back onto my feet, like you did. After all, you turned out all right!" So her mom just watches her daughter go through years and years of pain and tumultuous times unnecessarily and feels totally helpless along the way, until one day she notices her daughter is now fifty years old and has a twenty-year-old daughter of her own. She overhears a conversation between the two, only to notice the similarity to the conversation she had thirty years ago with her daughter, and at that point, she just smiles. Some things never change; the 50/20 rule has probably been in effect since the beginning of human existence and probably will remain in effect until we're all gone.

A Different View

I've characterized our willingness or resistance to change and our ability to become fixated by a substance, activity, person, or ideology as part of our dynamic nature. Our lives are comprised of what I consider to be "trance states," each representing the current position of our receptivity to suggestions, influence, and intuition. These states constitute what people vehemently believe to be true in their hearts and in some extreme cases constitute what beliefs people would be willing to die for. Some examples of trance states are addiction, anger, bigotry, fear, hatred, knowing, love, lust, greed, politics, religion, and resentment, just to name a few. These states validate a person's acceptance of something as being absolutely true; therefore, anything else to the contrary must be false.

One definition I found for a trance is "a half-conscious state characterized by an absence of response to external stimuli, typically as induced by hypnosis or entered by a medium." I found this definition to be only partially accurate. As a certified hypnotherapist, I recognize that, although a trance can be characterized by the absence of a response to a stimulus, it also is commonly characterized by the presence of responses to stimuli. In addition, a trance need not be considered a half-conscious state, but rather a dreamlike state that occurs most often in those fully conscious in which we either accept, deny, or attempt to distort reality.

From my many observations of those in trance states, I recognize that addiction is clearly also one of those states. An interesting definition by *Merriam-Webster's*

Collegiate Dictionary of the verb *to addict* is "to give oneself up to a substance or an activity." This definition may be entirely foreign to what many of us have heard regarding addiction. We've heard that it's something of an external force that takes over us against our will and renders us totally powerless. We don't consider it to be an inside job! We think of the word *addicted* as referring to something we become or get, instead of something we allow ourselves to be. So rather than seeing addiction as a disease of the mind, I see it undoubtedly as a state of the mind. A trance state, to be exact.

We are always in one state of mind or another and are constantly transitioning from either an open or a closed state relative to suggestions and influence from others and the acceptance of our own intuition or better judgment. The way this works is very similar to the functioning of an electrical light switch. With the switch open or on, electrical current flows effortlessly to the light, but with the switch closed or off, electrical energy remains stalled at the switch, preventing electricity from flowing to the light fixture. This stalled electrical energy represents latent energy or energy that is available but currently untapped and is there waiting to be utilized if you choose. That's what a trance state is all about, a deeply impassioned state of the mind that can change in an instant if you so desire, or one that can remain in position for as long as you live. You alone control your switch and decide when or if you'll engage it. Sometimes we just have to realize that things are going to get much worse instead of get better and flip the switch while that option still exists.

One Way Out

Recently, I had a very bizarre dream that really illustrated our power to change while within the trance state. I say the dream was bizarre due to its lack of details, which left me wondering what I was supposed to be doing in the dream. I wasn't certain as to where I was or where I was going or why. The scene was unfamiliar, and all I can recall are galvanized fences and gates and that I was walking hand in hand with my wife. The day appeared overcast, and I noticed only a few people in the distance. Somehow we were walking through this gated area, opening the gates and then closing them behind us. We weren't trespassing, but I can't understand why we were walking through so many gates. Suddenly I heard some dogs barking ahead of us and then saw four or five loose dogs behind a low fence growling and barking fiercely as they strained with all their might to get out. They looked like muscular pit bulls and Rottweilers, and I could see them foaming at the mouth and trying their best to jump over the fence. Immediately I grabbed my wife's hand hard and turned her around to get away before any of the dogs got free. I remember I pushed her ahead of me as I opened the gates in front of us.

Before I knew what was happening, one dog had grabbed my wife and was pulling her down to the ground right behind a fence as she was screaming for me. When I turned around, my heart sank to my feet as I saw the dog on top of her gnawing violently at her body. My head was on fire as I ran back toward her and jumped over the fence, landing with my foot squarely on the dog's neck. I heard it snap instantly under my weight as I rushed to lift my wife and get her back to safety. Before I could, all the other dogs were loose and charging us from only feet away. I felt completely helpless and unable to think of a solution...then suddenly, I ended the dream.

Intellectual Grappling

The trance state of "knowing" is one that's always in play, where we're constantly comparing what we believe we know with what we believe needs to be known, and we take quick exception with anyone who claims to know anything we do not know. You know.

We are constantly grappling or wrestling with others intellectually to bolster our mental positions. It's a defensive bluffing technique that looks more like an inferiority complex than one of confidence in one's knowledge. Nonetheless, it appears to make us feel better about ourselves. We bristle at any notion that someone is suggesting that our knowledge or training is inadequate in any way or that we could benefit from gaining more. Regardless of our level of training, we will rarely concede that we are not as smart as someone else or that we need more knowledge than we currently possess. And it doesn't matter who that someone else is. It could be Albert Einstein, and we'd still say, "What makes you think you're smarter than me?" That's why "knowing" qualifies as a trance state, because once you believe you already know everything, you become unable to learn anything. "Either we are pilgrims looking for answers in order to make sense of our world, or we are wanderers who have turned off onto byways of distraction or despair, alienating ourselves from wonder." This was how Blaise Pascal, a famous nineteenth-century mathematician and philosopher, put it as he sought to describe people as being either seekers or nonseekers. Which are you?

A common twenty-first-century mistake many of us make, is that we loudly profess to be seekers, while our actions clearly prove otherwise. John was a multibillionaire who searched the world over to locate someone who could bestow upon him the ultimate gift of true enlightenment. He searched far and wide until he heard of a high priest who lived in a remote cave in the Himalayas and who was renowned for his gifts of wisdom. Upon meeting the priest, John spoke incessantly about his business prowess, his trials and tribulations, and of all the evils of the world, never allowing the priest a word edgewise. Finally the priest placed two teacups in front of them and poured his tea first. Then the priest leaned forward and poured tea into John's cup, not stopping even when the tea reached the rim and spilled over the edge. John yelled, "What are you doing? You're spilling tea all over the place." The priest replied, "Your teacup is like you, already full; I cannot help you."

On a similar note, I recall speaking with an individual years ago who had had an opportunity to receive a first-class, Ivy League education for free as a benefit of his job but opted not to take advantage of that opportunity. He told me, "I already know all I need to know." Now, the confusing part was he didn't have a high-paying job or much money, and he routinely spoke of being unhappy with his life as a result, yet he passed up an opportunity to have all those things. I guess we could attempt to psychoanalyze what he said and then determine that he was probably using a defense mechanism and was instead afraid or insecure as to whether he could handle the rigors of college work and therefore responded out of misplaced pride when he said he already knew all that he needed to know. We could also guess that he actually believed what he said.

I'll Do It When I'm Good and Ready

There is something about someone telling us something! It all seems to depend on who is telling us, how we perceive the person who's telling us, and how we interpret what they're telling us. If for any reason we feel they're telling us something that they believe we don't already know, then we've got a problem and our response is always the same: "I'll stop/start [fill in the blank] when I'm good and ready and not a nanosecond sooner!"

An old colleague and friend of mine—let's call him Melvin—shared a story with me that really illustrates the untapped power we possess. I hadn't seen him in a while, and when I did, I realized he had changed significantly. He appeared to be full of energy and looked like a much younger version of his old self. When I re-marked that he looked different, he quickly stood up straighter and said with a big smile, "I lost fifty pounds!" As I congratulated him on his achievement, he added, "And it took me less than three months!" Of course I had to ask him, how did you do it? Mel told me his story.

It actually happened by accident. One day I surprised my wife and our seven boys by taking them up north to a popular water park. The weather had been great, nice and hot, so I thought it would be the perfect thing to do. We hadn't gone in a few years, and we had the time, so why not. At the top of one water slide, there was an employee standing next to a scale, and he said that the weight limit was two hundred and fifty pounds. He didn't need to weigh my son, but he asked me to step on the scale, and when I did, it read two hundred and fifty-three pounds. Immediately my son screamed, "You weigh two hundred and fifty-three pounds?" Instantly, I felt about two inches tall, and my face must have been beet red because at that moment it seemed like all the eyes in the pool were suddenly on me. The worker tried to ease my embarrassment by saying, "Even though you're a few pounds over, I'll let you go this time," but his words didn't even begin to erase the feelings I had.

As if I that experience wasn't enough, that evening I agreed it would be fun to go to dinner at a theme restaurant, notoriously known for their sarcastic waiters. After we had all finished our meals, our waiter asked my wife and I if we would like something from the bar, and I said, "No, thanks. I don't drink." He quickly responded with a smile, saying, "Oh, so you're just fat." All my kids and my even my wife broke out laughing as if it was the funniest thing they had ever heard. After I regained my com-posure, I asked for the check, and no, I didn't leave any tip. That night while I lay in bed, I recounted the earlier events of the day, and I made a promise to myself that this would never happen to me again. Starting the next day, I went for a run, ate a healthy breakfast, and decided to do that every day. Within days, the pounds started to fall off, and my wife and kids already noticed the difference. Then, in less than three months' time, I got on the scale in the morning and saw I had lost fifty pounds. It was easy!

Now, how was Mel able to do that?

That story brings to mind yet another story of a weight-loss client I met years ago—let's call her Linda. She weighed about 423 pounds, and she had told me that she really wanted to lose weight due to her declining health condition. "I have type II diabetes, poor circulation, fibromyalgia, arthritis in my shoulders and knees, and just feel terrible overall," she told me. Now up until this point, Linda and I had been talking over the phone, and she was contemplating making an appointment to come see me. She continued to tell me how she had come to hate going to her doctors because every time she saw them for the last ten years, all they ever said was "Linda, you have to lose weight."

"'Lose weight, lose weight' is all I hear from everyone—my mom, my sisters, and my so-called friends," she said. Well, Linda didn't make an appointment after all...at least not then.

About a year and a half after I had initially spoken with Linda, she called back and sounded elated. She said she had lost 120 pounds in the last three months and claimed the process had been relatively easy. Linda reported that she was feeling so much better now and that her diabetes had improved and her arthritis was significantly reduced. She stated that she wanted to come see me soon and continue to lose weight with the additional help of hypnosis. Finally we met. Linda was a lovely lady and still in the prime of her life. As I asked her about how she had lost her weight, she simply replied that she had followed the diet her doctor had been suggesting for the last ten years. Confused, I followed up by asking, "What changed? What made you all of a sudden decide to follow your doctor's suggestions?"

Linda said, "I don't know, I guess it was just time."

When I probed deeper into Linda's motivation to start following her doctor's suggestions, she said, "I had invited my six-year-old grandson to visit and stay with me for a few weeks during the summer, and one day after we'd climbed some stairs in my house, my grandson turned and looked at me and said, 'Grandma, you can't breathe.' After that day I just felt I had a reason to get healthy because I love my grandson and want to be around for him, and I believe he wants me to be around too."

Linda's story always reminds me of a little cartoon image that was taped to a wall in my doctor's office. The cartoon showed a man sitting on a hospital bed saying to his doctor, "Give it to me straight, Doc, how much longer do I have to ignore your suggestions?" Just as I finished reading the cartoon and started laughing, in walked my doctor. As I told him what I thought was so funny, he said, "Well, isn't it true?" I responded, "I guess it is."

My doctor proceeded to tell me a story based on something that had troubled him. He and I have a great relationship, so he felt very comfortable in confiding in me. He said, "I chose to be a doctor to help people, by sharing what I'd learned medically with them. Some years ago I remember this teenaged girl, this young woman, who was the daughter of some patients I'd seen for years. She was eighteen and a sweet girl and had just started smoking. I mentioned to her that cigarettes were real bad and that it would be good for her to stop now before smoking became a habit. She replied that she liked smoking and probably wouldn't do it for long but stated she wasn't ready to quit so soon.

"As I fast-forward, I remember mentioning her smoking every year at her annual checkups and commenting to her that she should stop. Ten years later, I couldn't believe that so much time had passed and that I hadn't been able to convince her to stop smoking. Regrettably, twenty years after she started smoking, I informed her of an unusual spot I found on an x-ray of one of her lungs. The spot turned out to be a malignant cancer and one that had spread to her throat and brain. I remember going home that night and crying to my wife as I told her what had happened. I told her how my longtime patients had entrusted their only daughter to my care, and I'd failed them."

At that point, I couldn't take anymore. I couldn't ignore the pain on my doctor's face or bear to hear the pain in his voice a moment longer. I said, "Doctor, you're a fine man and a great physician, but you're being way too hard on yourself. Do you know what Buddha would have said in regards to your predicament? 'No one saves us but ourselves. No one can and no one may. Our path is ours alone to walk.'"

My doctor thanks me to this day for having shared that saying with him then, when he needed to hear it most. Many times we forget our limitations, which are great in regards to changing others but which are nearly nonexistent in regards to changing ourselves.

You're Not the Boss of Me

It appears our pride and our egos know no bounds and require constant massaging to avoid feeling threatened and obligated to push our chests out to exert our control, no matter how unreasonable. Heaven forbid anyone direct us in any way; after all, that would just prove us to be weak and not in charge. This logic goes something like this:

$$no = yes$$
$$don't = watch\ me$$
$$stop = go\ or\ no$$

So our mental/physical response to them is "Yes, watch me go" because "you're not the boss of me." I first heard that phrase—"You're not the boss of me"—on a comedy show years ago, one starring real-life husband and wife team Jerry Stiller and Anne Meara. Anne would yell to Jerry to do something like "Take out the trash," and Jerry would yell back to Anne, "You're not the boss of me!" Then after Anne left, Jerry would mumble to himself and say, "Who does she think she is? I'll take out the trash when I'm good and ready." Moments later Jerry would say, "I think I'm ready to take out the trash now." It was a great show, and the scenes mostly ended with Jerry doing whatever needed to be done but not until he was "good and ready."

Marsha, aged thirty-two, shared her story of a trip home after a night of getting wasted on alcohol and benzos. She had been expected home after work at about 6:00 p.m. Marsha worked at local retailer located in a tough neighborhood, and her family always worried about her until she arrived home safely. Her family consisted of her husband and her three children, and they were all looking forward to seeing her, especially this evening. Six o'clock came and went, and so did seven, eight, nine, ten. Finally, Marsha arrived home a little after 3:00 a.m., staggering up the stairs and bumping into the walls leading up to their apartment. As she approached the door and fumbled for her keys, the door opened, and her husband yelled, "Where the f——k have you been?" Quickly she responded, "You're not my father, and you're not the boss of me, and I'll do whatever I damn well please!" One thing led to another, and within minutes after a major screaming match, Marsha was out the door, promising to resume doing what she'd been doing. As she left, she said, "Don't wait up." Four days later when Marsha finally returned, the apartment door was ajar, and everybody was gone. The closets were empty, and the only things left were some hanging birthday decorations and some uneaten birthday cake. Still visible on top of the cake were the words "Happy Birthday Mom. We Love You!" And alongside of the cake were three beautifully hand-designed birthday cards and some words from her husband written on a birthday napkin, saying, "Don't wait up!"

As Marsha recalled how she felt that morning, she said she had mixed feelings. "I was very, very angry, but more than anything, I felt extremely empty. It was as if my whole world had just been pulled out from under me and I knew it was my fault. It looked like my husband and kids had arranged a surprise birthday party for me and had invited quite a few relatives and friends. My kids had even baked me a beautiful five-layer birthday cake." Marsha said she cried for almost an hour and then drove back to the package store for some more vodka.

We're always so hell bent on not listening to people...just because. What is it? Is it the fact that their lips are moving, or that a sound is coming out of their mouths, or both? If someone is suggesting something contrary to what we're saying or doing, then automatically we have a disconnect? Have you ever done that, vow to continue to be destructive just to prove a point? We get ourselves into terrible situations just to show others that we can. It's just another trance that we enter into willingly to spite others. We create damage and destruction just to show someone that "you're not the boss of me."

CHAPTER 6

How I See It

Do I live in a friendly or a hostile universe?
—ALBERT EINSTEIN

"No good deed goes unpunished." Have you ever heard this saying? Well, just about every person I've met in drug treatment has. So, is it really surprising that they're in drug treatment, when they've been hanging around people who routinely say these things and probably believe what they're saying? When I ask these same people if they know where this saying comes from, they say they don't know where it comes from, but it makes sense. Does it? Does it make sense that for every good thing a person does, a punishment is sure to follow? Well, it makes absolutely no sense whatsoever to me! This saying happens to be a bastardization of a beautiful saying from the Bible. The original saying reads, "No good deed goes unnoticed." The first saying is apt to have people who believe it commit bad deeds, simply because it states there's no benefit in doing anything otherwise, unless they're masochists. The original saying, however, says uncategorically that no kindness will be left unrecognized.

Do We Know What We Want?

"As a population's food supply increases, its population increases, and as its population increases, its food supply decreases, and as its food supply decreases, its population decreases." This idea, which is tied to the ABCs of ecology and has often been communicated in discussions of population and agriculture, has perplexed humanitarian societies for decades. Boiled down, this law states that the food supply dictates the growth or the death of any population. As a population has more food available, the population grows, and as the population's food supply dwindles, the population declines. Certainly there are other factors to a population's survival, but few, if any, are more critical than the need for food and water. The dilemma that this law presents is in its circular nature. If giving a population more food will only lead to a growth in that population, which will then need even more food, how will the problem of their starvation ever end? But, if we don't give a population the food that it needs, then some of their people will die. Maybe there is more to this conundrum than just providing food. Most likely, there are other underlying, fundamental issues that also need to be addressed to permanently solve problems like these. If so, will we be willing to act on them once we recognize what they are?

A Case of Dumb and Dumber?

So this is where we are: if we want something to flourish, then we increase supply of the things it needs to flourish, and if we want something to perish, we simply decrease the supply of those same things. Flash back to 1933 and the repeal of the Eighteenth Amendment for the prohibition of alcohol. We fought vehemently against prohibition and for the right to be able to drink alcohol, and we won! The question is what exactly did we win? As you look around and see an increase in alcoholism, drunken driving deaths, and destroyed families as a result, ask yourself if you feel like a winner. I doubt the people diagnosed with wet brain or alcohol-induced cirrhosis consider themselves winners.

Now, fast-forward to 2016, and we're fighting vehemently for the right to smoke marijuana recreationally. Does anyone really believe that making recreational marijuana legal will help anyone other than the people who stand to benefit financially from it? As we continue to fight to exert our rights as human beings, we are forgetting to engage our common sense. As we continue to fight, we have to really analyze what it is we're fighting for. Are we fighting for something worthwhile or fighting just to be fighting? Can anyone say, "Déjà vu, all over again"? Is it a legitimate case this time, for something we truly need, or is it just another case of "you're not the boss of me"? In these very uncertain times, we don't need smarter phones, we need smarter people.

Technologically we may be at 7.0 or even greater, but evolutionarily we're still at 1.0.

So let's apply that law of ecology to the drug supply instead of the food supply. As a population's drug supply increases, its population of drug users increases, and as its population of drug users increases, its drug supply decreases, and as its drug supply decreases, its population of drug users decreases. It's a simple law to understand but apparently a difficult one to want to understand. Despite the growing number of people addicted to alcohol and other drugs and the destruction they leave in their wakes, we still have a very liberal attitude toward the use of those substances. Currently, some people are pushing hard for home delivery of alcohol and clamoring loudly for the legalization of recreational marijuana and other mind-altering drugs, not to mention the destigmatization of their use. But at the same time, I've never heard anyone say, "What the world needs is more alcoholics and other drug addicts on our streets and in our homes." The only people I expect to want that are the dealers of alcohol and other drugs...until, of course, the problem affects someone they love.

Let's be honest with ourselves, the more food that's around us, the more food we will eat; the more drugs that are offered, the more drugs we will take; the more guns we have, the more guns we will use; the more pornography that's accessible, the more pornography we will watch. It's really not complicated: the more available anything is to us, the more we will avail ourselves of it. Must we continue to debate these things that are already facts of human nature? We're wasting valuable time fighting fights that cannot be won, unless we use the facts we already have!

Living in a Bubble

"Hi, Joan. How are you?"

"The world sucks, and then we die."

Okay. This was an actual response I received one morning from a patient at a methadone clinic. Actually Joan had given this same response on quite a few mornings. Joan was always having a difficult time at the clinic and said she never felt anyone was trying to help her get better. She spoke about conspiracies between the nurses and the doctor and how they had colluded to water down her doses to save money. She mentioned how she noticed the color of her methadone was lighter than it had been and that she hadn't asked for any change in her dose, so there was no plausible reason for the change in color, other than water having been added.

One day I saw Joan screaming in the clinic lobby saying, "Everyone around here claims they want to help me, but I haven't received any help in the eight years I've been here!" As I passed her, I smiled, and she asked me, "Why are you smiling?"

I replied, "If you have a few minutes after you get dosed, I'll tell you why."

After Joan was dosed, (a term commonly used in the addictions field to denote that someone has been administered a medication) I asked her to come back to my office so we could speak in private. I told Joan the reason I was smiling was because what she said in the lobby was absolutely absurd. Joan's face turned bright red as she said, "Absurd? Why?"

I said it was absurd "because from the moment you walk in the clinic, you receive help. The administrative assistants greet you and update you on your account and provide you with any necessary clinical updates. Next, the nurses dose you with methadone so you can go about your day without having withdrawals. On certain days the doctor meets with you to review your medication status and how you're feeling overall, and then maybe you meet with your individual counselor or attend a group or even meet with the clinical supervisor or clinical director." I told Joan those were all forms of help, but for help to work it, has to be reciprocal. Help cannot be received by those who resist it.

We all have something called "free will," which serves as an impenetrable bubble around us that keeps out whatever we want and allows in only what we choose. So help can never enter our bubble unless it's given permission. Help is always around all of us. Maybe it's in the clerk at your local convenience store who asks, "Are you okay?" after seeing us not looking so good for whatever reason. Maybe it's on a billboard that reads, "Is now your time to quit? If so, we're here for you." Help is there at every turn; we just have to be willing to see it in order to receive it.

Dispelling Unlikely Theories

Ray was a guy who'd struggled with opioid addiction since he was fourteen. He was fifty-nine when he shared his theory about life with our group. As we discussed some ways to help prevent relapse and avoid all the horrific results of continuing to use despite all the consequences, Ray interjected that our efforts were all futile and that we couldn't change the design of the master plan. Ray suggested that there was an unalterable plan for each of us and that no matter how hard we tried, we couldn't change it. Ray claimed that each of us was born with an expiration date stamped indelibly on our behinds. He laughed as he said it and then changed the location of the stamp to different random spots, not just our behinds. Ray said that despite this notion sounding funny, he believed wholeheartedly that it was true. He gave some examples of friends who had never used drugs or drank alcohol but died young due to freak accidents and mysterious illnesses, while alcoholics and addicts he knew who did everything wrong lived to ripe old ages. I had responded to Ray's comment about the expiration date and our conversation went like this:

Me: So you truly believe that we're all born with an expiration date stamped on us, and that no matter what we do, we can't change that date?

Ray: Yeah, I honestly believe that.

Me: An expiration date like on a gallon of milk? You know, how it's stamped around the neck of the container with the date?

Ray: Exactly—just like a gallon of milk.

Me: Exactly like a gallon of milk?

Ray: Yes, exactly.

Me: So you're saying that if I had a gallon of milk in the refrigerator, it would expire by the same date as if I had that same gallon of milk sitting on the counter during a summer heat wave. It's that what you're saying, Ray?

Ray: Well, no, that's not the same thing.

Me: Why is that?

Ray: We're not milk.

The truth is, like milk, our lives are impacted by what we do to ourselves, despite any predispositions that may exist, and until we are open to realizing this fact, we are bound to act in ways that are reckless and irresponsible and dangerous to everyone. Clearly certain behaviors can speed up the process of our expiration, and we absolutely need to know this. To be under any delusions to the contrary will only serve to promote and accelerate our harmful behaviors.

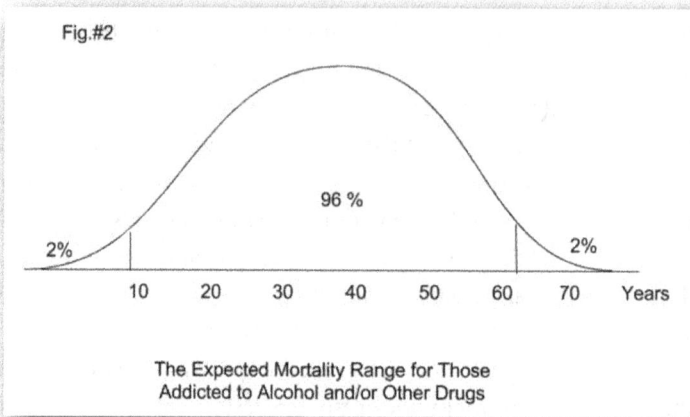

The Expected Mortality Range for Those
Addicted to Alcohol and/or Other Drugs

Figure 2 is a diagrammatic response to Ray's remarks regarding how healthy nonusers die despite their best behaviors. This diagram depicts how 96 percent of people addicted to alcohol and/or other drugs die within a certain age range, while only a few outliers actually make it to a ripe old age. Is it possible you could be an outlier? Sure, but it's highly improbable. Do you feel lucky? This diagram is only a loose representation designed to dispel the notion that users usually live long, productive lives despite their unhealthy lifestyle choices.

Stuck on a Myth

Liz was a client I saw at my office some years ago who was suffering from advanced emphysema and was still smoking. She said she thought it was time to stop and that her doctor has repeatedly suggested she stop smoking before it was too late. Liz added that the cost of her habit could pay for a new car that she really needed. She reported she'd been smoking since she was seventeen and that was thirty years ago.

Liz stated she had tried to stop in the past but said none of the things she had tried worked: the gum, the patches, Wellbutrin, Chantix, and even switching to brands she disliked. I told Liz that what she just said really wasn't fair to the manufacturers of those products because those products have all been FDA approved and have gone through rigorous clinical trials, and for the most part, they do what they purport to do. I said that what would be more fair to say when she talked about those products was "When I used [fill in the blank] and it interacted with my psyche, I was unsuccessful at stopping smoking." Liz laughed and I said,

"Yeah, that is what you should say, because with everything we use, the common denominator is always us, so we have to include us in all our successes and in all of our failures, just to be fair."

Liz said she had heard about hypnosis having worked for a friend, so she thought she'd try it. Liz stated that she wasn't sure she could be hypnotized because her mind was always racing and unable to shut down. After Liz and I spent about an hour talking and discussing all the ill effects and diseases caused by cigarette smoke, she began to smile. I asked her why she was smiling while I was talking about all the devastation smoking can wreak on the human body and even on animals. She said, "No reason."

I replied, "Liz, you have a beautiful smile, but why are you smiling now?"

Liz replied, "No reason," and I asked her again, "Please tell me why you are smiling now."

Liz said, "If you really want to know, I'll tell you. My grandmother was ninety-eight when she died, and she had smoked since she was eighteen, and she didn't die from any effects of smoking. My cousin, on the other hand, was twenty-seven and had never smoked and ran marathons each year, but dropped dead one day unexpectedly from cardiac arrest."

I said, "I'm sorry to hear about your losses, but what exactly are you trying to tell me?"

Liz replied, "I guess I'm trying to say, doesn't it all boil down to the luck of the draw?"

I replied, "Does it? The way I see it, you could barely climb one flight of stairs to my office and you're dragging around an oxygen tank with you, so clearly *you'll never be grandma* because you're already a mess and you're more than fifty years younger than she was when she died! The good news, however, is that you won't be your cousin either, because he died at twenty-seven and you're still here at forty-seven."

Instantly Liz's smile went away and her eyes glassed over as if in a trance, and before long we had hypnosis.

Liz stopped smoking after thirty continuous years of smoking. I saw her at the supermarket within the past year, and she reported she was now running 5k races and was determined to run a marathon. And as for the oxygen tank, Liz reported that her need for that tank went away within the first two years of not smoking. In Liz's case, it was imperative that we dispel the outliers in her mind before she could be successful at quitting.

This Isn't the Life I Want

My wife had a good friend named Kay who invited us over to her house one day before Thanksgiving a few years ago. Kay was sixty-eight and retired and living alone in a big house. While we were there, Kay said she had been depressed for a while and didn't know how to snap out of it. She said she had been reviewing the events of her life and realized she had nothing left to look forward to. Kay mentioned how she had been single for almost twenty years after her divorce and that she hadn't been on a date in all that time. She added that given her current obese weight, no one would want to date her anyway, and then she said she couldn't blame them.

Later in the evening, Kay complained about having some tingling in her right foot due to her type II diabetes and said that it didn't hurt necessarily, but was just irritating. I said, "You have diabetes?"

Kay replied, "What's so hard to believe about me having diabetes?"

I said, "Well, being that you were a nurse for decades, I just figured you would have known what to eat and not eat."

Kay looked at me angrily and said, "Can we just drop it?"

Since I was a guest at her home, I figured I probably wasn't being polite, so I apologized, and we changed the topic.

About two weeks after our visit, Kay said she was going to see her doctor about the discomfort in her foot, and within a week of seeing her doctor, her leg was amputated above her knee. I was blown away when I heard this because from the casual way Kay had spoken of her discomfort, I never anticipated her foot was that bad. Apparently her foot and leg had been black from gangrene before her doctor's visit, and she had been in denial regarding the severity of her problem for a while. When we saw Kay next, she was in the hospital shortly after her surgery and had just finished having breakfast. I remember glancing at her chart at the foot of her bed and noticing "AMA" or "against medical advice," written in regards to her menu. Kay had declined having food from the diabetic menu and stated that she wanted to select her meals from the regular menu. I mentioned it to Kay, and she said she hated diabetic food and wouldn't eat it, and then she asked why I was looking at her chart. Moments later a nurse brought in some black coffee. Once the nurse left the room, Kay opened the top drawer of her end table and pulled out a nearly full Styrofoam cup of sugar.

I flipped out and said, "What are you doing? Don't you know why you're here?"

Kay replied, "I can't drink coffee black. I've always put sugar in my coffee since I was twelve."

Fast-forward through another year of rehabs and hospital stays for complications due to her diabetes, and Kay was having trouble with her left foot. Before long, we had had déjà vu all over again, and Kay lost her left leg. The only thing that changed about Kay's eating habits was that they got even worse! She just would not listen to any suggestions from me or my wife and appeared bound and determined to just let herself go. Now, Kay had lost both legs, was two years older and was morbidly obese, and she saw herself as a considerably less desirable catch than she had been just two years earlier. Kay had no motivation at that point to do anything to help herself recover and to this day goes from hospital to hospital and rehab to rehab. Kay is sadly an example of someone who continues to be confused about the value of her life and who currently perceives no opportunities for happiness.

During this time with Kay, the Boston Marathon bombing happened, in which three lives were unfortunately lost and many people lost limbs. The amazing part is how those survivors, not victims, have rallied, and how they continue to demonstrate a resilience that is unfathomable. Some amputees even run in races today and participate in all types of sports events. Despite their injuries, fortunately they still can see a life worth living.

Are the Mind and the Body Really Connected?

Susan posed an extremely interesting case and had called my office only after her last doctor urged her to do so. Susan reported that she had been to ten internists and two podiatrists for an ongoing problem with her foot, and she said that the last podiatrist felt, based on his careful review of her past treatments and medical recommendations and after his thorough testing of her symptoms, that perhaps a hypnotherapist could be of assistance. Susan said she was very surprised to hear her doctor's suggestion but told him she would give hypnotherapy a shot, even though she didn't believe in hypnosis.

Susan arrived days later for her appointment along with her husband. As soon as they met me, they said almost in unison that neither of them believed in hypnosis, but that Susan promised her doctor she'd come. I smiled to hear how vehemently opposed they were to something that has helped countless people over the millennia. We must remember that our ancestors have been around for approximately six million years, and that's a lot longer than pharmaceuticals. And since the beginning of our time, hundreds of thousands of years ago, we have sustained many injuries and suffered much discomfort, but fortunately enough of us have managed to survive the tumult of life in order to be able to reproduce and allow the rest of us to be here today. What our predecessors did was no easy feat, but one that should prove, that our current debates regarding this subject are nothing more than a waste of verbal communications. This is the subject of the mind-body connection. Do you realize that as recently as the 1980s, if you had mentioned the mind-body connection to most of the doctors in any of the top-rated hospitals in our nation, they would have laughed at you? They simply did not believe in it. What's even more frightening is that many doctors still don't believe in it today!

Fortunately, Susan had met a doctor who ranked among the elite in his field and was eager to refer her to a certified hypnotherapist. After our awkward introduction, Susan and her husband both settled into their chairs and immediately folded their arms. It didn't take an expert in body language to tell me they were going to be tough clients to convince. I asked Susan to explain exactly what had been troubling her.

Susan spoke of her right foot, which had been stuck or paralyzed in the upright position for over two years. So instead of her foot resting flat on the ground, it was stuck in a forty-five-degree angle with just her heel touching the ground.

That was Susan's life, hobbling around on one foot and one heel for close to two and a half years, wearing one heeled shoe and one flat shoe and visiting new doctors almost every other month. I asked Susan to explain thoroughly how her problem began, and this is her story:

My husband and I went to visit the home of a new friend, and it was getting dark by the time we arrived at their house. As we were walking up the cement steps to their door, I misstepped due to not being able to clearly see the next step. There had been a chip broken out of the step, and the area was dark due to a lamp light overhead missing a few bulbs. I tripped and landed on my knees and on my hands, and feeling shaken and embarrassed, I waited a few moments before attempting to steady myself and get up. Just about that time, I looked up and saw our new friends Richard and Marjorie staring down at me on all fours in the grass alongside the cement walk. The first thing I heard Richard say was, "Boy, you're clumsy," and he laughed and so did his wife. Then they helped me up and ushered me into the house. I think my husband was shocked by the whole thing because he never said a word, but I could see the strange look on his face. Once inside we didn't mention my fall, and before long we were all playing cards and having a good time. About two weeks later, I woke up and I couldn't straighten out my right foot. It was just locked in an upright position! Immediately I called my doctor and was able to see her right away. That's how it all started.

Susan spoke of all the doctors she'd visited and all the tests she'd received and all the suggestions she had been given, but said nothing had worked. She said one doctor had even recommended cutting her tendon and then reattaching it after repositioning her foot, but no other doctors agreed, so she passed on that idea. Susan said the last two years had been a living hell due to the pain and inconvenience her paralyzed foot had caused:

I can't do anything I used to do, like take long walks, bowl with my girlfriends, and certainly not go out dancing like I did every Friday night. It's even a major hassle to do my job, and my job isn't that physical, but I still need to get around the office and help people with their returns and stand on my feet all day. I work in retail in customer service. So, I don't really think you can help me since all the doctors I've seen so far have pretty much given up on me.

Susan appeared very discouraged and not sure she wasn't just wasting her time rehashing what had happened to her more than two years ago. I asked Susan if she and her husband had ever seen those people again, the ones they had gone to visit. Susan replied that they saw them every week and sometimes even twice a week to play cards or to watch a sports event on cable. She mentioned that the cement step was still chipped and that the lights overhead were still out and added that they also frequently joked about her falling and what happened to her foot. They would say, "Watch out now, little girl, because you know you're clumsy," and then they would laugh. I asked Susan how she felt about their comments, and she said she didn't mind and that she laughed along with them.

I told her I was very confused and that I was getting a very strange vibe about the whole situation. I said, "Here you are, two and a half years later, walking on your heel, wearing two different shoes, unable to resume activities that you enjoy, and visiting doctors every month due to your chronic discomfort, and those people have the audacity to laugh at you. They haven't even shown you the common decency or the respect to repair the step or replace those simple lightbulbs, and you call them your friends! Despite you laughing along with them, I don't believe your foot is laughing."

Susan asked if I thought that how she felt had anything to do with her foot being paralyzed. I responded, "Since you came here for hypnosis, we might as well get on with it."

Before we began I asked Susan to remove her socks so I could see the difference in her feet. Clearly I saw a rock-hard tendon leading down to the instep of her right foot that appeared to be holding her foot hostage in an upright position.

Susan fell easily into a very deep, hypnotic trance, and as she did, I spoke of her encounter with her so-called friends and stressed that her foot was very unhappy with the way things had been handled and that it had become paralyzed due to her unreconciled differences having manifested physically. I added that now was the time to acknowledge the true relationship she's had and to get on with her life! As I continued speaking, I pressed down lightly on her right instep, and her foot abruptly relaxed into its normal, pre-paralyzed position.

I looked over at her husband and motioned for him to take a look at her foot, and he stared with a look of amazement. A few minutes later, I brought Susan out of her deep trance and directed her attention to her foot. As Susan stared at her foot lying flat on the floor, she sat motionless. I leaned in toward her and asked if she was okay.

Immediately Susan grabbed me and hugged me as she began to cry. She said she couldn't believe she could move her foot again as she tilted it upward, downward, and round and round. She and her husband both left shaking their heads and thanking me profusely. Susan called the following morning, still shocked with what had happened, and said, "This is the first time in more than two years that I can wear an actual pair of shoes, and today I'm wearing heels!" Susan has sent me quite a few clients since then.

You Don't Know Him Like I Do

Have you ever dated someone that your parents thought was wrong for you in so many ways, and the more they appeared to dislike the person, the more you told yourself you were in love with the person even if knew in your heart your parents were right? It's just one of those things we routinely do to show others they can't control us.

Here's Marilyn's story:

I was just nineteen when I met my first real boyfriend. He was twenty-eight and was the coolest guy I'd ever known. He was so different than the guys in my school and was so independent. He just didn't seem to care what others thought about him and was never scared to flip a middle finger at anyone that disagreed with how he saw things. I liked that in a guy! To me it meant he had his own mind and was his own man and didn't just listen to everyone trying to boss him around. Johnny had a nice car, and his parents had money and lived in a nice neighborhood. My parents didn't like him though; they said he was too old for me and that they didn't like the way he treated me. They didn't like how he spoke down to me and treated me like I was his child. They said he had a mean, angry face and he looked like he hated the world. I assured my parents that things were all right between us and that I didn't mind how he treated me because I knew he loved me.

I swore my parents were just jealous of Johnny because I spent so much time at his house. They had a huge house, and Johnny had his own side of the house far away from his parents. They couldn't even hear us from their side, so we always had plenty of privacy. As the months passed, things started to get bad between us after his father left his mother for another woman. He blamed his mother for the breakup and said had she just kept her big mouth shut, his father would have never left. I thought he was being pretty hard on his mom, but he told me to stay out of it and mind my own business. I realized that he was right and that she was his mom and that it wasn't my place to butt in.

Sometimes after he saw his mom and had been arguing with her, he'd come over and see me, and then we'd get into an argument, and then my father would overhear us and ask if everything was all right. Then Johnny would yell "Yeah!" and storm out of the house and get into his car and leave. A few times when my parents were away, he'd grab me violently and shake me and tell me how I didn't know anything so I should just shut up. I figured he was probably right; after all, he was almost ten years older than me.

Before long whenever I went over to see him, I could expect him to be in a bad mood and purposely pick a fight with me. One day we really got into it, and he punched me in the face. He hit me so hard I thought he'd broken my eye socket. My parents were livid when they saw my eye, but I told them not to get involved because I had really been the reason I was hit. My father had fire in his eyes and wanted to go right over and punch Johnny's lights out. I told him to stay out of it because if he caused Johnny to leave me, I would never forgive him. As time passed our fights got even worse, and once I wound up in the hospital with a concussion. My father said he had had it with Johnny and was going to beat him with a baseball bat. I stopped my father before he made it to his car, and I told him if he ever touched Johnny, he would never see me ever again, and I meant it.

My parents just didn't realize I was really in love and that I wanted to make our relationship work despite the rocky times. They didn't understand that Johnny was going through some tough times adjusting with his parents' divorce and that I just needed to be there for him and not keep aggravating him. One day when I came home early from my part-time job, I decided to go over to his house and surprise him. I noticed that his mom's car wasn't there, so I knew they couldn't have been arguing. They always left the back door unlocked, so I walked in. I didn't see Johnny in the living room or the kitchen, but I could hear him talking upstairs. I figured he must be on his phone. I went up to his room only to see him lying there naked with a girl I used to know from school, and from the looks of things, this hadn't been the first time. He looked at me and shrugged his shoulders as to say, you caught me. At that point I felt a switch turn off in my head, and all I could think of was what a fool I had been all this time taking all of his bullshit when he never even loved me.

Johnny had been playing me all along. My parents had been right from the start; Johnny was no damn good. From that very second, he was dead to me, and I no longer felt any love whatsoever for him. It's amazing how that worked; before that day I would have stood in front of a bus to save him, but after that moment, I was ready to drive a bus over him. I see him now around the neighborhood on occasion and just pass him like a total stranger, and surprisingly I feel absolutely nothing for him: no hate, no regrets, and certainly no love. I never knew love could just end like that, in an instant, but it can. I just had to wake up and finally see things as they really were.

Does It Matter How I See Things?

Our world is one of perceptions and interpretations of events, experiences, and things, animate and inanimate. They are what they are to us based on how we perceive them to be at any particular point in time, and we feel as we feel based on how we interpret those perceptions. Although we may look at the same things, we all have the tendency to see those same things in distinctly different ways, based on a myriad of uniquely individualized factors. And the ways we're interpreting those things are determining the paths we take and ultimately the journeys we'll experience throughout our lives.

Thoughts may appear to be random and sequentially come first, but actually thoughts occur due to perceptions and interpretations of past events, experiences, and things. Those perceptions and interpretations then lead us to make choices that determine our directions, which can become our paths. Those chosen paths then dictate the journeys we will take along our existence. Usually as interested parties, we begin by questioning someone's choices and then attempt to convince that person that they are headed down the wrong path based on our observations. Then we suggest, as a parent would suggest to a child (that's how it's usually perceived), that this other path would be more suitable for them. The problem with this approach is that children rarely even accept these suggestions, so why do we think adults will?

We could begin by acknowledging that our choices and our paths are neither right nor wrong but simply our choices and our paths. Surely some choices and paths will lead to pain and destruction, but that is our prerogative as individuals in a free country. Each of us will ultimately determine whether our choices and paths are leading us in the direction we want. If we ignore that fact as we attempt to help others, we may appear condescending as to suggest we know a better way for someone to live his or her life. Each person has the right to choose her or his own path regardless of where it might lead. All these suggestions, however, are mainly in reference to adults and not children, as children still require and expect guidance from us as adults, despite their seeming unwillingness in some cases to accept it or want it. Unfortunately, some children may believe they are adults before they reach adulthood developmentally and officially, and they may choose to accelerate their process and venture out prematurely down their paths.

Generally our paths run in parallel, so in our lives we meet relatively few people directly, relative to the world's population. Sometimes our paths merge, as in a family and in a marriage and also with close friends where the members usually strive to work in collaboration and bring mutual respect to the relationship. Occasionally, however, our paths neither run in parallel nor merge, but rather are on a collision course as our individual choices run in direct conflict and pose imminent threats to others. Herein lies the dilemma, not with our choices or our paths in and of themselves, but with the inevitable impact they have on unsuspecting others. And until our perceptions and interpretations of our lives change for the better, we will continue to see things as we do and continue to do those things that we're doing and remain on that collision course of destruction.

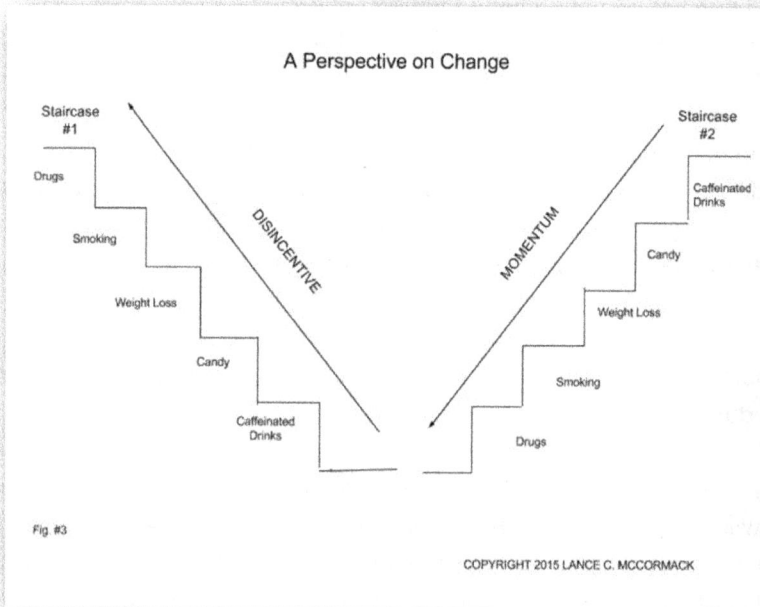

A Perspective on Change

Fig. #3

In figure 3 you will notice that all of the items listed under staircase 1 are the same as the items listed under staircase 2, and all for good reason. The difference is that they are in reverse order. The difference depicts how challenges are either easier or more difficult based on how we perceive those challenges.

Consequently, our perceptions or perspectives dictate our outcomes.

In staircase 1, the diagram illustrates the perceived difficulty in changing behaviors. It shows a staircase leading upward and lists challenges ranging from no longer drinking caffeinated drinks to stopping the use of other drugs like opioids, benzodiazepines, cocaine, and so on. Jeffrey, in this case, has repeatedly spoken about wanting to stop all the behaviors listed but repeatedly communicates how hard that will be. He claims the items on his list constitute an upward battle requiring relentless, steadfast diligence and ongoing feelings of deprivation. Jeff questions whether all his efforts will be rewarded and if there is really any incentive to work that hard. As a result, Jeff views his tasks as ones with no guaranteed payoff and ones that will likely never be achieved due to their perceived disincentives.

Staircase 2 represents Margaret's perception of her challenges. She too communicates a desire to stop drinking caffeinated drinks, stop gorging on candy, lose weight, stop smoking cigarettes, and ultimately stop using or abusing drugs. Margaret remarks that she will start her journey by stopping the easiest habit first and states that this will help her build her confidence that she can do this. Margaret adds that as her confidence builds, she will become stronger in her resolve, and as she becomes stronger, her successes will build momentum, and that momentum will make all her other habits that much easier to eradicate. She states that she expects to experience a snowball effect and then feel absolutely wonderful as a result.

Margaret and Jeff both communicated a desire to live fuller, healthier, and happier lives, but only Margaret appears to be on track with her communications. They both perceive their challenges differently and expect to experience different feelings along the way. I anticipate that their outcomes will be truly based on "how they see it."

CHAPTER 7

The Rage in Me

Never do something permanently foolish just
because you are temporarily upset.
—Anonymous

"Don't wait up!" Remember this phrase from chapter 5 that Linda said to her husband and that her husband later repeated back to her? Well, just to refresh your memory, Linda was so angry that her husband spoke harshly to her when she arrived home drunk one morning, nine hours after she was expected, that she stormed back out of the house saying, "Don't wait up!" Then Linda quickly resumed her drinking and drugging just to show her husband that he couldn't control her.

Control appears to be what we're all after: control of things and other people, and most of all, ourselves. So whenever we perceive someone's actions as being controlling of us, we balk. We act like donkeys kicking out our hind legs, attempting to shake whoever is on us. Unfortunately, sometimes we're shaking off the wrong people.

Sometimes we're interpreting their actions and/or communications incorrectly and reacting to them as threats and displays of superiority instead of signs of caring and love. I call this problem of impulsive reactivity as one based on content versus conveyance. The idea is that we benefit by looking for the content in all situations and not just by focusing on how information is conveyed. Many of us are not diplomats, so we are not trained in diplomacy. We have a tendency to get heated at times and say and do things based on our emotions that we wouldn't otherwise say or do and communicate in ways that are generally uncharacteristic of us. We yell and we scream and we shake our fingers at one another in the hopes of conveying the seriousness of a perceived situation and also to express the depth of our concern.

Unfortunately, once the yelling, screaming, and finger shaking begin, the accused generally shuts down and erects a barrier to all the content and the concern and hears only the conveyance. This is where the rubber meets the road. Once the barrier goes up, problems follow. The key to success in these situations is to simply take a breath. Taking a breath allows more oxygen to enter our brains and pacify our instinctual, primeval urge to react impulsively. This split-second exercise can change the course of history!

Let's revisit Linda's case and see how things could have turned out much differently had she only taken a breath. When she arrived home nine hours late, drunk, had she taken a breath when her husband yelled at her, she could have searched for content.

Linda could have acknowledged that she was nine hours late and said, "I'm sorry." Had she searched for content, she would have noticed her husband and her three small children standing there crying, happy to see her finally home and safely in one piece. Had Linda searched for content, she would have noticed all the birthday decorations on the walls and the beautifully wrapped birthday presents lying all around the house for her, along with the numerous cards and a delicious-looking five-layer birthday cake with candles waiting to be lit. Had Linda taken a breath and searched for content, she would have felt the fear her family had experienced in her absence and also noticed the love they had in their eyes for her. Unfortunately, Linda only heard the conveyance upon her arrival, and as a result, left the house immediately to resume doing what she'd been doing, only to return days later to an empty house and a brief, familiar phrase scribbled on a birthday napkin: "Don't wait up!"

A Rage to Live

A Rage to Live is a movie from 1965, directed by Walter Grauman and starring Suzanne Pleshette, a beautiful actress who passed away prematurely at the reported age of seventy from respiratory failure as a result of lung cancer from smoking cigarettes. She was a phenomenal actress who always captivated me. This particular movie, set in a very pivotal, tumultuous time in American history—the civil rights movement, Woodstock, and the unpopular Vietnam War—represented a time not unlike our present time. A time of tension and frustrations and of demonstrations of individualistic self-expression. A time depicting our distrust of government and our ongoing struggle for the American Dream and our unwillingness to settle for the status quo.

In *A Rage to Live*, our main character, Grace, portrayed by Suzanne Pleshette, is a troubled high school teen, not yet a woman but no longer a little child. She's the daughter of an extremely wealthy widow and the younger sister of a brother attending an Ivy League college. Grace is seduced and loses her virginity to a college-aged friend of her brother's. After this act of statutory rape, Grace becomes quite sexually active and involved with several older guys, much to her family's dismay. Once confronted by her mother, she lies and denies any allegations against her and says, "I'm not a baby, and I won't stay in a house where people think that about me, so either you take my word for it, or I'm going to pack my bags and leave right now." Fortunately for Grace, her lovely mother replies, "Very well, dear...I'll take your word for it."

That conversation marked a very critical juncture, one that many teenagers and adults face every day, where they either give or are given ultimatums. Many times the person hearing the ultimatum reacts impulsively, based on their emotions running high and from a position of hurt pride and stubbornness, and he or she responds very unlike Grace's mother and says, "Leave!" In this case, both Grace and her mother take it down some notches and concede that they both care for one another. Grace says, "I love you, Mama," and her mother replies, "I love you too, dear." That's beautiful, and that's in the movies, but unfortunately in real life, that doesn't happen nearly enough. Grace's mother has a heart condition, and after the stress of their talk, she passes out at the foot of their stairs. The family doctor is called, and he suggests that her mother take a long vacation away from the "central problem," alluding to Grace.

Grace's brother, Brock, is informed of the problem and confronts Grace regarding her actions and the stress she is causing their mother. Once again she denies all allegations and then finally comes clean, saying she didn't realize how her actions were affecting their mother. Brock asks Grace about the main boy (young man) in question and asks her if she loves him, and she replies that she hates him. He continues by asking, "Was he the first?" and Grace replies, "Yes, he was the first. I thought I loved him, but then I found out that I could feel that way about someone else, someone different."

The conversation continues this way:

Brock: Grace, that's not love.
Grace: No, but it's being wanted and needed and held close. It's almost love.
Brock: You don't need to settle.
Grace: I'm not settling.
Brock: You talk like a girl who has nothing else in her life, who nobody cares about.
Grace: No, but when I feel that way, I can't think of anything else. It doesn't matter who I am or what I'm supposed to be. Nothing matters. I can't help it!
Brock: Well, we've got to do something about this.
Grace: I know.
Brock: Maybe you can talk to a doctor.
Grace: No, I can't. I'm too ashamed.
Brock: They don't give you lectures; they try to help. You just said you can't help yourself.
Grace: All right, I'll think about it. Maybe after Mom's better.
Brock: That could be a long time.
Grace: I said I'll think about it! After all what will they tell me? "Control yourself." But I try, I do, but sometimes it just doesn't work.
Brock: Grace, from now on it has to.
Grace: I know, Brock, I know.

Now this last line from Grace is said very sadly, indicating her dismay in having to stop what she truly enjoys. This is the essence of "lust," claiming to want to stop a behavior, but at the same time being ambivalent about wanting to stop that behavior. That dialogue between Grace and Brock is classic, textbook addiction talk even though it's straight out of a movie. This talk, however, took place more than fifty years ago, and notice how nothing whatsoever has changed in our communications since then.

Let's fast-forward a few years and through a few more promiscuous affairs and to the death of Grace's mother. In the middle of the night, while Grace's mother is stroking out with a heart attack back in the hotel room they are sharing while on vacation in the Bahamas, Grace is out in the field behind the hotel stroking some waiter she met earlier. After Grace finds her mother dead, she plunges into a deep depression that lasts for some years, and then later she emerges from it to marry Sidney, an old family acquaintance. For several years their marriage blossoms, and Grace gives birth to their son. Things are going well until Grace once again succumbs to her desires and becomes dangerously entwined with a jealous farmworker. Grace tries to break it off when he tells her he's in love with her.

In this scene, Grace says, "We both knew what this was. Sure, I know I couldn't stay away from you, but I have a husband and a son that I love."

Her lover grabs her by the hair and says, "Who are you kidding?"

This stuff is classic! We do all kinds of things that we want to do, things that we feel like doing, despite knowing the consequences and knowing how those things are going to hurt people who love us. We go ahead and hurt them anyway, and then we have the audacity to tell them how much we love them. Exactly! Who are we kidding? Grace's husband finds out about her affair and confronts her. Their dialogue goes like this:

Sidney: Stop lying!

Grace: I swear. You have to take my word. I never loved him, not for a second. I don't know how it happened. I loved you, always. I couldn't help myself.

Sidney: So, you had to work it all out and make plans to meet. So, you knew what you were doing, but you went ahead and did it anyhow.

Grace: I know it was selfish and awful, but no matter what I've done, I love you. Can't you understand that?

Sidney: I'm not able to understand the kind of love that can turn around in a minute and kick your guts out. There's no love or regret here; you're just sorry you got caught. In this world you either learn a set of rules, or you don't, and if you learn them, you stick by them. They may be no damn good as far as rules go, but they're all you've got. Well, you said the hell with the rules and the hell with me, so the hell with you! We'll get through tonight somehow, but tomorrow it's good-bye, and I'm taking Billy [their son] with me!

Grace: For God's sake, you can't leave me.

Sidney: I'm sorry, but I can't live like this. I love you, but with any luck that will pass.

Grace: Do our lives all have to go up in smoke because I made one foolish mistake?

The last scene shows Sidney walking over a bridge and into the darkness as Grace repeatedly calls for him and cries. There you have it! It sounds like a soap opera, but this is also how it sounds in real life. I've heard almost these identical lines before from patients and clients I've met. We can apply this dialogue to any addiction, to anyone, anywhere, and it will all sound pretty much the same and all end pretty much like this one did, or worse. Yes, there are consequences to our actions, and having addictions doesn't make us exempt from them. For there to be a different outcome, the offender must truly acknowledge what they have done and sincerely want to change and then demonstrate their desire for change through their changed behaviors. It's called "walking the walk and not just talking the talk." Nothing else will suffice.

Too Angry for Our Own Good

We all get angry at times—that's just natural and a part of being human—but we don't have to allow our anger to get the best of us and replace our common sense with plain old stupidity. All it takes is taking a breath to change our perspective during any given situation. During a women's group I had hosted, I had spoken about the value of separating the content from the conveyance, and to demonstrate the possible opportunities lost in not responding properly, I yelled at a woman in the front row. I looked her straight in the eyes and yelled, "Take this million dollars!" Her face immediately turned beet red, and I asked her, "Did you hear what I said?"

She quickly replied, "No, because nobody talks to me like that. I don't care who you are. I'm not going to sit around and be yelled at!" She then stood up and walked out of our group.

Not at all surprised by what just happened, I asked the other women in our group, "Did you hear what I said to her?"

Immediately several women replied, "Sure. You were going to give her a million dollars, and since she didn't take it, can I have it?"

A few minutes later, the first woman returned, and I apologized for having offended her and softly asked, "Couldn't you use a million dollars?"

She said, "Yes, but I just don't like being yelled at."

Could you imagine having passed up on such a rare opportunity, especially when accepting the money could have positively changed your life forever? Have you ever allowed your angry response to cause you to lose something or someone very dear to you? Well, this is what many of us do every day, allow our anger to get the best of us and then lose out on valuable opportunities to improve our lives.

Stop it...Stop it! Now, will me telling you to stop it, propel you to continue it, because no one tells you what to do?

We'll See Who Has the Last Word

I met with a woman who had suffered with COPD (chronic obstructive pulmonary disease) for several years and who had said she wanted to stop smoking. When she called, she mentioned that she had been smoking for nearly fifty years—ever since she was eighteen. Anna stated that she wasn't sure if it was even possible to quit at this point, given that she had been smoking almost as long as she'd been alive. She reported that the cost of cigarettes was just too much and she could barely afford to continue to buy them. I asked Anna if there would be a problem if the monetary cost wasn't a factor, and she replied, "No."

It was amazing to see Anna barely drag herself up one flight of stairs to our office carrying an oxygen tank at her side, and then only minutes later tell me that the only reason she'd like to quit smoking was because of the monetary cost. Some would say, "It must be the addiction talking." I would say, "No, it's just Anna." So, here's Anna's story, since we all have a convenient story ready to give anyone who questions why we're doing what we're doing:

> I had just turned eighteen when I met my future husband, Rick. He was twenty-one and appeared even older. I had been smoking for about two months already, and Rick had been smoking for about two years. Within a year I became pregnant and had our first son. I tried to quit smoking during the pregnancy but couldn't, but I did cut down quite a bit. Rick was working and supporting us and never missed an opportunity to remind me that he was the breadwinner of the family.
>
> Rick demanded certain things: that I keep a clean house, take care of our son, and have his meals on the table and his clothes clean for work. He

also told me quite clearly that I should be ready to give him sex whenever he wanted it, because I wasn't working and because I wasn't contributing anything to the household. That used to really burn me when he said that, and sometimes we got into pretty bad fights as a result, but I would always end up giving in because Rick would threaten to throw me and our son out of the house if I didn't do what he said. It was always his way or the highway. Everything I did had to meet with his approval: where I went, what I ate, what I wore all had to be reviewed by Rick before I was given permission to do it. I felt like a prisoner in our own home, but I had no money of my own and nowhere to go.

Rick constantly complained about my cigarette habit even though he had one too. He said he couldn't continue to pay one dollar a pack for my cigarettes forever and that my habit was taking him to the poorhouse. He complained all the time about why I had to smoke so much, but the more he complained, the more I smoked. I guess I just smoked to keep my anxiety and my stress down. I wasn't going to stop smoking, especially since it was all I had. Without smoking, I probably would have killed myself!

Honestly. Rick was driving me crazy and I needed cigarettes just to calm my nerves.

Twenty-five years and two more kids into our marriage, Rick just stopped smoking one day and told me to stop too. I said that I would, but not today. Each year Rick got worse with telling me to stop smoking. He said, "I stopped smoking, so why can't you?" I told him that I could but that I didn't want to. Rick said how he hated to come home to a house that reeked of cigarette smoke and a wife that smelled the same. He said that I hadn't contributed a penny all these years to our house and that he was sick and tired of paying for cigarettes for me. We went round and round for years about my habit, until I couldn't take it anymore, so one day I got a part-time job babysitting. I wanted to make enough money to cover my cigarettes so I would never have to hear Rick's mouth again. That was a year ago, and since then I was diagnosed with advanced emphysema, a form of COPD, so here I am, trying to quit. That's my story.

After hearing Anna's story, I said, "I get the picture. Your husband tells you when to get up, what to eat, where to go, what to wear, what to buy, and when to go to sleep. Clearly he controls you. My question to you is, are you willing to go to your grave to prove a point? That he may control every aspect of your life, but he can't stop you from killing yourself if you want to, and you're going to prove to him that you can. It sounds like the old saying 'cutting off your nose to spite your face.'

Anna stopped smoking after fifty years of a having a habit fueled by anger!

You Remind Me of Someone I Hate

Suzanne stopped smoking after thirty-two years of lighting up, all on her own. No gum, no Wellbutrin, no patch, no Chantix, no nothing...except a thought. Suzanne had come to see me not for smoking cessation but for something else, and she just happened to share with me how she had stopped smoking. She had met the father of the first of her three sons some twenty-seven years ago, when she was only seventeen. Suzanne said she had been smoking since she was twelve and had smoked every day without fail until she finally quit.

After having two more relationships and having two more sons, Suzanne had decided to see how life would be as a single, nonattached woman. "Men have screwed me over my whole life and have given me nothing but grief," she said, "and now I'm just going to focus on me for a change. I hate the fact that I have to do it all alone, but I can't trust men to be there for me when I need them. I had three sons all needing a father, and I had to be both a mother and a father to them, and it just wasn't right. The worst part is that I already see their fathers in them, in the ways they act, and I hate it! You know, I love them and all, but I already see them mistreating girls and talking to them like dogs. I raised them the best I could by myself, but I think they're going to be exactly the same as their no-good fathers."

After a brief silence, I asked Suzanne, "So how did you stop finally smoking?"

She replied that she had adopted a really cute, female puppy, just a few weeks old, from the pound almost a year ago. She stressed the fact that the puppy was a female and said, "The last thing I needed was another male anything in my life." Suzanne then spoke about driving down the street one day with her puppy sitting in the passenger's seat.

She said she noticed the puppy stretching her neck and climbing up from her seat, scratching at the window like she was trying to get to the top. "I almost had an accident because I was looking at her and wondering what she was doing." Then, Suzanne said she realized what was happening: her new little puppy was trying to get air from the little opening at the top of the window. She said she could see that her cigarette smoke was choking her little, innocent puppy, and she thought to herself that her puppy didn't deserve that. "I knew I had to stop smoking; otherwise I would harm this precious little pup who does nothing but love me. I threw my cigarettes out the window and never picked up another one."

I said, "That's quite a story, but I'm confused. You had three sons, and you had smoked all throughout your pregnancies with them and then continued smoking throughout their lives, and at some point, when they were merely infants, you were smoking as you drove them around in your car and they probably gasped for air just like your puppy did, but their struggles for air didn't make you quit. Why?"

Suzanne replied, "I don't know. I guess I was just wasn't ready."

Now, do you think it was simply a case of Suzanne just not having been ready to quit, or was it possibly something more?

A Life Unfulfilled

Jason thought the world was out to get him and that he had been born to be tortured.

Every day, thoughts of "Why me? Why me?" crowded his mind and colored his behaviors. "So many people have what I want, and they all seem happy to have it. They laugh, they sing, and they all seem to get along, but not me. I'm different, and nothing is going to change that. So I might as well get used to it...get used to being laughed at and made fun of because this is my life. I'm deaf and I can't speak. I was born this way. Nothing is wrong with my vocal cords, I'm just unable to talk because I've never been able to hear. If I could hear, my life would be perfect, and I would be happy!"

Jason said this to me on the first day we met as he stood in line to get dosed. He had been a patient on methadone for nearly twenty years and had never seriously contemplated getting off of methadone. Jason said methadone helped him forget all the bad things in his life and helped him stay calm and able to raise his family. He had four girls and one boy from two different women. Jason said he loved his kids and was happy that all of them could hear and talk. He said he would never wish being deaf and unable to talk on anybody.

I asked Jason about how he started using opiates, and he said he'd been smoking pot first and then sniffing glue. Jason said that when he was about sixteen, a friend told him that heroin made him "feel like a king" and said he should try it, so he did. Jay said he remembered that when he first sniffed heroin, he felt like nothing bothered him and that he didn't even feel like he was different. "Now, things are different though," Jay remarked. "If I take heroin now, it just doesn't feel the same, even if I take a lot, not unless it's really good stuff. It's hard to break through methadone. Now taking heroin just makes me feel irritated because it doesn't work the way it used to, and then I get in trouble at the clinic because I piss dirty!"

Jay and I spoke many times after our initial meeting even though I wasn't his assigned counselor. I just happened to like him, and I guess vice versa. The great thing was that he had been assigned an interpreter at the clinic, so our communications were much easier. Apparently Jason was some kind of mechanical/electrical genius, because ever since he was a little boy, he had been building and fixing things: electrical motors, car engines, pipes, and anything else that needed fixing. Jay had many opportunities for work due to his amazing talents, but drugs always got the best of him and before long unfortunately disabled him and left him unable to do all the things he was born to do.

It seems Jay was one of eight and the only one with a handicap. He hated his siblings for that and tried to hurt them however he could when given the chance. He'd turn off the television volume when he was watching TV with his younger siblings and tell them, "Since I can't hear it, you're not going to hear it." Sometimes Jay would even lock them in the closets when his parents weren't at home and not let them out until he saw the custom-installed light flashing at the door, indicating his parents were back. He knew his parents would never believe his siblings if they told them what he had done, because they felt sorry for him and felt responsible for his handicap. It wasn't that his siblings were bad to him, because they weren't, it was just that he felt bad for himself and felt he had to get even. No matter how his family tried to love him and compliment him on his talents, Jay saw only what he lacked. Up until our last meeting, Jason talked incessantly about his anger and how if he wasn't always angry, he wouldn't still be using drugs, but that he expected he would always be angry because being born the way he was had robbed him of his chance for happiness.

Girl Gone Mild

Rachel was a miserable woman by all accounts, always complaining and always in a foul mood. She could find a dark cloud if she was sitting on the sun. I'd asked her why she was always so unhappy, and Rachel replied, "People that smile a lot are only fooling themselves, because no one else believes what they're selling."

"Okay," I responded.

"Life is hard, and life is miserable most of the time, and if you can't be honest about that, then you're only lying to yourself." This was Rachel's reply on one of her more positive days.

A few months passed, and I noticed Rachel standing in line for our group that was about to start. She was smiling! I almost passed out. I couldn't believe my eyes. In the four years that I'd known her, I'd never seen her smile, and guess what? She had a beautiful smile! Our topic for the group was "Road Rage: Why It Occurs and How We Can End It." Immediately Rachel's hand went up, and she asked to respond. Rachel said she had had a terrible case of road rage until only a month ago.

"I was an animal on the highway. I cut people off, laid on my horn, screamed at people, and gave the finger to anyone that looked at me sideways. I even bumped bumpers with cars that were traveling too slow in front of me. I was a wild woman...was!"

"What changed?" I asked.

"I was coming back from an appointment with my doctor for some female problems. She had just told me about the results of my recent tests and said I had cancer in my ovaries and recommended I have a complete hysterectomy. I'm only thirty-three, and that would mean I could never have any kids. I couldn't believe what she told me, and I was in shock when I left her office. I got in my car, and I didn't even realize I was driving. My mind was somewhere else.

"Next thing I knew, some red-faced guy was shaking his fists at me from the next lane. Usually something like that would have caused me to go berserk and not stop until we were pulled over and I'm beating him with a baseball bat. This time was different though. When I saw his red face, it reminded me of myself when people have cut me off, but this time I realized I hadn't done it on purpose. I realized that I had not been paying attention to my driving because I was too busy thinking about having cancer and what would happen to me if the doctors were unable to keep the cancer from spreading. At that moment, I knew that other people could have had serious things going on in their lives too when they did whatever they did on the road to me, and that probably most of the time none of them intentionally set out to do anything to me, because they didn't even know me. They were probably doing it because they were distracted by some problem they were having, like I was."

"Wow! That's pretty astute, Rachel."

I saw the faces of other group members go numb as their jaws dropped from amazement. They all knew Rachel, but they never knew that Rachel!

There's Another Name for It

Fear! Yes, that's what anger is, fear in disguise. Anger is systemic and intense and a derivative of confusion, frustration, and pure, unadulterated fear. Sure, some fears can be helpful, and some can even save our lives, but anger for the most part manifests destructively. So, do you even know why you're always so angry? Of course you do.

You always knew, but were just too afraid to admit it, even to yourself. Afraid to admit what, you say? Everything! Afraid to admit that you're afraid, afraid of not having what you want, afraid of not getting what you want, afraid of not being what you want to be, afraid of not being able to be what others want you to be, afraid of not knowing what to do, afraid of not knowing how to do it, afraid that no one understands you, afraid that no one listens to you, afraid that no one respects you, afraid that others will get what you believe you rightly deserve, afraid that you are not smart enough, afraid that you are not strong enough, good-looking enough, assertive enough...afraid that you are a loser and that you'll never succeed. How's that for starters?

Imagine having so many fears and so much anger and no solutions. It's a catalyst for disaster! Fear leaves us always in a state of anxiety—this uncomfortable, self-terrorizing state that continually disrupts our lives and, as a consequence, the lives of those around us. Fear derails our best intentions. Fear masquerades as strength but is quite the contrary. We cannot experience true happiness until we understand and then allay our fears. Until we do, they will always stand in our way and prevent our best selves from prevailing. It's like placing a large refrigerator directly in front of yourself and attempting to walk forward. You can't; it's impossible, until you move the refrigerator.

Become what it is you desire to be, and let nothing stand in your way! Do what you must, learn what you must, train, work, and most of all, listen to the suggestions of others who have no personal motivations other than to offer you helpful insights. Despite what you've been told or what you've believed up until this point, you and you alone decide what you will become! You will either allow anger to define you, or **you** will define you!

CHAPTER 8

Setting the Bar

Self-expectation is a promise we make to ourselves.
—A LANCEISM

"You get what you expect." I'm sure you've heard that saying before. I happen to believe there's a lot of truth to it. It's about setting the bar as to what we expect to achieve in our lives. Michelangelo said, "The greater danger for most of us lies not in setting our aim too high and falling short; but in setting our aim too low, and achieving our mark."

Mary and I had this very insightful conversation one day, and I think it gets to the essence of what many of us know to be true about expectations:

Me: Mary, you continue to say that you want to stop drinking alcohol and using other drugs, and I've said to begin by reading the Alcoholics Anonymous book, also known as the Big Book, and consider doing the twelve steps. You said you would months ago, but you still haven't even obtained the book. Why?

Mary: I don't know why.

Me: No, tell me why. Months ago you'd asked me to help you, and I gave you some suggestions that I believed would help you, but you didn't take those suggestions, and now you're asking me again for my help. I'm confused! So again, please tell me why you haven't obtained the Big Book by now or inquired about the twelve steps.

Mary: I'm afraid.

Me: Afraid? Afraid of what?

Mary: I'm afraid to read the Big Book and do the twelve steps.
Me: Why in the world would you be afraid to read the Big Book or do the twelve steps?
Mary: I'm afraid they may work!

Now, that makes sense—perfect sense! Let's face it. The truth is, we don't expect to change until we're ready to change, and some of us are just not ready to change regardless of what we're saying to others. It's not that we can't change now; it's simply that we don't want to change now. We have all had glimpses of the power of expectation throughout our lives, and we already know it works, but we also know it demands commitment and that it requires that we make a decision. We also know that sometimes those decisions will be contrary to what we currently want. So we don't readily decide to employ any new expectation unless we believe we have exhausted all other options and that we have no other choice and until we believe it's absolutely necessary, which unfortunately may be too late in some cases.

Chicken or Fish?

If you've ever been invited to a wedding or a holiday party at a hotel or a similar venue, you've been asked this question. Chicken and fish appear to be the main choices of caterers because they're relatively easy to prepare and mostly everyone likes one or the other. In regards to making choices, Martin, a former client of mine, shared something with me that a previous substance-abuse counselor had told him upon their first meeting. The counselor said, "You look like a nice guy, so I don't want to waste your time, and I don't want you to waste mine. So right now, I want you to pick a side."

Martin replied, "Pick a side? What do you mean?"

And the counselor said, "Pick a side. Decide whether you want to be the best damn alcoholic or drug addict you can possibly be or the best son, brother, father, husband, friend, man, person you can be, because you can't be both. Don't be that person in the middle that keeps on talking about wanting to stop drinking or drugging but keeps on drinking and drugging, because they're the ones that are messing up everything for everybody. I don't care which decision you make; I'm not judging you either way. All I ask is that you make a decision. Don't spend the rest of your life vacillating in the middle, unable to make a decision, because that person wastes everyone's time. That person gives people that care about them the false impression that they want to stop their behaviors, when they know deep down in their hearts that they don't. Their loved ones naively are expecting something from them that they're not expecting from themselves. It's just not fair to them."

I thought that what that counselor said was brilliant, and I couldn't agree more. In order to achieve a new outcome, we must choose a new expectation!

Talking is easy—it always has been—but the doing demonstrates what you really want. There's a monumental difference between watching sports and playing sports, and just because you can watch sports 24/7 doesn't mean you're prepared in any way to play them. In order to be successful at achieving what you expect, you must be aligned! So many times we hear people talking about what they want to change. Sometimes we hear this talk for years, even decades. They talk about how much they hate what they're doing and about how hard it is to stop doing what they're doing, despite not wanting to do what they're doing. What you can't hear, though, is what their brains are thinking or what their hearts are feeling. If you could hear their hearts and brains talking, you'd hear them saying how much they love doing what they're doing and how they couldn't ever imagine wanting to stop doing what they're doing. That's what you call a huge communications gap! These two communications, from the brain and the heart in this case, are diametrically opposed to the communications from the mouth; they're complete opposites and 180 degrees apart, with entirely nothing in common except for the fact they're all coming out of the same body. One of the three communications is misaligned with the other two, but the people in this case are in perfect alignment for what they expect. These people expect to continue to do what they're doing, and they are; therefore, they have achieved complete success. Although there are three forces at work here, only the brain and the heart must be aligned in order to achieve one's expectation. Ideally all three—the thoughts from our brains, the verbal communications from our mouths, and the feelings from our hearts—should be aligned, but due to the staggering myriad of games we humans are capable of playing with words, the verbal component is not a necessary prerequisite for success at achieving expectation.

Expectation mobilizes an internal directive that exerts an energy unwilling to accept defeat. This force can be either linear or nonlinear in its approach or even present as a combination of the two, but once this force is in motion, it can be neither stopped nor deterred unless the expectation itself is altered. Therefore, it is imperative that we are both aware and honest about our expectations and any hidden agendas we may have, as they will manifest as they are directed.

Closely related to expectation, we discussed some popular perspectives of addiction in chapters 2, 3, and 4, and by now I am certain you've been thinking about your own.

Maybe you fully believe in one perspective or another, or maybe you disbelieve all of them and you have already formulated some unique perspective of your own. However, whatever you currently believe, please remain open to consider yet other possibilities.

Emotions Rule

Words are powerful! How many times have we heard this phrase? Imagine we were sitting in a small room together, just you and me. Written around the perimeter of the room like crown molding were words, just random words. I asked you to look at the words, and you did, and you didn't appear to have any reaction from having looked at the words. Next, I constructed sentences from those random words and then directed the sentences to you. Within moments, everything changed! Within moments, I had control of your physiology: your pupils, your heart rate, your blood pressure, and even the largest organ of your entire body—your epidermis. Honestly, I probably had control of even more things of yours, but this a good starting point.

The moment I constructed those sentences and directed them to you, everything changed. By directing the sentences to you, I gave them context, and by giving them context, I made those sentences personal. The moment those sentences became personal, you exhibited feelings based on how you interpreted those sentences. You looked at my face when I said them to you, you contemplated my word selection, you listened to my voice and its inflection as I spoke, you noticed my body language as I sat, all in an attempt to determine what I meant by what I said. Based on your determination, maybe you laughed, maybe you cried, maybe you felt like strangling me, or maybe you felt embarrassed by what I said and just wanted to slink down into your chair. In any event, you had a visceral reaction, whereby your body's functioning changed as your pupils dilated, your pulse quickened, your stomach tightened, and your skin reddened. I had control of your physiology, all due to some words I said to you, and that doesn't make sense at all.

Still, we act as if the words we use are unimportant, by continuing to use words that set us up for failure. Based on the concept of expectation and how "expectation is essential" to achieving success, do the words we select actually set us up for success? What if we are consciously choosing certain words in order to ensure that we continue to get what we want or to ensure that we continue to remain as we are? What if we're accepting labels for ourselves in order to continue doing exactly what we want to do? It reminds me of a man who was reading the back of my business card aloud and who then asked me, "Why would anyone want to end a sex addiction?"

"I'm an addict. I'm an alcoholic. I have an addiction. I have a disease." Why on earth would anyone accept these labels for themselves and then fight vehemently to hold on to them? Have you ever wondered why so many people would stand up in front of so many others and announce that they are addicts and alcoholics? Some might say, "Because that's what I am, and that's who I am. I'm no longer in denial, and I've finally come to accept this is who I am and this is what I have." My response is, not so fast! I can see the value of acknowledging that you have a problem, but reaffirming that you have a problem and that the problem is you, day after day, year after year, is itself a problem! It's self-serving and highly counter-productive, unless of course your goal is to relapse.

Just about now, some people may be taking umbrage to my questions and to my statements, fearing they don't like the direction I'm heading. Sorry, but I'm going there anyway. Because this game of brainwashing in our society has been going on for far too long. I've hosted countless relapse-prevention-type groups and have repeatedly heard people introduce themselves by saying, "Hi. I'm so-and-so, and I'm an alcoholic/addict." The words flow effortlessly from their lips...too effortlessly. Remember, in order to be someone else, you have to first see yourself as someone else.

What to Affirm

We are going to dissect some labels and get to the bottom of what they really mean and also get to the bottom of what you mean when you say them. Early on in my training as a hypnotherapist, I read about a psychiatrist by the name of Dr. Émile Coué from Paris, France, and his writings regarding the power of affirmations. Dr. Coué noted that he often prescribed different remedies for some of his patients even though those patients all had claimed to be suffering from the same maladies. He decided to give prescriptions for medications to some and prescriptions of positive affirmations to others. The patients who received his positive affirmations were to recite them daily: first thing in the morning, again in the afternoon, and then as the last thing before going to bed. Surprisingly, Dr. Coué found that in more cases than not, those patients who were prescribed the positive affirmations to recite fared better than did their counterparts at feeling better and recovering sooner from their maladies. This account is not designed to undermine the effectiveness of medications but rather to underscore the fact that medications are not the only way to effectively treat human concerns.

Affirmations are statements we make about ourselves and to ourselves. These are statements that we attest and affirm as being true about us. These attestations validate our beliefs as to who we are and who we aspire to be. When we say, "I am an alcoholic," or "I am an addict," or "I am both," we are speaking as salespeople, and we are actively selling. We are aggressively selling ourselves an idea of who we really want to remain being!

If you've ever been in sales professionally, you've probably been taught to speak of your sales aspirations by using the present tense, as opposed to the future tense. For example, during your first week with the company, you're already repeating to yourself, "I am the top salesperson in my company." We both know that you haven't even sold one thing yet, but you know that you expect to sell a whole lot of things real soon. Now, this may sound crazy to those of you not in sales, but to the salespeople, it makes perfect sense.

Salespeople know that in order to achieve success, they have to think as though they have already succeeded. They know that this kind of thinking creates an energy that will drive them to succeed. Dr. Émile Coué knew this back in the 1840s, but we struggle as a society to understand it now in 2016!

"I am" are words that constitute an affirmation. The most powerful sentences in the world also begin with the words "I am," so we can't take these words lightly. "I am well," "I am sick," "I am dying"—all these phrases indicate states of being and how we perceive ourselves to be.

An affirmation affirms and attests to what we believe to be true in our heart, in our soul. An affirmation conveys what we believe ourselves to be at present and what we aspire to be in the future. So when we say "I am an alcoholic" or "I am an addict," we are saying that this is who we believe we are down to the very core of our being, and this is who we expect to remain. You can't keep saying "I'm a drunk" and not be a drunk. And we all know what drunks do...drink! The moral of this story is, if you want to continue to drink, then continue to call yourself a drunk.

It's interesting to note that the definition of the infinitive *to addict* in *Merriam-Webster's 1984 College Edition Dictionary* reads, "to give oneself up to a substance or an activity." In 2012 their *Collegiate Dictionary* reads, "to devote or surrender oneself to something habitually or obsessively." So the noun *addiction* would pretty much mean "the result of having given oneself up, devoted oneself, or surrendered to a substance or an activity." Neither dictionary definition suggests that the addict is someone who has been taken by force or coerced in any way, but instead both definitions state that the addict is one who has given himself or herself up voluntarily to something.

My definition of addiction is "the desire, *above all*, to reproduce past pleasurable results over and over again." And although I am fond of my definition, I really love the image of someone giving herself or himself up to something because it makes the cure that much easier. Because if we've voluntarily given ourselves up, then at will, we can simply take ourselves back. This is totally contradictory to the notion that addiction is something that has taken hold of us against our will, in which case, we have to wait patiently and pleadingly until addiction decides, if ever, to release us. And, like a potential client asked me once before, "Why would anyone want to end a sex addiction?" Are the answers to this question any different for any other addiction?

"I have a disease called addiction." Why is that? I mean why is it that you say you have a disease because you've given yourself up to a substance or an activity? Is it like Alzheimer's disease or macular degenerative disease, or is addiction less like a disease of the mind and more like a state of the mind...a "trance state," specifically. Unlike diseases, trance states are fluid and can change easily as deemed necessary. Trance states exist once we meet certain conditions, and once those conditions are met, the trance continues until new conditions are met. So maybe addiction and disease both could be considered "'conditional"? However, a disease in many circles today describes a condition that is bound by science to worsen without proper medical interventions and one that may even worsen despite those interventions. The problem with diagnosing addiction as a disease in America, lies in the conveyed erroneous definitions of what a *disease* is. Thus, patients and caregivers unfortunately make erroneous interpretations. Rarely has the actual true dictionary definition for *disease* been used in our recovery communities, but rather we've heard highly customized, hyperbolic versions of the truth. Fortunately, the truth is much tamer than its fictional versions and, yes, we can handle the truth. The reason the need for this distinction exists is because words are very powerful to human beings. The way we interpret words can make the difference between life and death. Words move us to actions, so it's imperative that we use the proper definitions in order to derive the proper actions.

I've always been amazed by how patients describe addiction and disease. So many of them have very similar interpretations, probably based on having heard similar things. Surely, patients may spread many mistruths among themselves, but in many cases, they are also told mistruths by members of the recovery community, including their medical and clinical professionals. I know this to be true because I have personally heard these mistruths proliferated throughout recovery groups, forums, seminars, and other professional discussions. So, based on these mistruths, it's no wonder that patients have such erroneous definitions for addiction and disease that they continue to spread throughout their families and communities. Here are just a few of the definitions that I've heard:

Addiction: "something you got from your genes."
Disease: "something that does not go away 'cause you either did it so much that you can't stop, or you built a tolerance for it, which makes it a disease you can't stop doing; it just stays with you forever."

Addiction: "something mental or physical that takes over your life."
Disease: "something that keeps on getting worse until you go for treatment."

Addiction: "needing something to survive."
Disease: "something that will just get worse if you don't take what you need."

Addiction: "In my case, I caught a habit by using pills and then needing more pills."
Disease: "something that needs medications to fix."

Addiction: "being born with something that's in your blood."

Disease: "not your fault, something that has been waiting inside you for the right moment to come out."

Addiction: "only some people get it if they have the special gene."
Disease: "only medications can deal with it because it's so strong."

Addiction: "to be born with something that mentally and physically controls you."
Disease: "like a worm in your mind that keeps on growing that you never can kill."

Addiction: "compulsive behavior to do something, something that makes you unable to control yourself regardless of what you do."
Disease: "something that can be deadly if left untreated."

Addiction: "the inability to control one's own behaviors."
Disease: "the inability to change yourself."

Addiction: "a demon inside your head that keeps telling you to do the wrong things."
Disease: "a problem with not being able to not follow what the demon says."

Interesting! All these accounts are from patients who were receiving some sort of medication—methadone, Suboxone, naltrexone, Vivitrol, or Antabuse—were enrolled in a substance-abuse treatment program, or both.

Now, back to those dictionary definitions. As I mentioned before, the definition for *addiction* is "the result of having given yourself up to a substance or an activity." The definition for *disease* is "the condition of the living animal or plant body or of one of its parts that impairs normal functioning and is typically manifested by distinguishing signs and symptoms." Neither of these definitions sounds scary to me or gives me the impression of lifelong agony, unlike those given by the patients. The point I'd like to make is, that the more devastating we make anything sound, the more difficult we make that thing to overcome. We must begin by turning down the rhetoric and turning people onto the facts, minus the dramatic effects, in order to combat addiction effectively.

Do you consider smoking cigarettes an addiction? Okay, then as a smoker, do you also have a disease? Now, you may have a disease from having smoked—such as COPD, lung cancer, and so on—but does the fact that you are smoking mean you have a disease?

Have you ever heard of anyone who has stopped smoking cigarettes on their own and never returned to smoking? Do those people incessantly talk about being in recovery from nicotine, or do they just say they stopped smoking? People stop giving themselves up to substances and activities every day without medical interventions. Do you honestly believe that people are bound by science to continue their destructive behaviors, or could they actually be continuing their destructive behaviors based on lust?

Again, expectation is what sets up future orientation. Based on understanding the power of affirmations, we should conclude that calling ourselves addicts or alcoholics, especially beyond the point of accepting and no longer denying that we have a problem, only sets in motion a future orientation for that problem. As we cement in our minds the notion that we expect to always be alcoholics and addicts, we make that expectation reality.

If you must say you are an alcoholic or an addict and you truly expect to remain one for life, kindly disregard the following sentences. As I stated in the beginning of this chapter, "You get what you expect." I have coined a term that will get you free, if that's what you expect. But first, I will share with you the definition of that term: "someone who is convinced unequivocally that alcohol and other drugs have no place in their body." The term is *a believer*. Just about now you're probably saying, "You mean I'm supposed to stand up at an AA/NA meeting and, after my name, say I'm a believer?" Yes, that's exactly what I mean! I know, it's against what everyone else there is saying, but I don't care, and neither should you, because that meeting is *your* meeting designed to keep you sober. So what others say and do is their business, just as what you say and do is yours! So I ask you, are *you* a believer?

An Unfortunate Exposed

Rick was very articulate and always quick to express his opinions. One day during a group, he responded to our conversation by disputing the power derived from reading the Big Book of Alcoholics Anonymous and downplaying the success of the those following its twelve steps. As Rick continued vociferously stating his argument, other members of our group very noticeably became agitated while listening to his rant. I intervened and asked Rick why, since he had so devoutly read the Big Book and so meticulously followed its tenets, did he suspect he was still having problems remaining abstinent? I added that since he had read the book so many times from cover to cover, he must recall where it states that the book will work for everyone, even for those with mental disabilities, but "not for the few unfortunates, those people that are constitutionally incapable of being honest with themselves." Rick nodded that he had read that passage, and then I asked him point blank, "Are you one of those unfortunates?"

Rick appearing stunned as he looked around the room. He stared at the ceiling for what seemed like minutes and then responded by asking me, "Have you ever seen the movie *The Shining*?" I responded that I had. Rick spoke of how he had that movie on Blu-ray and how he occasionally fast-forwarded it to the part where the main character walks into a bar that's about to close. Meanwhile, our other members looked on quizzically as Rick continued to recount the scene from the movie. He spoke of how Jack, the main character, talks the bartender into setting him up with a bottle of his favorite before closing the bar and then proceeds to get smashed. Rick added that at that point of the movie, he pours himself a drink, and then another...and another.

Simultaneously several group members yelled out, "Why do you still keep that movie?" and "If I were you, I'd go home tonight and destroy it!" I then asked Rick, "Will you, I mean will you, go home and destroy that movie tonight?"

Rick looked back at me with a smile and said, "Remember when you asked me if I was one of those unfortunates?" I said yes, and Rick replied, "Who am I kidding? I love to drink. That's what I do. I love to drink!"

I replied, "Bingo! There you have it. You're finally telling the truth and being honest with yourself."

You know, we never saw Rick again. I hope he's doing fine. If he's not, we know at least that Rick is doing what he wants and that he's no longer pretending. And as long as Rick shares his truth and his decisions with the people in his life who love and care about him, they can in turn make their decisions as to their continued involvement with him. I guess it proves once again that honesty is the best policy.

Done!

Mike had smoked for forty-one years, five packs of cigarettes a day. That's virtually having a cigarette in your mouth all day and all night. To many, what Mike had was an addiction. To Mike, what he had was an unwanted, filthy habit that was depriving him of being the person he wanted to be. He wanted to be energetic, healthy, and calm and present to others the image of being in control. After all, he was an upper-level manager in a Fortune 500 company. Unfortunately though, Mike was none of the things he had hoped to be when we first met. His prior actions had undeniably confirmed the fact that hope has nothing to do with success.

Scenario: Imagine it's the deep of winter, and you just got off of work at two o'clock in the morning. It's dark as you walk through the icy parking lot to your car, only to find out that your car won't start, no matter what you do. You're cold and tired and just want to go home. You call someone you consider to be a friend and explain your predicament. Your friend states that he understands your situation and that he will try to come and pick you up, and he adds that he hopes he can. You hang up feeling unsure as to what he meant exactly, but after several hours pass, you realize he's not coming. You're angry because you're freezing and have no way to get home. You call another person you consider to be a friend and again convey your situation. She replies, "I'll have to get dressed, but I'll be ready to leave in ten minutes, and I should be to you within an hour. If I'm going to be any later, I will call you back, but I don't anticipate having any problems."

Now, in the first scenario, when your so-called friend didn't show up, you were probably angry, but you shouldn't have been because he never promised you anything. He spoke about trying and hoping, and as a result he didn't do anything. You should have expected that based on his choice of words. Sorry! As for the second person you called, if she didn't arrive to pick you up, you'd have every right to be angry with her because she made a commitment to you, she made a promise to you. Big difference!

Back to Mike. He communicated over our session how he was ready to quit and how he no longer was playing the games of saying he wanted to stop smoking when he had known full well in the past that he had never had any intentions of doing so. Mike stated that he had been "stupid" long enough and he had finally realized it was time to take his life back. So he did. Mike fell deeply into hypnosis moments later and awakened a nonsmoker. That was seven years ago. About five months ago, I ran into Mike at a sporting goods store, and not only was he still not smoking, he was participating in the Senior Olympics and was in the store looking to purchase a discus. Are you kidding me? A sixty-four-year-old man who had been smoking five packs of cigarettes a day for forty-one years is now competing in a discus event. That's beautiful!

So why was Mike so successful at stopping smoking? The answer is that he was truly committed. Just like in our scenario, Mike had made a commitment and a promise to himself. Mike wasn't trying or hoping, and he wasn't indecisive or ambiguous about what he wanted. Mike was in full alignment with his goals. His head and his heart and his communications were all aligned, saying the same thing. Do you know that the day after Mike quit smoking, he called me and said he felt great! Now, how was that possible? How could anyone who smoked five packages of cigarettes a day for more than four decades just stop one day and not even feel any withdrawals? How is that scientifically possible? I'm glad you asked. Once again, Mike demonstrated what results when a person is truly committed to making any significant change. In the figure below, you will see what science claims to be true and what our physiology proves to be true.

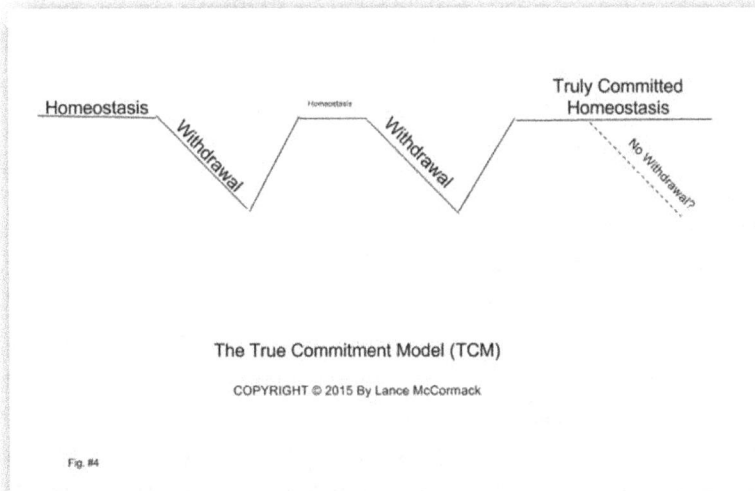

The True Commitment Model (TCM)

COPYRIGHT © 2015 By Lance McCormack

Fig. #4

Science would have us believe that anyone who abruptly stops any addictive behavior, especially those involving taking drugs or any chemicals, is certain to have a negative reaction or withdrawals. The medical profession and science would also lead us to believe that human beings are protracted by nature and wired to make changes very, very slowly. They also attempt to convince us that human beings possess little willpower and require their constant medical and pharmaceutical interventions in order to accomplish anything. As a result, the pharmaceutical industry has had a field day with manufacturing products for every aspect of our lives. Now, we have products to wake us up, keep us up, make us feel happy while we're up, keep us more alert while we're up, keep us erect while we're up, and then fortunately more products to help us fall asleep, and better still, others to help us stay asleep. You must be kidding me! The worst part is that we've fallen for their sales pitch, hook, line, and sinker.

I always have to laugh when I recall an old television commercial. It features this guy about to walk past a diner window, when he stops dead in his tracks and pastes his face against the glass as he watches the cook grilling a large steak-and-cheese sandwich. The background monologue speaks about how this guy has some type of gastrointestinal reflux disease and how he really pays the price when he eats greasy foods. Moments later, here's our guy sitting at the counter of that diner with a large steak-and-cheese sandwich on his plate. He's got an ear-to-ear grin on his face as we notice a bottle of medication off to his right. The monologue continues with some facsimile of "now you can go for it." The inference is that, although you have a gastrointestinal disease and feel the ill effects of that disease when you eat greasy, fatty foods, you can rest assured that by drinking their medication, you will not suffer the consequences of having eaten that food. Now, does anyone think we're that stupid?

Yes! Because we know we have reflux disease; regardless of whether we can feel the effects of eating fatty foods or not, we still know we have *reflux disease*. But they know that all we care about is not feeling the effects of reflux disease, because they know that we just want what we want.

How many times have you heard someone talk about taking baby steps in regards to stopping a behavior? I've heard it said so many times it makes me want to barf. Where do you believe they first heard it? You guessed it—from the medical community. In many of these cases, what they're saying is just nonsense, and it undermines our ability to exhibit the dynamism that we possess. Now, I am not suggesting that we should abruptly stop taking our heart medications or any medications that have been legally prescribed to us. What I am suggesting is that when we're discussing addictions to food, caffeine, tobacco, stimulants, hallucinogens, marijuana, gambling, sex, pornography, and a host of others, we can be dynamic in our approach and feel fine in the process. I only say this because I have seen this to be the case whenever people are truly committed to stopping any behavior. If I hadn't seen this accomplished countless times with my own eyes, I wouldn't be making these assertions...but I have! Now, I didn't mention drugs like alcohol, opioids, benzodiazepines, barbiturates, and some others only because they generally require some sort of detoxification process first that may also include the aid of other medications. Nonetheless, users of those drugs can also act dynamically in their approaches to end their addictions, and we'll discuss those ways specifically throughout this book.

Now I'll explain how the true commitment model works. I'm sure you're already on the right track as to how you think it works, so I'll make my explanation brief. Many of us who talk about stopping a behavior really don't want to stop that behavior; we just want to convince others that we do. During this process of attempting to convince others, we may take all kinds of medications and agree to all kinds of tests, studies, and treatments, only in the effort to support our claim that nothing can be done. The smoker says, "I've done everything you've asked. I've tried to stop cold turkey, I've taken the gum, the patch, Chantix, Wellbutrin, and nothing has worked!" My response, when you say you've tried everything and nothing has worked, is that you're not being fair to the makers of those products because they've all been clinically tested and scientifically proven to do what they purport to do, whether it's inhibit the reuptake of serotonin or whatever. So what you're saying isn't fair to them. What would be fair in your communications going forward is to say, "When I tried, [fill in the blank] and it interacted with my psyche, I was unsuccessful." Now, that's being fair, because you acknowledge the common denominator in all of those failed attempts: you!

Many of us are already aware that we possess natural painkillers in our bodies. These natural painkillers are our bodies' very own opiates. We know these as endorphins that produce a pleasurable, analgesic, pain-relieving effect. These are powerhouses, and they don't cost anything, so we don't have to go looking for a dealer in the middle of the night in order to experience them. In addition to these endorphins, we have dynorphins. Dynorphins have been known to possess an exponential painkiller effect and exhibit a strength in excess of seven hundred times that of morphine. That's more powerful than any opiate you could find anywhere, from anyone on the planet! Although some recent studies of dynorphins suggest reasons to block these powerhouses, the fact remains that we have tremendous untapped painkilling powers within us.

Back to the true commitment model. We as human beings are always working subconsciously to maintain a level of stability, a level of balance, a level of homeostasis. As best we can, we strive to consume foods and drinks daily in order to achieve and maintain this equilibrium. Again, using an example of a smoker, in the TCM (true commitment model) diagram, you can see where homeostasis declines and then again where it returns each time after resuming smoking. At the far right in the diagram, you'll notice that when you'd expect withdrawal to occur (represented by the intermittent line) it doesn't, but instead homeostasis is maintained. The question is, why? Homeostasis is maintained because the person (the smoker in this case) is truly committed to stopping smoking. And since he is truly committed to stopping smoking...a miracle occurs inside of him! I say "miracle" because we are all miracles, designed from miraculous things.

The sooner we become aware of this, the sooner we will experience these miracles. When we are committed to changing any behavior, our bodies know we are serious, and they come to our rescue, then and only then. Remember those dynorphins? Well, those dynorphins come to us when withdrawals would have otherwise come to us. It's as if they are saying, "Don't worry—I've got you!"

SECTION IV

The Second Element of Addiction: An Energy Imbalance

It never feels quite comfortable walking on an angle.
—A LANCEISM

This section explores energy, as it applies to human beings. The following chapters will cover how energy works for us, how our energy can become unbalanced, and how readers can regain their energy balance and as a result strengthen their resolve for abstinence.

CHAPTER 9

What's Energy Got to Do with It?

The energy within us will determine who we are.
—A LANCEISM

Everything...that's what energy has to do with it! Energy is everywhere and in everything. Whether it's in motion or has the potential to be in motion, energy is available in many forms, like in the radiant energy in the sun we see as light, or in the thermal energy surging through our radiators that we feel as heat, energy is at work all the time. Energy happens to be measured by its ability to do work. Logically then, directed energy has the ability to do much more purposeful work than energy that is undirected or misdirected.

Energy...we all want it, and many of us will go to extraordinary lengths to get it. Energy comes in many forms and can be utilized in many ways. Energy imbalances in any form present challenges to the user and can create agitation, anger, confusion, damage, discomfort, dissatisfaction, fear, frustration, pain, perilous conditions, withdrawals, and even death. We are all painfully aware of what happens when hydropower regulated through a dam exceeds the dam's capacity for that energy or when the electrical energy demands of an electrical circuit exceed the circuit's ability to provide that demanded energy. What if energy works the same way in the human body? What if energy imbalances in our bodies and in our minds could lead us to being predisposed to addictions? It could be a bad thing, a very bad thing, but it also could be a very telling thing that's absolutely something worth knowing and understanding. The great news is that most imbalances can become balanced as long as there's an honest desire to do so.

Measured by more than just the ability to do work, we are the flow of energy that courses through our veins. We are the energy that ignites our soul to do miraculous things. We are the energy that creates in us the desire to be more than appears humanly possible. We are truly wondrous things! This energy is the basis of life and can also be measured in a subject's ability to experience pleasure through neuroelectrical processes, and pleasure can be a beautiful thing as long as it remains in balance. Whether we're trying to stimulate our minds and bodies or trying to calm our minds and bodies, energy is the medium we tweak in order to derive the pleasurable feelings we seek. Sometimes, very innocently, an energy imbalance can begin and develop into something very, very dangerous.

In human beings, energy is a result of hydroelectrical intercellular activity. It's the outcome of synthesized materials in a fluid form interacting with electrical impulses. What exists in that synthesized material dictates the level of electrical charge produced and transmitted and ultimately the level of communications expressed. Therefore, we can control to a large degree how we feel, how we think, and how we act through what we take into our bodies.

Think of all the things we consume every day: all the things we drink, all the foods we eat, and all the medications we take. All these things provide some kind of energy, and in return all these things create demands for that energy. Once our bodies get accustomed to having something, a demand for that something exists. It just makes sense. So we have to be extremely careful as to what we're consuming because we may be quickly getting in over our heads by creating bodily demands we can't possibly sustain. Please review the following list of some of the things and activities that can create questionable energy demands in our bodies, and note if any of these things would be on your list:

- alcohol & other drugs
- nicotine
- caffeinated coffee
- excessive sugar consumed by itself or in foods & drinks
- Red Bull
- Mountain Dew
- 5-Hour Energy drink
- Monster Energy drinks
- diet pills
- candies
- cakes
- cookies
- pies

- gambling
- exotic dancing (stripping)
- pornography
- sex
- shopping
- dangerous extreme sports
- video games

As you can imagine, the list of things that can create energy demands is quite long, so I've just mentioned a few of some well-known, commonly consumed items and activities, so we all can have some familiar examples. Since all these things create energy demands in our bodies, it would stand to reason that the more of these things we have, the more demands our bodies have for these things. Additionally, all these things cost money, and what happens when we run out of money and can't afford these things every day? An energy deficit happens, and then we're stuck like a motorboat without an engine, searching for a way home. We're left to our own devices to find satisfactory alternatives, whatever they may be.

In the meantime, how do we feel with this built-up, unfulfilled demand for energy, this energy deficit? For starters, we feel weak, disoriented, agitated, and depressed. As you might suspect, these feelings of disequilibrium will not go un-addressed or unsatisfied for long. During this time, it's as if we are focused almost entirely on reestablishing our internal chemical balance, and this focus will not dissipate as long as we know there exists ways, albeit temporarily out of our reach, that will satisfy our imbalance. If we were glasses of water, we would look like this:

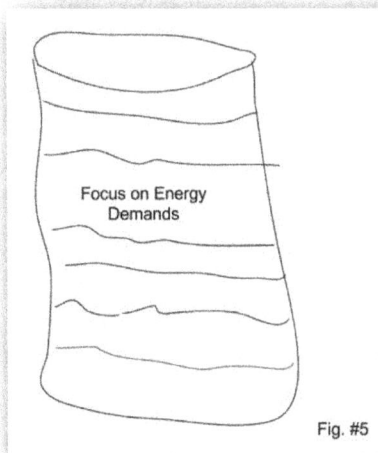

Focus on Energy
Demands

Fig. #5

Yes, we'd be a wobbly glass of water! Imagine that this glass has a tight lid on it and the water inside has no way of escaping, so the energy inside the glass (you) just keeps on building up pressure. That's exactly what happens to us, and that pressure in us comes in the form of a bodily tension, an alarming discomfort that keeps us feeling we're not quite whole and that we're missing something very important.

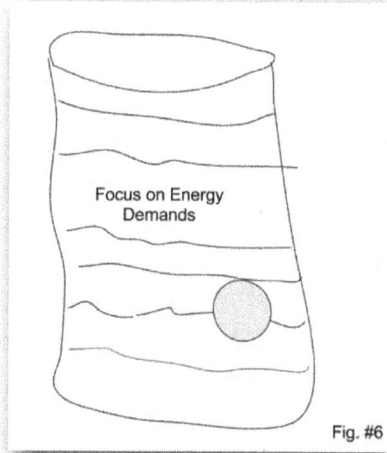

Focus on Energy
Demands

Fig. #6

In figures 6 and 7, you can see that there's a hole in the glass now, and that hole allows energy to escape and be diverted to other things that give us energy, like exercise, physical work, interesting hobbies, other people, and of course healthy foods and drinks that provide us with clearer thinking, greater feelings of calm, and less extreme surges of unsustainable energy.

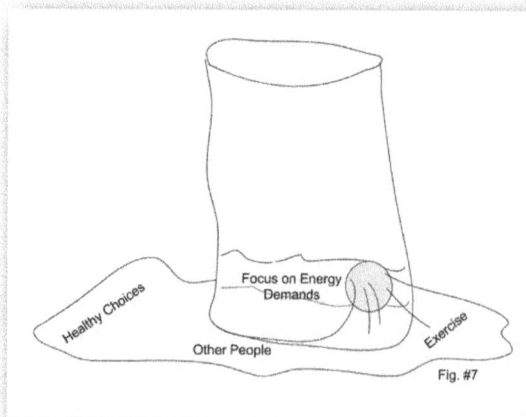

Focus on Energy
Demands

Healthy Choices

Exercise

Other People

Fig. #7

Diversion is but one way to redirect misguided energy. We will discuss diversion again, along with several other strategies, thoroughly throughout the course of this book. They all work, but it's still up to you to decide whether you're ready to do your work!

In this chapter we've lightly touched upon what energy is and how it works in our bodies, and we briefly covered how energy demands are created and one method by which those energy demands can be satisfied in healthy ways. In the following chapters, we will expose what it really feels like to be chemically imbalanced and how our sensitivity to life in general changes dramatically once we choose to cross over and disregard the power of energy.

CHAPTER 10

Unaware and Unprepared

Simplicity brings more happiness than complexity.
—BUDDHA

The simple solution is often overlooked as we search for complicated answers.

Many times we find ourselves concocting convoluted stories, when the truth could have easily served us better. Routinely we adopt new constructs, new beliefs, new memes about how things work, without any deeper investigation. We just nonchalantly accept things as if they were truths, and many times from people we don't even trust. Science uses a method, the scientific method, in which people first have ideas or hypotheses (educated guesses about how something works), and then they experiment, and based on the outcome of their experiments, they draw conclusions as to whether their guesses or ideas are valid. The question in our case is in the validation. Are we attempting to validate our need for using mind-altering drugs or trying to validate our lives through the use of these drugs?

The sad part is that some of these ideas, these constructs, are seriously flawed, and many others are downright wrong. Imagine living your entire life based on life-threatening misconceptions. If nothing else, make a promise to yourself to keep things simple from this point on, and rely more on what your body is telling you and less on what those in your sinking boat are saying. Remember, there are no bunk beds in a casket.

Life can be challenging enough without adding all the unnecessary drama and misinformation. If we can listen more and talk less, we can seize opportunities to emerge victorious from the chaos we've created. I remember working at a methadone clinic some years ago, and one day just before our usual group started, a new guy to our group looked at me and said, "Man, not another group. No offense to you, but for more than thirty years, I've been coming to groups, and there's nothing you can say that I haven't already heard before," and I replied, "Perhaps, but maybe this time you'll listen."

There's a big difference between hearing and listening. If our hearing is sufficient, of course aural sounds and words that are made and said will be heard; it's just a function of hearing. Listening, on the other hand, is much more interesting because, although the sounds and words are entering our physical pathways through hearing, it's not until we listen that we have the opportunity to, at minimum, consider value in what we've heard and make a decision as to how to utilize that valuable information; otherwise it's just white noise.

That gentleman whom I spoke of was a little taken aback by my reply, but later he actively participated in our group and then became a regular participant in our subsequent groups and even began talking about tapering off of his methadone dose and having a life again after thirty years on methadone. How's that for the power of listening!

Now, as we've already discussed, everything around us consists of energy. Whether it's chemical energy, mechanical energy, thermal energy, nuclear energy, kinetic energy, or latent energy, it's all energy. And in the world of drug use, our energy is all focused on drugs. We know that energy can be neither created nor destroyed—that's just one well-known law of physics—but we also know that energy can be diverted, converted, transferred, or transformed. Think of focusing your energy away from drug thinking for just a moment, and then imagine that same energy directed elsewhere. How powerful that would be! The great news is that it can be done, and you can do it!

Before we continue, we must admit to ourselves how this all began. Back in chapters 2, 3, and 4, we touched on some of the ways society believes you came to be as you are and how you've bought into some or all of them. I'm saying there were and there are other things contributing to your predicament, and energy is at the root of them. Have you ever seen a parent either carrying an infant or pushing an infant in a stroller? Sure you have. Have you ever seen that parent give that infant a bottle?

Again, sure you have. Now, have you ever seen that parent give that infant a bottle filled with soda or another sugary soft drink? And the answer is…? I've seen it happen on more occasions than I care to remember. This is one of the simple pieces to our puzzle. As we've agreed, we will keep things simple and listen to our bodies and respond accordingly and not concoct convoluted stories when the truth would serve us better.

Many times in drug treatment facilities, I have found parents or a single parent giving soda to an infant and/or a young child or children, and that's the drink they all consume. Sugar-laden, caffeinated sodas and caffeinated drinks in general. According to *Webster's New World Dictionary College Edition*, "Caffeine is a stimulant to the heart and central nervous system and a substance formerly used in chemistry." A substance formerly used in chemistry also qualifies as a drug, and another definition of a drug is "any substance used as a medicine or an ingredient in a medicine." As for sugar, they may not call it a drug, but it certainly is a psychoactive substance "which has a physiological effect when ingested or otherwise introduced into the body." So some of us have become accustomed to giving these drinks to our children without realizing we were giving our children medicinal drugs. Now, for what reason exactly are we continually drugging and medicating our children? The answer may terrify you!

For children already used to sugar and caffeine, we as parents continue to drug and medicate our children with sugar and caffeine to combat their withdrawal symptoms.

Their symptoms of withdrawal by definition are "distressing physiological and mental effects" that sound a lot to me like uncontrollable crying, kicking and screaming, and being unable to be calmed down easily. Imagine what comes next after months or years of this behavior: a trip to the doctor to discuss the uncontrollable, unwarranted behaviors of your child. And after careful consideration and deliberation (sorry I'm being a little facetious here), the outcome is routinely a diagnosis of ADD or ADHD (attention deficit disorder or attention deficit hyperactivity disorder).

Now what disorder is complete without a prescription of medication or medications? Methylphenidate hydrochloride, better known by its popular brand name, Ritalin, has been widely used and widely documented as an overprescribed medication for developing children diagnosed with ADD or ADHD. When I was a kid, we had overactive kids too, but Ritalin was not readily available, and those kids were directed to play more sports and engage in other physical activities that took advantage of their overstimulated minds and bodies. Times have changed considerably, but children have not.

As a younger man, I worked at a Sheraton hotel as a front desk clerk, and sometimes I moonlighted as a limousine driver for a popular classic car and limousine service. On one particular day, after having worked an eight-hour shift at the hotel, I went home, changed into my suit, picked up the limo, and traveled about twenty minutes to pick up a couple who were looking to travel to New York. I was selected for this particular job because I was born in New York City and was familiar with a lot of the surrounding area.

My passengers were going to attend a function at a hotel in Rye, New York. The function was to begin at 10:00 p.m. and last until 3:00 a.m. The drive took roughly three hours, and we arrived at our destination by 9:00 p.m. At about 11:00 p.m. while I was sitting in the car and just staring out into the darkness, it dawned on me that I had been a little overzealous in taking the assignment. After all, I had worked all day, picked up my passengers, driven for three hours to our destination, and now I'd have to wait six hours until their convention ended and then drive another three hours to get them back home. What an idiot! I was already exhausted and it was only 11:00 p.m.

I never was one for taking drugs, but that night, based on being so tired and knowing that I still had a long night ahead, I started to consider the option. My rationale was that I didn't want to have an accident on the way home and kill us all in the process, so I knew I needed something.

Finally, I made the decision, against my better judgment, to go looking for drugs. Back then, Rye, New York, wasn't that happening a place late at night, so it took me a while before I spotted a neighborhood that would likely have some. After almost an hour of searching, I wasn't about to back out now. I bought what I thought I needed, and I took it without hesitation.

At 3:00 a.m., when my passengers returned exhausted to the limo, I was ready for them. I opened the rear door and ushered them into their seats with a big smile and began to bombard them with questions about their evening as I drove off. It probably sounded more like an interrogation. I couldn't stop talking. I remember just staring at them as they looked at me, horrified and probably wondering what in the world had gotten into me to be so talkative. I even pushed aside the divider between the cab and their seating area and said, "I want to hear everything about your convention, and don't leave out a detail." I talked incessantly all the way home. My passengers couldn't have been happier to arrive at their door!

Three days later, after not having slept a wink since New York, I was back to my job at the front desk talking with some hotel guests when my hand started to shake uncontrollably. I remember the guests looking at me and looking at my hand shaking as I pushed it down to the counter. Once the guests left, I looked at my right hand again, and it was still shaking. I didn't know what was happening to me, but I didn't like it.

Suddenly I knew why my hand was shaking. I asked myself, "That did this?" Right then and there was the defining moment. I recognized that I had two options:

Option one: "That did this? I guess I need some more of that, and I'll feel better."
Option two: "THAT did this! I must NEVER have THAT ever again!"

Selecting option one would have meant awakening each day for the rest of my life to trembling hands before taking that drug. Selecting option two meant that once I waited out my discomfort, my hands would never tremble again due to that drug. So, what was that drug?

This was the eighties, so coke was big, and crack was huge! Amphetamines and methamphetamines were the craze, and hallucinogens were widely used. My drug was in, my drug was hip and wildly popular. My drug was caffeine. On that fateful night in New York, I had ingested two large Styrofoam cups full of black coffee and sugar. Those were my first cups of coffee ever, and my last!

Dehydrated and Malnourished

Most of us believe we're good parents, and we honestly believe we're doing everything we can to raise healthy children. The truth is that we only know what we know. The problem is, we may not know enough! Proper nutrition is imperative, especially for the developing child. It's not that we deliberately set out to sabotage our children's health, but we ourselves may not know what good health really entails. We can only pass on things that were passed on to us or things that we have learned along the way. This is not about blaming; this is about becoming aware, so that we don't continue to do the wrong things and so we don't continue to communicate the wrong messages.

In earlier chapters we touched on some views about addiction as a disease that's genetic, and we'll talk more about that in coming chapters, but for now I'd like to float another idea about addiction. A woman once said to me that she was sick of people disputing addiction as a genetic disease when clearly it is. She stated that it's been proven over and over again, but still we have this ongoing debate. She reported that almost everyone in her family tree is either an alcoholic or a drug addict and that she just was born to be addicted like all the rest before her. She said, "With that kind of history, how can addiction not be hereditary?" What do you think? Do you think she has proven a case for causation, and that since almost everyone in her family has battled addiction, she was genetically predetermined to be addicted? Maybe, or maybe not.

Imagine a child being raised from birth in a family that didn't really understand much about good nutrition. They were good people, just not well versed in the facts that all foods are not created equal. They believed that as long as their kids were eating and drinking something, they were getting adequate nutrition. After all, kids are known to be picky eaters, and sometimes we're lucky if we can get them to eat at all. Now, since this family doesn't know much about the nutritional differences between different foods and drinks, it may be safe to say they're also unaware of their respective energy values.

They're unaware of the benefits of nutrient-dense foods or the dangers of nutrient-deficient foods. Say their children didn't drink much water or milk or consume many water-dense foods like fruits and vegetables or eat many proteins like chicken, fish, meat, or vegetable protein sources, but instead either drank sugary drinks and drinks with caffeine or drank nothing at all, while they regularly consumed simple carbohydrates like french fries, pancakes, and waffles. Now, many of us know that a diet of soda and other caffeinated drinks and processed foods like pancakes and waffles may not be the best things for our kids, but did we know we could be setting our kids up for addiction?

Simple-Carbs-to-Water Ratio

This ratio measures the proportion of simple carbohydrates to water. The higher the ratio of simple carbs to water, the higher the tendency for an elevated blood sugar level. The higher the blood sugar level, the greater the risk for dehydration and malnutrition.

Here's an interesting story about sugar. Its details may not be 100 percent accurate, but I believe they're close enough to illustrate my point. In 1793 a cargo ship carrying barrels of sugar, rum, and apparently some water, ran aground with five sailors on board. After nine days stranded on a deserted island, the sailors were rescued but were found to be in terribly emaciated condition. Every one of them was severely dehydrated and malnourished.

Upon return to their home port, the sailors were treated and questioned as to what they had consumed on the island that would have contributed to their sickly condition. The sailors reported they had consumed a steady diet of sugar, rum, and water. François Magendie, a renowned French physiologist, was eager to understand why these sailors had become so malnourished when they'd had the luxury of sugar, rum, and water. Magendie decided to conduct some experiments on dogs, giving them a similar diet of sugar and water. After approximately thirty days on a diet of just sugar and water, all the dogs were dead.

What was learned from this experiment was that humans and animals cannot survive long on a diet of sugar and water or just sugar. Conversely, both humans and animals can subsist on just water for quite some time. So the moral of the story is, if you're ever on an island with just sugar and water, forget the sugar and drink the water!

This is not to say that human beings don't need sugar, because that's absolutely not the case. In fact, our bodies need sugar to survive. Our energy comes from sugar, and our sugar comes primarily from both complex and simple carbohydrates. Complex carbohydrates from natural foods like fruits and vegetables metabolize slowly and methodically, while simple carbs in processed foods like french fries and pancakes metabolize quickly and erratically. Just like automobiles need gas as their fuel, we need sugar as ours, but we need the right types of sugar and the right amount of sugar. And like cars, our bodies also need other things, all in the right amounts, in order to run efficiently. Besides fuel, both cars and humans need oxygen, and if there's too much fuel and not enough oxygen, our car engines don't start, and our human engines run poorly. And besides air, car engines also need water to cool them down, and so do we. All these elements—sugar, water, and oxygen—are needed in our blood. If there's too much sugar in our blood and not enough oxygen, we have problems, and if there's too much or too little water in our blood, we have problems. With too little water and an excess of sugar in our blood, the effects from consuming simple carbs in particular are dramatically intensified, not only creating dehydration and deoxygenation, but also creating a pleasurable effect and a bodily demand for more sugar. How do dehydration and deoxygenation affect the development of addiction? Directly! They affect the development of addiction directly. The more simple carbs we give our children in proportion to the H_2O we give them, the more we predispose them to develop anxiety and depression, and as a result, greater cravings for simple sugars.

Another Important Ratio

How about the proportion of simple carbohydrates to complete proteins—do you think this ratio has any bearing on addiction? Sure! How can it not? Few of us will dispute that water plays a crucial role in our cell environment and blood volume, but have we given much thought to the role of complete proteins (the ones with all the essential amino acids) in regards to our cell development and nutrient absorption? We need these essential amino acids daily in order to function and perform efficiently, otherwise our enzymes and other important cell structures begin to degrade and cause muscle breakdown and atrophy. This process is somewhat complex, but the basis of it is very easy to understand. Without our necessary daily intake of essential proteins, our bodies begin to cannibalize themselves in order to survive. Unlike the nonessential proteins that we make internally, we must consume these essential proteins from external sources. So if our diet consists mainly of simple carbohydrates from processed foods and caffeinated, sugar-laden drinks, besides dehydrating and deoxygenating our cells, we are destroying our bodies' ability to grow and develop normally, both mentally and physically. This means that all the things that make us human, stand at risk, and as we attempt to live our lives in this extremely fragile, weakened state, alcohol and other drugs stand at the ready to fill the void.

By the way, what do you think is usually the first psychoactive substance an infant consumes? For that matter, the first psychoactive substance a fetus consumes? Wouldn't it be sugar? In most cases it would be. What if this same infant or fetus was given copious amounts of sugar regularly as part of her diet? Would she develop a ravenous bodily demand for sugar? How do you think she'd feel if she went a day without it? We spend so much time debating whether tobacco, alcohol, or marijuana is the gateway drug, but who is talking about the most logical choice for that coveted position of the ultimate gateway drug—SUGAR! Perhaps the mother of all addictions!

Yes, it can give birth to all the rest. Well, I know I'm stepping out on a limb as I'm boldly suggesting that sugar is the gateway drug. Here I've said it, and I'm not taking it back.

I'm saying that consuming inordinate amounts of sugar in relation to water—and, for that matter, also in relation to the consumption of complete proteins—predisposes human beings for addiction. It makes no difference if that human is a fetus or a senior citizen—too much sugar in a person's diet will lead to anxiety, and anxiety will lead to searching for solutions to quell that anxiety. Whether that solution is alcohol, food, opiates, benzodiazepines, cocaine, crack, gambling, methamphetamines, marijuana, sex, shopping, or something else, there will be a hole that develops inside of us that needs to be filled, and we will ultimately fill it with something.

So, parents, stop what you're doing, pull that bottle of soda out of your baby's mouth, and never put it back in. Replace those sugary drinks with water and freshly prepared fruit and vegetable juices, not store bought, and begin feeding your children fresh fruits and vegetables. Add low-fat, complete proteins and good sources of healthy fats to their diets, and redirect your children's palates while you still can to get them onto the road to a healthy and happy life free of sugar cravings!

CHAPTER 11

Buckle Up, 'Cause Here Comes the Roller Coaster!

Controlled is what we claim we don't want to
be, unless of course it's our decision.
—A LANCEISM

So now that our kids are thoroughly dependent on caffeine and copious amounts of sugar at a young age, what do we do? That's the big question. We've created this energy demand in them, and now it needs to be satisfied. Caffeine appears innocent enough at first glance, until you feel the effects of not having it: headaches, irritability, shakiness, dizziness, the inability to concentrate, and other unsettling side effects. And yes, those all disappear after you have your fix, but those withdrawal symptoms only stay away until caffeine's pleasurable effects wear off. What exactly are caffeine's pleasurable effects to a person who has already become dependent on caffeine?

To the new imbiber of caffeine, the effects are powerfully apparent. Something has clearly changed within you; you feel more stimulated than ever before, and it feels exciting to be that exhilarated. But, is that the way you feel now as a seasoned caffeine drinker? The likely honest answer is no, because although you feel better after having your first cup of "joe" in the morning, or after your first soda or energy drink, you mainly feel better because you're getting rid of the withdrawal symptoms you created by your last use of caffeine. Who wouldn't be happy to get rid of uncomfortable feelings or preemptively head off symptoms before they come?

And who couldn't easily mistake getting rid of or preventing these uncomfortable feelings for pleasure?

And besides quelling your withdrawals, you're "chasing the dragon." That's a familiar phrase in the drug world, meaning that after you become enamored by a drug's initial pleasurable effects, you can spend the rest of your existence subconsciously chasing the high you initially experienced, but never finding it ever again. It's like someone just played the biggest joke on you, and now they are laughing all the way to the bank because they've just hooked another "custy" (slang for customer) for life, saying, "You'll be back!"

So these so-called pleasurable effects of caffeine on a caffeine-dependent person are really nothing more than the feelings they would have felt naturally before they became dependent on caffeine: no headaches, happy, calm, stable and alert, and cognitively in control. We have gained nothing by becoming dependent on caffeine and have only jeopardized our ability to maintain homeostasis normally. It is critical, especially for the developing individual, that we understand where this road leads. There is nothing mysterious about chemical dependency; it is all very calculable, logical, and methodical.

Sure, some dependent caffeine drinkers contend that they're not dependent on caffeine at all but simply like the aroma or the taste of their drink and maybe enjoy the coolness or the warmth of their beverage, and that's understandable. Freshly brewed coffee smells terrific, and many caffeinated soft drinks taste delicious. What's not to love? Whether we as adults choose to acknowledge that we're dependent on caffeine is not important, since we as adults are making the choice. What is of dire importance is that we realize we are also making these choices for our children, who are completely unaware and totally unprepared. This is not intended as a diatribe against caffeine, but as a wake-up call to how we are unconsciously creating problems where there were none, especially in children and young individuals who look to us for proper guidance.

As time goes on with the use of any mind-altering drug, whether it's caffeine or methamphetamine, what we've become used to, at some point, no longer has the same effect. This phenomenon is known as tolerance, needing more of a drug to derive the same desired effects. But actually tolerance is only one part of the cycle of use: sensitivity, tolerance, desensitivity, and then resensitivity constitute the steps in the progression of use. First, we begin using a drug and become sensitive or sensitized to its stimulating or narcotic effects, and we like it, so we keep on using it.

At some point, either sooner or later, we become tolerant or used to our drug's effects—so used to its effects that we experience no real effects at all from the current drug, and we don't like that. After becoming tolerant to our drug, we welcome the return of all the bells and whistles. We acknowledge at this point that since what we used last time didn't ring our bells, we have become tolerant or used to the current amount of our drug, and we determine from that assessment that we will need more of that drug or something more powerful next time to experience that feeling we first fell in love with.

That leads us to desensitization, which is somewhat similar to tolerance but much more destructive. It's similar to tolerance in that being desensitized also means you no longer feel the drug's effects as you once did, but it differs greatly in the scope of its impact.

Tolerance defines the chemical changes, whereas desensitization defines the overall visceral changes. Desensitization sets the stage for anhedonia. Many of us are very familiar with the term *hedonist*, that person who seeks pleasure above all else. Well, the term *anhedonic* or *anhedonia* means just the opposite: that person who, according to a 2015 edition of *Merriam-Webster's Dictionary*, is someone who has "a psychological condition characterized by inability to experience pleasure in acts which normally produce it." Some other definitions describe *anhedonia* as "the loss of the capacity to experience pleasure" and "the inability to gain pleasure from normally pleasurable experiences."

This is huge, and this is a game changer! This means that life in general will never, ever feel the same, and it predicts with certainty that life will eventually lose all its luster. This means that the more we continue the cycle of using psychoactive drugs, the more desensitized we become to life itself. Experiences like looking forward to your favorite meal, or really enjoying the intimacy of sex with your partner, or even feeling that special love that melts your heart when you gaze into your newborn child's eyes will eventually disappear, and you'll be left instead with feelings of only emptiness. Then you find yourself being diagnosed with having depression when what you really have is anhedonia that you caused yourself, but unlike depression, anhedonia isn't so easily remedied.

The big problem here is that you don't even see anhedonia coming; it's like a stealth bomber that slides in during the night and blows up your entire city while you're sleeping. So instead of stopping your use of alcohol or other drugs, you gleefully proceed to the next step. This next step is resensitization, when we consciously make a decision to up the ante and use more of what we've previously used, or we decide to gather input from other users about what's really "kick ass" these days, and we consciously choose to take the plunge and become resensitized at whatever cost.

These four steps, from sensitization to resensitization, constitute what I call the "hamster wheel of lust," the beginning of the "rat hole." I call it the hamster wheel of lust because this continuous, hedonistic, lust-driven, selfish existence will be your life until you decide you no longer want it to be, or until your lust for alcohol or other drugs takes your life, whichever comes first. Unfortunately, these four steps of mental processing usually do not occur in young children, at least consciously; they just know they want to continue to feel good, and unfortunately they have few tools with which to express to us what they're feeling, so they act out, a lot.

Now, we've been talking about caffeine, but this also applies to the excessive use of sugar in all forms: foods, drinks, candies, cookies, and so on If it's something used to alter our moods or our activities, it has the potential of being abused and being something that can punch our ticket to the hamster wheel of lust. Imagine having anything that constantly requires you to have more and more of it in order to get the feeling you used to get. Imagine having to find a way to get that thing as you need more and more of it just to feel "normal" again. Imagine this is the problem your eight-year-old is facing, but the child doesn't know it, and neither do you.

So what happens next? After months or years of trying to get your out-of-control child under control, you're worn out and open to any solutions, whether they have side effects of not. Now that soda and candy no longer seem to do the trick of mitigating your child's bad behavior, you realize you are in way over your head, and you have no idea what to do next. For the spankers out there, a so-called "good spanking" used to solve the problem, but now not even that works at calming your child down. Before, you were willing to cause your child's overstimulation with sugar and caffeine because at least she appeared happy and wasn't whining and crying all the time, but now she is cantankerous whether she has her regular caffeine and sugar or not.

Time for professional help. Something is wrong with your child, very wrong, and you know that unless you get help, she is only going to get worse. After talking with family and friends and just getting blank stares when it comes to any solutions, you decide to ask for professional help. Seeing a school counselor sounds like the ticket since they're somewhat familiar with your child and with other children who may be experiencing the same problems. The problem is that the counselor is likely to suggest the same solution he or she has suggested for all the other children with similar symptoms. So without knowing your child's in-depth family history or dietary habits, that counselor is focused on treating your child's symptoms, not their root causes.

This is nothing whatsoever meant against school counselors; they are fine people, working extremely hard, especially these days with the kids we give them. Another problem is that these counselors are inundated with kids that have many problems, and more problems every day. Some of us believe we can drop off our kids with our problems, and somehow they will be returned to us all fixed. In the course of a school day, counselors are supposed to identify, correct, and/or refer our children with problems to all the necessary resources,…and, let's not forget, also collaborate with teachers as they attempt to teach our children all they need to know.

Scenario: Consider for a moment what you do when you purchase a new car (I know, another car analogy). It doesn't matter whether it's brand spanking new and has never been used or if its odometer reads many miles, as long as it's new to you. When you first get this car, you can't believe it's yours, and you're so happy to own such a fine vehicle. You want to know everything you can about it: what kind of engine it has, how fast it can travel per hour, how many miles it gets to the gallon, all about its features and amenities, and even about the amount of octane it requires in its gas (87, 89, or 93 super unleaded).

So we are very interested in what our new car needs to run efficiently, and we wouldn't dare think of putting something in it that doesn't belong there. Imagine being late for work, running down to your new car, and then realizing when you jump into your car that your gas gauge is on "E" and you've already learned that "E" in your new car means there's absolutely nothing left in your tank. Suddenly, you remember that you have a fresh gallon of Tropicana orange juice in your refrigerator. Now, do you think you would you be inclined to get that orange juice and pour it into your gas tank? Why not? You're in a rush and have to be somewhere important. You may even know that chemically the orange juice could break down into metabolites sufficient to power your new car the distance required to get to your destination, so why don't you use it? The reason you don't use the orange juice is because you know that it doesn't belong there in your tank. Regardless of whether it can get you to where you want to go or not, you know there'll be major consequences to using it; maybe your filters will clog, your ignition system will fail, or maybe even your engine will seize up, but in any case, whatever happens, you know it won't be good. Whatever happens, you know there'll be a price to pay for having used that orange juice, and you know that the car you love will no longer be working as it should.

So, I'm asking you to show yourself and your children at least the same consideration you would show your car, and acknowledge the fact that some things belong in you and some things don't! This isn't a matter of our mothers, our spouses, our doctors, or our anybody else telling us anything. No one is trying to control us or direct us in any way. This is simply a nonemotional, nonjudgmental fact: some things belong in our bodies, and some things just don't! We ingest harmful things into our bodies in all kinds of ways and demonstrate no consideration as to what ultimately may result as long as the immediate result is gratification. And to make matters even worse, we also exercise this lack of respect toward others whom we are entrusted to protect...our children.

People, let's get back to keeping things simple and providing our children with the proper care and nutrition they need, so they can be prepared and available each day at school to learn and in general to develop as individuals without having to cope with a multitude of unnecessary challenges. That means we must stop medicating our children with caffeine and copious amounts of sugar before they feel the need to graduate and go searching for the next best thing that will help them feel normal.

Journey into Nothingness

In the pleasure sensitization model illustrated in diagram 4, you can clearly see how a chemical imbalance can begin and how anhedonia can result and change your life forever.

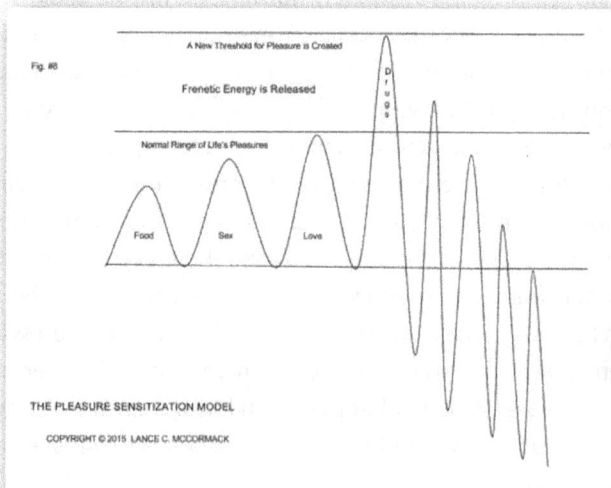

THE PLEASURE SENSITIZATION MODEL

COPYRIGHT © 2015 LANCE C. MCCORMACK

In figure 8, we see that food, sex, and love constitute the range of life's normal human pleasures, and along with that range of normal pleasures comes a relative energy level. That means there's a certain amount of energy derived from having these things, and thus our bodies over time come to demand that level of energy regularly. Food, sex, and love are human needs like water and air, and when we don't have them, we crave them…we deeply "desire that something, generated by a sensation arising from the lack of it in our bodies." Once that desire is fulfilled, we feel satiated and able to focus our attentions on other things, but until that desire is fulfilled, our attentions continue to be distracted as our focus continues to be directed solely on fulfillment of our desire.

Imagine what occurs when we stray beyond the "normal range of human pleasures" and add new things that expand our range of sensations. We create a new range, a new threshold for pleasure. And just as with the original, normal range of human pleasures, we have now created an energy demand that is relative to the new pleasures we've just added to our list. And like those pleasures in the initial range, which are actually human needs, we now crave those new pleasures as if they too were human needs. Now we have a problem—a major problem! How do we at this point actually distinguish between those new pleasurable sensations and our original pleasurable sensations that are actually human needs? The lines between the two have become blurred and are no longer distinguishable.

Notice in figure 9 how things have changed. Along with a new threshold for pleasure comes a new level of energy I call "frenetic energy" or "frantic energy." This energy is experienced whenever your desires are unmet. In your original range of pleasures, frenetic energy was released when your desires for food, sex, and love were unmet, but now the intensity of this frantic energy has increased exponentially with your new threshold for pleasure. From this point, whenever you attempt to enjoy your old "normal" pleasures of food, sex, and love, you instead feel a sense of nothingness, an emptiness, that leaves you only wanting more. More of everything: more food, more sex, and more love. This nothingness marks the dissatisfaction between what you have and what you want. Your favorite foods are no longer appealing, sex with your partner is no longer exciting, and even the intense love you'd felt each time you saw your beautiful baby's face no longer exists.

As I discussed earlier in this chapter, this loss of pleasure is also known as anhedonia. These feelings of nothingness, as you can imagine, cannot be left unresolved; they must be addressed and fulfilled somehow. We as humans are feeling beings, and as feeling beings, we will generally not stop seeking those feelings we desire until we can no longer feel. Fortunately, there are exceptions!

Now we will need more of everything just to feel the same. In the following pages, we'll reintroduce some of the substances and activities that will help satisfy our new energy demands and discuss why this particular replacement strategy will always end badly.

THE PLEASURE DESENSITIZATION MODEL

COPYRIGHT (c) 2015 LANCE C. MCCORMACK

How to Feel Something Again

Remember this list from chapter 9 where I said things would end badly if we don't get a handle on our frenetic energy? Well, here it is again. Once we stopped using our drugs of choice, we developed an energy deficit. To fill that deficit, unconsciously, we either started using other things or increased our use of other things to replace that energy; things like:

- alcohol & other drugs
- nicotine
- caffeinated coffee
- excessive sugar consumed by itself or in foods & drinks
- Red Bull
- Mountain Dew
- 5-Hour Energy drink
- Monster Energy drinks

- diet pills
- candies
- cakes
- cookies
- pies
- gambling
- exotic dancing (stripping)
- pornography
- sex
- shopping
- dangerous extreme sports
- video games

Although you may see the things on this list as energy sources, I see them as "bodily energy demands." What that means is that once we get used to them, our bodies demand them regularly, just like our bodies demanded our drugs of choice. The problem with this strategy is that it's a strategy destined to fail. We will continue to need more of these things until the cost becomes prohibitive and the cost of our past drugs of choice seductively appears to be a better value. Even people on methadone and Suboxone have the tendency to consume these things and participate in these energy-demanding activities because they still aren't where they want to be.

You would think that their medications would be sufficient, but those medications are only designed to stabilize patients, not to replicate their new thresholds for pleasure.

Energy Exchanges Continued

The state of nothingness is a very dangerous place to be, especially when we know there's "something" out there. Since we can agree that everything is composed of at least potential energy, we know we have at least the potential to escape our state of nothingness and feel something again—something that reminds us that we want more out of life than just mere existence, so we search for energy substitutes. As I've previously discussed, all energy has some quantitative value. In humans, everything we do and everything we consume has an energy value. As such, we can always exchange things of equal values as necessary to maintain balance and feelings of control. Please review the model below, as I have assigned some arbitrary values or energy units (EUs) to some common items, just to illustrate my point. My concept is called the energy substitution model and is commonly used by humans to restore and maintain feelings of normalcy.

In the energy substitution model:

    1 slice of bread = 1 EU
    40 slices of bread = 40 EUs
    1 twelve-ounce bottle of beer = 40 EUs
    10 twelve-ounce bottles of beer = 400 EUs
    1 bag of heroin = 400 EUs

In my illustration, you can see how any product can be substituted for another based on having comparable energy units or EUs. I came about this realization after years of meeting with patients in substance-abuse settings who were not our traditional drug users; by traditional, I mean users who had started using years ago and had progressed to their current level of use. These nontraditional users had not been alcohol drinkers or drug users for most of their lives and then at a certain point became raging alcoholics and drug addicts.

I must have met nearly one hundred people, mainly women but also a few men, who qualified as in my mind as nontraditional. All of these people had been considered either obese, morbidly obese, or superobese and had undergone gastric-bypass surgery. Their stories were nearly identical: they had never been drinkers or used other drugs, and some had held down considerable jobs, while others were on some form of disability. Most maintained that they came from loving families, and many stated that they had children, and some even had great-grandchildren. All of them stated that their drug habits didn't begin until after their surgeries. Now, it wasn't like we had all these people together in one group; most of them never met one another, so they didn't have the opportunity to put two and two together, but I did.

What I determined from the stories of these individuals was that this was no coincidence. Imagine being superobese and having an appetite that demanded forty slices of bread daily. As I show in my model, forty slices of bread equals 40

EUs. One twelve-ounce bottle of beer also equals 40 EUs. The difference is that, after gastric-bypass surgery, this person can no longer consume forty slices of bread. Since her surgery, her stomach is only a fraction of its former size, with only a fraction of its former capacity. But, what about this person's desire for forty slices of bread? Just because her stomach is smaller anatomically, meaning she can no longer physically consume forty slices of bread daily, doesn't mean that her psyche's demand or her body's feelings for the energy derived from forty slices of bread have diminished. So here comes the energy substitution model: since her body can easily tolerate a twelve-ounce bottle of beer, her energy demand for 40 EUs is easily satisfied with alcohol. To make matters even worse, alcohol just happens to be a diuretic, causing her to urinate more frequently and thus feel dehydrated more often and feel compelled to drink more alcohol. Can you see where we're going with this? Next, she's drinking ten twelve-ounce bottles of beer and those equal 400 EUs, which just happens to be the equivalent of one bag of heroin, based on our model. I think you know how the rest of the story goes and I think you also realize that based on our model, the choices for substitution are virtually endless!

Based on the substitution model, you can readily see how habits can grow to monstrous proportions and surmise how easily a soccer mom or dutiful dad can turn into a gloryhole mom or dad in order to satisfy their ever-increasing energy demands. Unfortunately, this is happening every day, all across America, and with no signs of abating. By the way, a gloryhole is a hole in a wall-like structure where men can stick their penises through and have some stranger on the other side of that wall suck them. What a world we've created, all in an effort to derive pleasure and feel comfortable in our own skin! This world of substance abuse will take us undoubtedly down the seediest roads that exist, so never say never, until you quit.

Not Only for Food, Drink & Drugs

You may believe that the energy substitution model only applies to things we can ingest, but you'd be wrong. As I said earlier, everything has an energy value, and all energy values can be exchanged. You could exchange using cocaine for gambling, or an eating addiction for a shopping addiction, or a porn/sex addiction for a methamphetamine addiction, or a methamphetamine addiction for an addiction to extreme sports, or maybe you could even combine them all together. It's possible; if you've built up a tolerance for enough energy units, the sky's the limit, literally.

Behaviors also qualify for earning energy units. Did you think for even a minute that all that screaming and yelling, smacking, and abusing could go undetected on the EU scale? After all food, alcohol, and other drugs aren't the only psychoactive sources of energy we receive. Just as we take in energy from those sources, we take in energy, both good and bad, from other people. And just like we get used to the energy derived from foods, alcohol, and other drugs, we get used to the energy derived from others.

That means that once we accept these things into our lives, we develop an energy demand for more of these things. At first, many of these intense behaviors make us feel uncomfortable and rightfully frighten us, making us want to run for the hills, but if we allow these volatile behaviors to continue, something very self-destructive can occur from an energy standpoint, and we can begin to demand this abusive energy just to feel normal. At this point, calm energy can feel unnatural, and we can feel uncomfortable and even neglected if these abusive behaviors stop.

Did you ever wonder why some people go from one abusive relationship to another and seem to steer clear of all the nice people? The reason is that they tend to subconsciously select new partners with energy values comparable to their energy demands, who not surprisingly turn out to be similar to their past partners. As a result, they enter into volatile relationships over and over again. This method of energy selection applies not just to personality traits, but also to the *division of labor* or power within a relationship. Our tendency as humans is to be attracted to others who complement our total energy and who make us feel complete. This is because we are always working with 100 percent energy as a total to be divided among any couple, family, group, or pairing of friends. However, just because this complementary tendency exists, doesn't necessarily mean that the relationships developed will be either acceptable, beneficial or equitable. This pattern will continue until individuals recognize the reason for this pattern and decide to learn new constructive ways to fill their energy demands. For more information on energy, kindly review chapter 9.

How Can We Know the Energy Values of Everything?

We can't, but we know our energy unit exchanges are close when we feel better and have less inclination to continue our prior destructive behaviors. There is no list to consult in regards to energy values because there are too many sources of energy, too many combinations of sources of energy, and too many individuals, each with their unique metabolic peculiarities, to even begin to think of compiling any such list. Some people might argue that we do have such a list already, and it's based on a scientific measurement of energy called joules or on a more commonly used measure known as calories. I would respond that I am aware of that list but would add that even that list won't be able to give us a reliable qualitative energy exchange rate for three bags of heroin or five hours on the one-armed bandit. The reason is that in math and science, we're used to measuring things quantitatively and not by feelings. However, in life, we don't usually say, "I could really go for 790 calories right now." Instead we say, "I sure would love a cheeseburger with fries about now." So reliably I would say that we will subjectively know that we are there energy-wise, when we feel better and our behaviors change as a result.

CHAPTER 12

A Street Chemist Is Born

You should have seen me coming; after all, you made me.
—A LANCEISM

From apple juice to crack. It seems like quite a leap but not necessarily. If you're weaned on fruit juices and soda, crack cocaine may just be a natural step in the process of trying to continue to feel normal. You may think this correlation is a little dramatic, so just ask around...ask your adult siblings or close friends with kids as to what they gave their children to eat or drink as infants, toddlers, and developing preschoolers, and then inquire as to how their kids are doing now. You'll have your answer, and I doubt you'll like it!

In our last chapter, we spoke about infants and developing children being given sugary, caffeinated drinks, and we highlighted the powerful effects of coffee, but look around you now as an adult, and see what your adult relatives and friends are drinking and eating. We are having a very difficult time as adults: alcoholism is rampant, many of us are struggling to maintain a healthy weight, and opioid drug abuse and dependence is impacting us daily, and all we seem to want to do is lower the drinking age, eat and drink more sugary foods, and legalize more drugs.

Chemical imbalances are created every second of every day. Sometimes we hear someone say they have a chemical imbalance, and we think of them as having something that's highly unusual, but it's not—it's extremely common. Imagine the impact of a caffeinated drink on the body of a two-year-old. Picture the disruption caffeine causes to their delicate chemical makeup, the veritable electrical firestorm that's created in every one of their cells (and not just in their nerve cells), and then consider what damage is likely to occur as a result. A chemical imbalance, at the very least.

Recently I watched an episode of *Toddlers and Tiaras* (and no, I don't watch it all the time). As you probably suspect, this show is about beauty pageants for toddlers and little girls. During this episode, a mother was preparing her three-year-old daughter to go on stage. As they were still in the dressing room, to my horror, the mother handed her daughter a can of Red Bull to drink before her performance. Now, let's take a minute here and evaluate this. If you read the warning on the back of a can of Red Bull, it clearly states, "Not recommended for children under the age of nine." I wouldn't want my child drinking this at any age, but this girl was three! What her mother did to her was nothing short of criminal. When this little three-year-old toddler finally went on stage, she appeared to not even remember what she was there to do. She stood there in a daze as the judges remarked to themselves that something was wrong with her. After this little girl was escorted off of the stage, her mother appeared disgruntled with her performance, at which time, the girl reached for another sip of Red Bull. The question is, if she's used to drinking Red Bull at age three, what will this little girl need by age six? Do you see her being that little girl sitting quietly in her seat in class, or do you see her being unable to sit still in class as she disrupts all the children around her?

So here we are with a ten-year-old girl who's been acting out for years now and who has been on a medication like Ritalin for about four years. She seems somewhat better but is still not feeling quite normal. And as her little body continues to grow, so does her need and desire for more medication. Now she's old enough to realize what makes her feel better, and she knows exactly how to push your buttons to indicate when she needs more. Remember that hamster wheel?

No Longer a Baby, But Still Not an Adult

Before long our little girl is in her teens and socializing with other teens who have been going through similar mind and body disturbances. Someone shares an experience of drinking some of their dad's alcohol when he was away and says how it "suddenly gave me a reason for being on the planet." I heard this sad line from a young woman in recovery recounting her first experience drinking alcohol as a fifteen-year-old girl. So, our little teenager is still on her meds and drinking alcohol as often as she can. Where's Mom? Where's Dad? They say they're working to put food on the table. I say that's fine, as long as they're also taking the time to look up from the table to notice the faces of their kids. Parents only have to look at their kids to see that they're having problems and that they need their undivided attention.

We must remember that we are all opportunists by nature and are always seeking opportunities for homeostasis or balance through deriving pleasure. What may have started as our daughter's naive attempt to balance a chemical imbalance has turned into the creation of yet another street chemist. Now our teenager knows more about how to bring her moods up and how to bring them down with chemicals than we will ever know, and she is just getting started!

Ritalin…That's a Kid's Drug

Our teen has now outgrown the medication that seemed to settle her down as a little girl. She knows it; she feels it. Back then, it appeared to help her concentrate and focus her attention on school and on whatever else people were saying to her. But as the years have passed and as she's added a few new drugs to her menu, like alcohol, marijuana, and maybe some party stimulant drugs, her tolerance for Ritalin has grown dramatically, and when she just has her regular dose of Ritalin, she is "off the wall." From the outside it appears that our girl is just going through a growing phase, or maybe it's just her "time of the month"—that's what her parents think, anyway. Sure teenagers are known to be unpredictable and hard to handle due to their raging hormones and overall teen angst, but there is a difference here—a huge difference. Our girl has developed a tolerance to her dose of Ritalin, and she's experiencing withdrawal symptoms.

Back to her doctor for an update. Of course she doesn't tell her doctor that she's been drinking alcohol and smoking whatever; she just says her meds are no longer working. "Fine, we'll put you on something stronger, something more suitable for a young woman your age," her doctor says. Adderall, the drug some may call Ritalin's big brother, is now her medication, and she loves it! She has energy again and can focus again, especially whenever she has too much to drink or smoke. After all, alcohol is a depressant drug, and one that can therefore cause depression. The rate of depression is extremely high in teenagers and even higher in teenage girls. That high rate is also associated with the increased risk for suicide among teens. There is only one other age category where these risks for depression and suicide are even comparable, and that's with people in their sixties. Then, to make matters even worse, marijuana, a cannabinoid, is also a psychoactive drug that is known to impair the nervous system and cause symptoms of lethargy and decreased energy and motivation. So between alcohol, marijuana, and normal teenage hormonal disturbances, we have a pretty unmotivated, depressed, suicide-prone young woman, and these are supposed to be her wonder years. So, Adderall will be just the ticket to get her out of those doldrums, except for the fact that besides causing feelings of elation, it too can bring on feelings of depression.

Just Adding Fuel to the Fire

Adderall to the rescue. I sure hope someone has bothered to give this girl a breathalyzer or urinalysis test, because if they did, they'd know more of her story and not just be relying on the bogus story she's been giving. Maybe they'd even discover that she may not need Adderall after all and her behavioral issues may be symptoms of other problems that can be addressed in other, nonmedicative ways. It's bad enough that her mom and dad have no idea what's going on with her, but now they've entrusted their precious teen to a physician who may not thoroughly realize her individual risk factors.

Adderall is nothing to play with; it's a powerful psychoactive stimulant drug prescribed for people diagnosed with ADHD (attention deficit hyperactivity disorder) and narcolepsy, a certain type of sleep disorder. It's a brand name for a combination of the stimulants amphetamine and dextroamphetamine, and it's designed to help restore chemical balance in the brain. Adderall has many side effects, especially when not taken as directed. Here are just a few, according to some reputable online sources:

- powerful cravings for more
- being unable to feel normal without it
- sleep disturbances
- alternating between having insomnia and sleeping too much
- intense hunger
- anxiety and irritability
- panic attacks
- lack of energy, fatigue

- inability to feel happy
- depression
- phobias or panic attacks
- suicidal thoughts
- nervousness
- dizziness
- restlessness
- headache
- stomachache
- decreased appetite
- dry mouth
- nausea
- weight loss
- constipation or diarrhea
- loss of interest in sex
- changes in vision
- seizures
- chest pain
- trouble breathing
- fainting
- severe weakness or numbness
- uncontrolled movements or voice sounds
- hallucinations or delusions
- aggressive behavior
- uncontrollable behavior
- severe skin rash
- swelling of face, lips, or tongue
- difficulty swallowing or talking
- irregular heartbeat

These are just some of the side effects your child could experience. Some teens, especially girls, may see Adderall and newer, similar drugs like Vyvanse as wonder drugs to help them lose weight without ever thinking about all of the side effects.

Although Adderall and other drugs may suppress appetite, they should never be thought of as a diet pill. There are many safe ways to lose weight, and this is definitely not one of them. This choice comes with the risk of severe consequences like cardiac arrest, psychosis, and stroke, not to mention addiction, and our girl is already at a higher risk for Adderall addiction simply because she's already been abusing alcohol and other drugs. And please, let's not forget one last consequence: death.

Something Else to Consider

As for the numbers, teenage girls are quickly catching up to their male counterparts with addiction. And in addition to being quite competitive, females are also considered to be more vulnerable than males to addiction from a biological and physiological standpoint, due to several factors. Now, I know there are female readers out there saying, "That's total BS—I can drink or drug any guy under the table," and that may be true, but what's also true is they're going to pay more dearly for that talent. Okay, now that we're past that bravado, females are known to have in general less muscle mass and more fat on their bodies. As a result, our girl may experience greater concentrations of Adderall, alcohol, and other drugs into her bloodstream since muscle can help absorb some alcohol and other drugs, but fat can't. This means that more of the drugs will pass directly through her blood and into her vital organs, causing a greater impact and likely resulting in earlier signs of damage.

If that wasn't enough, our girl may also experience more vulnerability from a hormonal perspective. Due to regular fluctuations in her hormones, namely estrogen and progesterone, she may experience the tendency to crave more sugar in the form of simple carbohydrates (like Skittles and Twinkies) during certain hormonal phases. The more she opts for sugary foods, the more anxiety and depression she'll experience. Her responses to these cravings must be controlled in order to reduce her future cravings and drastic cyclic changes. Knowing that her cycles will be forthcoming, she can prepare in advance for them by purchasing the right foods (complex carbohydrates and complete proteins) that will not only provide her with relief from future cravings but also help reduce their intensity. Imagine your daughter being in the middle of that cycle experiencing drastic hormonal shifts and being offered alcohol or other drugs. Don't put her in that position of weakness when you know how to make her strong! Help her learn about her body so she can control her body with the proper nutrients.

Back to Adderall...we had mentioned before that our girl had experienced bouts of depression, but paradoxically Adderall is known to possibly increase her risk for mental health disorders like depression and bipolar disorder. So over time she can become more depressed while using it and more depressed if she's withdrawing from it—the "Adderall crash." So what we have here appears to be a conundrum, a dilemma, a very confusing problem, and our girl may be smack dab in the middle of it. She wants to stay high and never feel the crash, but not so high that she's geeking (all messed up) all the time, so she's got to constantly work to balance her mood states.

But Drugs Cost Money!

How is our little girl going to maintain her habit when she doesn't have a job and couldn't hold down a job if she had one? She's guzzling coffee, Red Bull, and Mountain Dew and smoking cigarettes throughout the school week, and drinking alcohol, smoking pot, taking more Adderall than prescribed, and popping Ecstasy on the weekends.

This stuff costs money!

What can she do to make enough cash to keep her habit going and stay in school so her parents don't find out that she's a total mess? She could apply at Walmart for an associate's position, but I doubt they'll be willing to pay her $300 a day, especially since she's new and untrained. Instead she could start stealing from Walmart and their competitors—that would probably be more likely. She could start turning on other students at her school so she can get her stuff for free. She could start breaking into cars and houses and snatching pocketbooks and purses and robbing little old ladies.

She could start seeing decrepit old men and women in seedy motel rooms, back alleys, and back seats. She could do a lot of those things or all those things, but one thing she's extremely unlikely to do is stop!

You know what? We haven't even mentioned heroin yet. Prices have come down a lot on dope, and it's become a lot more affordable, especially once you catch a big habit. I always find the phrase *catch a habit* to be amusing. A young woman about twenty years old once said that to me about how she'd been using heroin for about a month when she realized she was hooked. She said, "How was I to know I'd catch a habit?" Is anyone out there even awake? The talk about drugs is everywhere—everywhere! How can anyone today say "How was I to know?" unless they've been living under a rock with their hands over their ears?

When Price Matters

Opiates, opioids...It doesn't matter; they do the same thing, and that is take away your freedom under the guise of just taking away your pain. Hydrocodone, widely known by its popular brand name, Vicodin, along with its big brother oxycodone, affectionately known by its brand name Percocet, are usually the prescribed opioids that get the ball rolling. Then "big daddy," OxyContin, a timed-release version of the narcotic analgesic oxycodone, very similar in nature to the illegal drug called heroin, comes to town just to be with his kids, Vicodin and Percocet, and our party really starts rockin'. As part of a commonly communicated law of physics states, "Energy in motion tends to stay in motion." This is very appropriate in this case, because once this ball, this drug ball, starts rocking and rolling, it's going to take nothing short of an act of God to stop it.

Prescription drugs are becoming increasingly more difficult to get because of stricter regulations after more than two decades of unregulated, overprescribing mayhem. Each state is moving at its own snail's pace to meet federal mandates, but still few are focusing on the real problem, and we'll talk plenty about that later. So now it's becoming much more difficult to get these prescriptions with all the scrutiny involved. Even if you have a legitimate medical need for this level of pain relief, you're going to have to prove it with adequate diagnoses and documentation, as it should be. So what does one do with a raging drug habit and no legal way of getting the drugs? Go to the streets! Can't afford those hefty prices for Vicodin, Percocet, and OxyContin? Our girl has found that heroin will suffice quite nicely and at a much lower price...well, at least financially.

Yes, there are many pieces to this rotten pie: pharmaceutical companies; lobbyists; commission-motivated pharmaceutical salespeople (that is, pharmaceutical reps); overworked, naive physicians trusting those commission-motivated pharmaceutical salespeople; woefully inadequately trained physicians; and their misguided, medically trained but greed-motivated colleagues who have completely betrayed the Hippocratic oath they initially swore to uphold; confused and unscrupulous drug dealers just out to share their misery with anyone else willing to gamble; and finally, those preoccupied parents, the ones not taking time out to listen and know their children but instead wasting their precious time just talking at them. Yes, there are many pieces to this rotten pie, yet the solution is still as simple as it's ever been for all parties concerned. Learn what the right thing is, and do it!

As I think about physicians and pharmaceuticals and overprescribing I can't help but recall my own situation back in the eighties, with a serious injury. I had been a fitness instructor at a popular health club and along with my duties of helping patrons reach their fitness goals, I was assigned to monitor the chlorine levels in our pool and whirlpool. Hey, someone had to make sure all those bathing beauties weren't developing eye irritation! Well, despite this obvious perk of the job, one day I saw a heavy set, paraplegic man drowning in the whirlpool. I quickly ran in, reached down and grabbed him under his arms and lifted him straight up and out of the whirlpool. Whoa!!!! Instantly, I felt a lightning bolt-like pain strike me from my neck all the way down to the toes of my right foot. I was taken quickly to a nearby hospital and later diagnosed with having three herniated discs; one cervical and two lumbar, and for the pain I was prescribed an opiate called Talwin. I took this opiate everyday as prescribed for three months while I was out of work, and once my prescription ended, so did my use of Talwin. This opiate was exactly what I needed; no more and no less. Have you ever heard of Talwin? Probably not. The question is, why not? The answer is, it's not as strong and it's relatively less expensive than comparable opiates and physicians would rather prescribe OxyContin, which is just the opposite! Now, please don't take what I'm saying as an endorsement for Talwin, because that's not my intention, I'm just relaying my personal experiences with Talwin, so you can make more informed decisions. Additionally, what I'm saying is, I never developed an addiction, so my belief is, if you're prescribed the appropriate medication, and you take it as prescribed, neither should you. Nonetheless, the buck always stops with us, as it should, and it's always up to us to do our homework before we blindly accept any medications, regardless of who's suggesting them.

We as parents need to exercise our due diligence, and that means we must truly care for our kids by investigating everything about what they drink, what they eat, who they hang out with, what medications they are prescribed, and what effects each of those medications will have on their bodies. We are no longer in the sixties when doctors used to hand us prescriptions and we just took them, no questions asked. If you have a doctor who balks at your questions about the safety of the medications they've prescribed for you or your children, you need to run out of that office as fast as you can and find a new doctor. Now, in the year 2016, we have the right to collaborate with our physicians regarding the decision on which medications we are willing to take, without the fear of reprisal by our physicians. This is not just our right; it is our duty, to ourselves and to our children.

It's time to wake up and acknowledge that our daughters and our sons have raging drug problems and that those problems aren't going away without our intervention. We must forget about our pride and the fact that we let it happen right under our noses, and instead we must get to work and fix what we've broken. A baby bottle of apple juice or soda seemed so harmless then, but we see now how one thing can lead to another and how time can turn a little so-called harmless habit into a lifelong energy imbalance.

Yes, we've converted calm, tranquil energy into the human version of the kraken (pronounced "crackin"), this gigantic, legendary sea monster with many powerful arms that destroys anything and everything in its path. But just like in the movie *Clash of the Titans*, the kraken can be killed, but we must be swift and steadfast in our approach.

We as parents aren't the first to be blindsided by our kids' drug use or the first to lose focus on what's most important, and we won't be the last. Just realize that we must get moving in a new direction now, in order to stop this runaway behemoth of a beast, because otherwise whatever bad happens will be mainly our fault because we saw it coming, and we just stood by and did nothing!

SECTION V

The Third Element of Addiction: A Drug Introduction (The New Equation)

Although we've only just met, I do believe our
relationship will be extremely memorable.
—A LANCEISM

n this section, several chapters will be devoted to highlighting the reasons for drug use and the tradeoffs involved with drug use. This section constitutes the third element of addiction.

CHAPTER 13

So You Like Getting High!

*If you are willing to be lived by it, you will see it
everywhere, even in the most ordinary things.*
—LAO-TZU

" What is it? It's not a what. It's not a who. It's what it does to you. It strips away your compassion, it takes away your empathy, your capacity for love, eating away at your soul, until all that remains is darkness." The funny thing is that these lines were from an episode of *Vampire Diaries*, a show chronicling the challenges of vampires with human emotions trying to fit into society. We know it as addiction. I swear the story lines from that show are based on true stories of addiction.

Like pages of time, addiction peels back thousands of years of evolution and exposes the naked *Homo sapiens*, ones that are driven solely by their primitive instinctual desires to serve their own needs, regardless of the impact on others. Addiction allows us to feel nothing but the desire for more of that which is desired. As we introduce drugs of abuse into our lives, we are making a monumental statement. A statement that our lives are not what we had expected and that any momentary attempts toward departure from our lives are only in an effort to make them somewhat bearable. As sad as it may sound, it's still just a cop-out, a simple ploy to take the easy way out, while others around us step up to life's challenges on life's terms.

Those in favor of drug use say, who are we to deny another of these wondrous pleasures? They say, if we can derive pleasure or relief from a drug, why not? That is the question. As one protester said upon being arrested at Woodstock back in the sixties, "Who is the government to tell us what we can eat, drink, or smoke?" If we want to destroy our lives, who has the right to deny us? That's true, but what about the rest of us? We are the masses damaged by the reckless among us who must protect ourselves from their callous indulgences. Perhaps the questions of the reckless would be valid if our individual lives took place in vacuums, instead of within a society where all our lives are inextricably connected to the lives of others. But since this is normally not the case, these careless acts prove to be more selfish in nature than acts of individual expression. So, "I'll do what I want" turns out to mean "what I do may harm you, but I simply don't care."

As we decide to use drugs of abuse, we must also acknowledge that there will be a departure from the lives we knew and an entrance into new lives that may appear more exciting but that have proven to be highly predictable and quite the contrary. These new lives mark the creation of a new equation. This new equation of drugs and us produces an exponential effect. It's like getting married and nine months later giving birth to sextuplets. We were two, and now suddenly we're eight, and we are dealing with an entirely new, extremely challenging equation. But unlike a new marriage between loving couples faced with the wonder of having a large family almost immediately, we have a new equation between two parties, each driven by distinctly different agendas. While your agenda may be just to have a good time and a few laughs, your drug of choice's agenda is to bring you to your knees and render you powerless. So, the race is on! In the meantime, the rest of us will just have to take a seat in the bleachers and see who wins.

We, as willing participants, will be asked to sign an actual agreement attesting to our willingness to participate in this drug-use undertaking after having been presented with a complete list of the inherent risks. We will then be asked to give this signed agreement to our loved ones, communicating our full intentions to destroy our lives and the lives of everyone around us. Our loved ones are to acknowledge receipt of the contract and attest to their disapproval of our intentions with their signature.

So as we boldly consider taking drugs, despite the reasons we have chosen to take them, we must also boldly consider the immeasurable damages that will be incurred as consequences of our choices and be prepared to take full responsibility for those outcomes as we embark on this perilous journey. As we have been told by countless people before us, drug taking is not to be considered lightly, as it comes with a lifestyle all its own, and one that will change us forever. So as educated drug consumers, we must be willing to make an agreement and sign a contract, forfeiting our lives as we knew them and agreeing to adopt a new, solitary existence focused solely on craving and self-satisfaction. So without any further ado, the contract!

Desire to Destroy Lives Agreement

This Desire to Destroy Lives Agreement ("the Agreement") is hereby made and voluntarily entered into by and between _____ ("the Destroyer") and __ ("the Affectee"). Both parties mentioned herein agree to be of sound mind and body and to be of legal age and under no duress in regards to the terms of this agreement.

Offer: The Destroyer will willingly and unapologetically engage in activities, lawful and unlawful, in the attempt to derive self-satisfaction and pleasure. This self-serving pleasure seeking will not stop until such time as deemed suitable by the Destroyer. The Destroyer will provide at no time any consideration for the impact of its actions on the life of the Affectee. No promises, implied or otherwise, are made as to when the suitable time for cessation of said pleasure-seeking activities shall be reached.

Claims: The Destroyer claims full responsibility for its actions and attests to having been given adequate education and specialized training from which to formulate well-educated decisions. The Destroyer at no time will hold accountable any parties other than itself for decisions it has made. The Destroyer recognizes the inherent dangers of its intentions, both to itself and to the Affectee, and waives all regrets in that regard. The Destroyer understands and accepts the burden of any and all pain and suffering resulting from its decisions and wholeheartedly avows no shame or guilt for its actions.

Consideration: The Affectee promises to always love and hold in its heart the best interest of the Destroyer, and at no time will the Affectee forget the wonderful times shared with the Destroyer and not desire a return of the Destroyer to those times. The Affectee promises to pay a sum incalculable in other than human terms for the loss of a relationship apparently not worth maintaining.

Acceptance: The Affectee accepts with deep regret the decisions deemed necessary by the Destroyer and agrees to remain justly bound by law, unless otherwise severed by law to the Destroyer. In regards to the intent of the Destroyer, the Affectee promises to remember its own life and not forgo its responsibilities or its own interests in lieu of the decisions and interests made clear by the Destroyer. The Affectee accepts no responsibility/indebtedness for the actions or the consequences of those actions by the Destroyer and waives all but legal responsibility to the Destroyer.

Mutual Intent to Be Bound: These are the terms of this agreement, upon which both parties mutually agree to be bound. All consideration herein will commence as of the signing of this agreement by the aforementioned parties. Shall any provision of this agreement be determined by a law to be unenforceable, that provision shall be revised and made enforceable without compromising the integrity of the remainder of the original agreement.

Agreed on this_____day of _____, 20__.

Destroyer,_____, and Affectee, _____

This agreement is to be given to anyone in your life whom you love or care about as a written acknowledgment that there exists a formidable problem or at least the potential for a formidable problem within the said individual. It's designed as a preemptive measure or as a considerate interventional tool to put the said person on notice that their behaviors are not going unnoticed. It allows the person to recognize their impact and your perceptions of their actions as well as the consequences of those actions. It asserts that you fully understand their rights to make their own decisions and attests that their decisions will undoubtedly impact your decisions. This agreement affirms that your desire for the person's well-being will never cease, despite any potential severing of the contact or any termination of the communications between you.

Let's Talk Stigma

I remember being a kid living in Harlem and enjoying the beautiful, hot summer days. Some of the kids would find a wrench and remove the nuts from fire hydrants and then play in the water as it was powerfully discharged. I know it wasn't the right thing to do, but it happened! Living on a hill, I could see all this water rushing down the gutters and carrying with it all kinds of debris: bottles, cans, paper, and all kinds of other trash. Somewhere along the line, I would always see IV drug users catching water in their hypodermic needles and then sticking those filthy needles into their arms and releasing that vile concoction of whatever drug and gutter bacteria into their veins and into their bodies.

Every few days I would see these same drug addicts, along with their alcoholic counterparts, staggering to our neighborhood blood bank to sell their blood for money to buy more alcohol and other drugs. Some would walk in with blood still dripping from their self-injections, yet walk out with their cash. I know it sounds crazy because it was! This is absolutely true, and it was a common practice all throughout New York City. As a result, New York City's blood supply became very unreliable and downright toxic, leaving countless patients, in dire need of blood, highly susceptible to contagions. These facts are testaments and reminders to the reality that many of our medical practices, our so-called best practices, are based on trial and error and not necessarily on common sense. Those thousands of patients who received tainted blood back then served as the unfortunate ground-layers for the blood-collections practices and guidelines of today. And into the foreseeable future, we can reasonably conclude that our current healthcare practices in general will only change after some future medical malfeasance has been exposed.

Due to endless paperwork, regulations, politics, wayward thinking, and hindsight conclusions, these outcomes are inevitable. We presently have the opportunity to break this cycle and enter a new era of human evolution; all we have to do is awaken to the reality that what we're doing now in regards to drug addiction is completely wrong. That is why we are in the midst of a growing opioid epidemic. Like football wide receivers, we're running quickly with the ball, but we're running toward the wrong goal.

Stigma—"a mark of shame or discredit." Most of us know what the noun *shame* means, but the noun *discredit* is a little tricky: "loss of credit or reputation." Both of these are definitions from a *Merriam-Webster's Dictionary*. Another definition of a stigma from an online source is "a mark of disgrace associated with a particular circumstance, quality, or person." At some point, we must recognize that some things we do aren't good, and that some things we do are just bad. Some things are bad for everyone concerned, and we shouldn't expect to get patted on the back for the bad things we do. This doesn't mean that we shouldn't expect to be treated with compassion, empathy, and reasonable care when we need help, but we shouldn't expect to have our bad behaviors accepted either. Now, I say "reasonable care" because some of the things we're considering as a nation go well beyond that.

Let's consider our opioid overdose prevention initiative to provide Narcan, the brand name for naloxone, an opiate antagonist, to our police officers and fire-fighters and all direct healthcare workers and educators. This humanitarian effort is in the hopes of reducing fatal opioid overdoses. Narcan is known to block and reverse the effects of opioids, so the user goes almost immediately into withdrawal after its administration and comes back from what could have been a fatal over-dose. The providers of this life-saving care are true heroes and should sincerely be applauded. This altruistic initiative sounds reasonable at first, until you hear from the users themselves.

As someone who has counseled thousands of patients known to have abused opioids, I've heard extremely disturbing testimonials from them in regards to their Narcan experiences. Many of these patients speak of being "Narcanned" as many as ten times over the course of a month. These same patients go as far as blaming Narcan for their overdoses. They say that since they know they will most likely be brought back and not die from an overdose, they feel more confident to push their use to the limit.

They communicate no concern that they have 911 on speed dial and that each time an ambulance races to pick them up due to a suspected drug overdose, it can't race to the care of someone else experiencing a heart attack or another emergency. They speak of all the family members and friends who have Narcan and how they are all well-trained in its use. They even add that if Narcan wasn't so readily available, they know they would be more cautious in their using. Do you think this an argument for arming all men, women, and children across our nation with Narcan? Don't we have more important things to do as a nation than waste our time and money on medications and training regarding those medications that sound reasonable but only cause an increase in bad behaviors? Just asking.

As agencies, governments, and people of power and status fight to remove the stigma of drug use, they are only making matters worse. When drug use was considered as something only the poor, disenfranchised people from urban eth-nic groups did, there was no race to remove any stigmas. Now that Main Street and millionaires are heavily involved in drug use, along with their kids, the move is toward destigmatization. Let's not allow the addition of this new class of drug users to cloud our better judgment. As history has shown, stigmas aren't always bad things. In fact, stigmas can be very good things and act as strong deterrents to bad behaviors.

Destigmatization is equivalent to acceptance, and acceptance is equivalent to an increased prevalence of any behavior.

We must not rush to satisfy the will of those embarrassed by the fact that addiction has hit home, but instead emphasize the fact that no one is exempt from its allure. Once again, we must not resort to ignoring the use of common sense and instead continue to utilize failed strategies of trial and error while expecting positive outcomes. Back in the sixties, when parents pulled their children away from drug users on the streets and told them how dangerous drugs were and how never to use them, they were sending their children clear messages: "I don't want you to be a drug addict, and a drug addict is not something you should want to be either!" We must return to sending our children and our loved ones clear messages, not messages clouded with ambiguity.

Think back to whatever example you can conjure as to how stigmas work. As a stigma persists, the likelihood of that behavior continuing decreases, and as a stigma fades, the likelihood of that behavior continuing increases. Let's take teenage pregnancies. There was a time not too long ago when they were frowned upon or stigmatized. Pregnant teens were ostracized, and some were even sent to live with distant relatives. Many of these teens returned years later mysteriously without any children. How many pregnant teens do you think they had then in comparison to the number of pregnant teens we have today? Yes, you guessed it, a lot less. Now, I'm not condoning those particular practices, just giving you an example of how stigmas work.

How about the old stigma of having babies out of wedlock? I know it's not even a term that's used these days, but it was once, not that long ago. Now that it no longer presents a stigma and it's commonly accepted, the number of unwed mothers has dramatically increased. Rarely do you hear about people feeling compelled to marry because they have children. Of course it's still an option, but it's no longer viewed as a requirement. In some cases it's even seen as cool, not having to commit to someone just because you have a baby with them. Maybe this thinking all started in Hollywood with actors, where they didn't want to jeopardize their wealth by marrying someone? Nonetheless, most of us aren't actors, and most of us aren't rich, so all it means for mainstream America is more single parents on public assistance and more children without fathers in their lives.

Do you remember when type II diabetes was called adult onset diabetes? It was called that because type II diabetes usually didn't occur until adulthood. Now that we have children in nursery school weighing one hundred pounds developing diabetes, they had to change the term. And as we work to lessen the stigma of being obese or "fat," we're seeing more fat people in general. There are even shows on television celebrating being fat. Yet we all know that the quality of life and the overall life expectancies for people considered fat are lower than those of their healthy-weight counterparts. I'm not saying they're not good people; they're just doing bad things for their health. Many times people just have to hear the truth in order to make changes. Please don't hate me; I'm just an observer.

Everyone has heard of the AIDS epidemic of the eighties and knows of how stigmatizing that was, yet years after the miraculous advent of antiretroviral medications, the prevalence of AIDS in some groups has actually increased. Due to a lessened stigma and numerous examples of celebrities living well with AIDS, we no longer consider contracting AIDS as a death sentence, and as a result, those risky sexual behaviors of the eighties have returned with a vengeance, and the number of AIDS patients among some groups has steadily increased. Here again, I'm not demonizing the patients; I'm addressing the increased behaviors due to relaxed views regarding those behaviors. Just because a disease has gone from being considered fatal to chronic and manageable shouldn't mean we can act with impunity.

Just in case you need another example of how destigmatization can increase the prevalence of a behavior, I'd like you to think back, if you're old enough, to a time when the Internet didn't exist. Sure pornography, peep shows, and prostitution existed, but mainly in very controlled environments (for example, certain sections of town, adult bookstores in those sections of town, and racy magazines kept behind the counters of obscure convenience stores and sold in brown paper bags). Going to those places and engaging in those behaviors weren't things you were proud of or that you discussed openly. They were things you did in private and didn't want anyone to know. There was definitely a stigma around being known as someone who frequently slunk around seedy parts of town doing God knows what. As a result, fewer people did it. Fast-forward to 2016 where pornography is rampant and bright-colored adult stores sit prominently on street corners in cities and suburbs alike. Teens and adults sit affixed to computer screens watching porn 24/7 and have indiscriminate sex with strangers in bookstore backrooms with every opportunity. Employees are routinely reprimanded and fired for being caught porn surfing when they should be working, and it's become accepted as something almost everyone does in the workplace. And the more it's accepted, the more it continues.

Watching pornography is so prevalent now, it's become an addiction for many people that requires counseling. I see men all the time seeking hypnosis to help them stop watching porn. Those same men, many of them under thirty years old, are complaining about erectile dysfunction. Put two and two together, and we have a large population of young men with erectile dysfunction due to watching too much pornography. It's that simple. There's nothing complicated about it! The problem is, the energy they're deriving from the things they are viewing online cannot be easily replicated in normal relationships. Their partners would have to be Olympic gymnasts with doctorates in the Kama Sutra in order to be close to satisfying their desires. These practices of seeking nonstop sexual gratification are tearing relationships and families apart all across this nation, and we see those problems only steadily increasing. This slope has always been slippery, but now we're slipping away! I remember traveling with my wife to Key West, Florida, some years ago and being welcomed by its sign, "Welcome to Key West!" In the background in the near distance, almost in line with that sign, was a huge store sign with letters written in bold print, clearly visible from the main road, reading, "FREE LUBE WITH EVERY VIBRATOR." Really, is that the second thing you want visitors to see upon entering such a beautiful city? The more we accept these kinds of things, the more of these things we can expect to see!

Think of how we view pedophilia today in our society. The idea of adults having sex with children, or even contemplating it, is abhorrent to most of us. Sex offenders are routinely stigmatized in many ways: with their pictures and their names in the papers and on television, and even their personal information listed for neighbors so they can be aware that a sex offender lives in their neighborhood. All these measures are designed to send the message "We do not accept sex offenders." No one wants to be classified as a sex offender, as they are people whom we've said we do not we want. Now, what if they said what they have is an addiction—would that make a difference in your mind as to how you view them? Probably not. So what you're saying is, you accept certain addictions but not others. You have empathy for people addicted to certain things but disdain for people addicted to other things. Why the difference? We feel badly for people who are addicted to some certain things, and we feel certain people are bad for being addicted to other certain things. It's confusing!

Despite the seemingly humanitarian efforts by our governments to eradicate stigmas against those involved in drug use, I urge you to use your common sense, because I suspect that if you do, you will arrive at the same conclusions as I have. Although they purport that the motives for their actions are to bring those afflicted with the disease of drug addiction out of the shadows and into treatment, it's an extremely naive theory and one not based on the facts. First of all, the people in question aren't afflicted with a disease, at least not in the sense that an illness has been communicated to them; they have willingly given themselves up to substances and/or activities. The word *affliction* implies that something has happened to them and not that they have brought something upon themselves. By using the proper words, we are more apt to arrive at our desired outcomes. This age of enabling practices and rhetoric must stop if we are to have any chance at all at mitigating this rapidly escalating problem. Secondly, no one is breaking down the doors to enter treatment, and the reason they're not is because many of them don't want treatment, and the reason they don't want treatment is not because of any stigma that presently exists. The reason they don't want treatment is simply because *they want to continue using drugs!*

I have yet to encounter this stigmatization that we hear about. All the people I've worked with over the years in the substance-abuse field have been caring and empathic in their endeavors to help those struggling with addiction. As for the general public, they will continue to make their own conclusions about addiction based on their experiences, and we don't need to bankrupt our future in an attempt to brainwash them into believing that we need a treatment center on every street and a Narcan holster on every hip. It will be a sad day in America when city workers are going door to door asking residents if they need buprenorphine, naltrexone, or Vivitrol. We as a nation are better than that! I agree that there is much work to be done to curb our opioid epidemic, and I also agree that we must continue to hold pharmaceutical companies and the medical profession accountable for their recklessness in their manufacturing and their overprescribing of medications, but I wholeheartedly maintain that we must hold individuals ultimately accountable for what they decide to put into their bodies.

CHAPTER 14

So You Like Feeling Numb!

*Thoughts are like plants, and in our gardens, we must select
with great care which thoughts we allow to take root.*
—A LANCEISM

To desire numbness is to desire disconnection from the world. Whether it's to dull the pain we cannot bear or to deaden the reality of our existence, the desire for numbness communicates a state of discontent from which we are eager to escape. This desire indicates that we are under conditions greater than our perceived capabilities and that we have conceded that flight is our only option in this "fight or flight" scenario. But when we unwittingly welcome this numbness now, we only set the stage for feeling more of the same when we no longer want it. To like feeling numb is to like feeling nothing, but to always feel nothing leaves us always longing to feel something.

After we've tried whatever it is and arrived at the point of desiring numbness on a regular basis, we have turned a corner, a very critical corner, a corner in which seduction has taken hold and promised us lifelong, toe-curling satisfaction. This is the point at which we transition from just fooling around with a drug or an activity to becoming a shareholder, a person with a stake in what we're doing. And as anyone with a stake in anything, we become very protective of that thing and very aggressive to anyone opposed to that thing.

When we reference phrases like *turning a corner* or words like *transition*, we are highlighting the fact that a sequence is involved. Behaviors like seeking something to feel numb are just that, part of a sequence of events leading up to creating a new habit. These behaviors don't automatically become habits; they must be cultivated systematically and then allowed to germinate in our minds and bodies.

Once these behaviors germinate and take root, they must then be sustained by desire in order to maintain a foundation.

So as we venture out to experience new things, we learn quickly how easily routine behaviors can turn into habits. As with any new habit there is always a beginning, a time when we decide we are not fully content as we are. And with any new habit comes a new understanding that new adjustments must be made and new allowances taken into account in order to accommodate this new habit. In this chapter, you will be given information and an accompanying diagram explaining the psychological processes involved in starting new habits and a roadmap as to how established habits can be permanently changed.

I use the conscious, subconscious, unconscious model (the CSU model) of habituation to convey how our thoughts become habits and how our habits, good or bad, can become our lives. *Merriam-Webster's Dictionary* gives one definition of a habit: "an acquired mode of behavior that has become nearly or completely involuntary." I see a habit as simply something we've become used to doing. I don't give habits any power, as they can only derive power from us. An example *Merriam-Webster's Dictionary* gives for a habit is "waking up early as a force of habit." I will show you in the CSU model how even behaviors like waking up early because you've done it for the past fifty years can be easily stopped once you choose to follow the steps.

The CSU Model of Habituation (Habit Forming)

The Sequence of Communications between the Mind Involved in Starting or Stopping a Behavior

Conscious	Subconscious	Conscious	Subconscious	Unconscious
Hears that Sees that Reads that Discusses that	Thinks that Believes that Trusts that Feels that	Does that Does that Does that Does that	Likes that Wants that Needs that Loves that	Is doing that Speaking that Living that Being that
Receives information	Formulates thoughts, ideas, perceptions and interpretations	Creates rituals, patterns and roadmaps	Solidifies thoughts, ideas, perceptions, interpretations, rituals, patterns and roadmaps	Automates responses
Habituation begins here	Most critical step to habituation	Seduction begins Decision made	Desire blossoms **Lust is unleashed**	Establishes a new concept of self
Stage 1	Stage 1	Stage 2	Stage 2	Final stage

Figure 10
(Copyright © 2015 by Lance C. McCormack)

The CSU model of habituation has been created from countless hours of listening and communicating with people struggling with habits and self-proclaimed addictions. Although this model is likely to apply to all habits, this information relates specifically to habituation in regards to psychoactive substances and activities (alcohol and other drugs, food and caffeinated beverages, and gambling and sex). Just like the lower forms of animals, we too can become easily conditioned or habituated. That is just part of our instinctual makeup; like it or not, it resides within each of us. The differences between us and those lower animal forms, however, lie in our ability to be self-aware and use reason, emotions, and integrative processes as tools to help us make better choices and in effect recondition and decondition our responses to old triggers. These unique attributes of self-awareness allow us to look introspectively at our lives and behaviors and analyze what we're doing and what we need to change. Our problems only exist when we are unwilling to engage the higher mind and constantly resort to the default: the primitive, instinctual mind. For those willing, life begins again, fresh and beautiful as it was intended, but for those few "unfortunates" as described in the Big Book of Alcoholics Anonymous, pain and suffering will be their reality. In the following pages, I have outlined the steps of habituation in great detail in hopes that you will take these to heart and utilize them to understand why you are doing what you are doing and to realize happily that you can change whatever it is if you're willing to follow the steps.

Conscious Mind—Stage 1

I say "stage 1" to distinguish it from the processes of the entire conscious mind. It's the initial part of our conscious mind that is focused on speaking, viewing, hearing, reading, and discussing. It's that part that receives information from all sources and that serves as a holding area of stimuli waiting to be deciphered. So this is a very, very important part of habit forming in that if you're hanging around in the wrong places with the wrong people, seeing and doing all the wrong things, the wrong habits can begin quite easily. I guess the easy answer would be to just not put yourself in the wrong situations to begin with, but that's not any fun, now is it? On the flip side, we could be hanging around the right people in the right places and doing all the right things, and that would also begin the process of habit forming. By now, you must be saying that life is just not that cut and dry, and you're right, because life can be downright sticky and more of a combination of levels leading up to the ideal mixed with the circumstantial, so that the right people can sometimes find themselves in the wrong situations and not know what to do.

Here is where strategy meets common sense. First, do you have a strategy, a planned defense against developing the wrong habits? Many people don't, and then they find themselves caught with their pants down—literally in some cases—as a result. Recognize the challenges that face you, and decide what and who you want in your life and what and who you don't. Decide what you'll do for what you want and what you won't do.

Decide who you are and what you are, and who and what you want to be. Proceed.

Subconscious Mind—Stage 1

Many people speak of the subconscious as lying somewhere beneath the conscious mind, but since neither has been physically located, their positional relationship can only be viewed as conjecture. I suppose this idea or hierarchy was created to convey the sequence of thinking, and I have no argument with that. However, I suspect the subconscious to be a most critical step to habituation as it formulates everything taken from the conscious—what it's heard, seen, read, and discussed—and then makes subjective sense of it. This is where we interpret what we've encountered and where we perceive what those things we've encountered mean to us. This is where our thoughts of who we are and what we want and where we are headed come into question. This is where our ideas of ourselves and of our world are scrutinized. In a flash we will decide, are these things that we've heard, seen, read, and discussed a call to action or an alarm to flee?

Conscious Mind—Stage 2

Now, after we've formulated our thoughts, ideas, perceptions, and interpretations, we are ready either to act or not act or possibly wait until later when we have even more information on which to draw. If we decide there's no real reason not to act, then we proceed and start doing whatever behavior and keep doing it, doing it, doing it. And as we do it and keep doing it, whether it's alcohol or other drugs or sex, gambling, eating, or whatever our choice, we create rituals, patterns, and road maps that make it easier to do each time. These rituals, patterns, and road maps become a welcomed part of the habit. They create an anticipatory response, because we know we are doing these things in order to get paid. This payday comes in the form of getting high, and the rituals, patterns, and road maps leading up to getting high can eventually become even more powerful and exciting than the actual getting high. But for right now, we are completely enthralled by getting high. In this conscious stage, we confirm our decision as being the right decision, by our choice to continue to do it, do it, do it, despite any consequences or outside urgings, which are just seen as interferences. This stage is where seduction begins. It's like the beginning of a romance novel starring two unlikely characters who enter into a sordid romance that everyone knows deep down is going to end badly.

Subconscious Mind—Stage 2

We agree that we like what we're doing, we agree that it's what we want to do, we agree that we need it in our lives, and we agree that we simply, undeniably love it! So now that we're in agreement and we've made this critical decision to continue along this path, the courting process proceeds swiftly and unabated. It's as if mariachis with their song and flowers appear at our doorstep welcoming us into the fold. The problem is that our new family is highly dysfunctional at best and deadly at worst and promises us nothing but to steadily take more from us. As our subconscious mind consents to being part of this family, we consent to enter into a trance that will solidify all the reasons why we should and dispel all the reasons why we shouldn't. In this stage, we solidify and confirm our previous thoughts, ideas, perceptions, and interpretations regarding our new decision and delight at our new rituals and patterns and impress ourselves with our clever new road maps. In this stage, we willingly commit all of these things to the deepest recesses of our souls, with the hope that they remain for as long as we shall live. With each passing event, our desires blossom greater, until ultimately *lust* emerges and outstretches its powerful arms and locks them tightly around us. At this point, we have bought into a new way of living, into a new lifestyle, hook, line, and sinker. And the only difference now between us and a fish that's hooked is...we want to remain hooked!

Unconscious Mind—The Final Stage

Happy and content with our new friends and family, we don't even notice that our routines have become second nature and no longer require any forethought. Our new habits are nearly all automated by now and are becoming more deeply embedded with every breath. At every opportunity we are doing that new thing, speaking about that thing, living that life, and being all the things that constitute a person who does those things: a liar, a sneak, a thief, and most of all, a liability. During this final stage, in the unconscious mind, all the dreams we had as kids vanish as if they never existed, and only one dream prevails. A new concept of who we are is firmly established, and the dream to never let this dream end is born!

Here we have it, all the steps involved in starting a new habit. Note: these six steps are not to be confused with the five stages I've described earlier. Follow these steps to create whatever and whomever you'd like to become. Also follow these steps if you're already someone who has created a new, unhealthy persona and now wants to become someone new and improved:

Step 1: Stop what you're currently doing!
Step 2: Begin with stage 1, and follow through until you've reached the unconscious final stage.

This is how that looks: if you're a smoker, stop smoking, start listening to non-smokers, start hanging out with only nonsmokers, start reading about all the benefits of being a nonsmoker, and start discussing how great you feel now that you're a nonsmoker.

Step 2: Think like a nonsmoker, believe you will always be a nonsmoker, trust that you've made a very wise decision to be a nonsmoker, and feel the difference in your body now that you're a nonsmoker.
Step 3: Seduction takes hold, and regardless of what happens to you, good or bad, you've made the decision to be a nonsmoker, and nonsmokers continually don't smoke.
Step 4: Like that you're a nonsmoker, want all the benefits of being a non-smoker, need to remain a nonsmoker, and love that you're a nonsmoker.
Step 5: Breathing fresh air, talking about healthy subjects, living a healthy lifestyle, and being someone who values health, you are now someone new!

Now, if you're currently a nonsmoker and desire to begin a smoking habit, simply reverse these steps.

These are the five steps to habituation. The only additional thing you'll need for success in creating a new habit is a sincere desire to change. Based on how easy it is to create a new habit, we may want to reconsider "liking to feel numb" as the chapter title suggests. Because although habits can be changed just by reversing the steps outlined, desire remains as the devil in the details.

CHAPTER 15

So, You Like "Not Giving a F——k!"

Your body is the harp of your soul. And it is yours to
bring forth sweet music from it or confused sounds.
—Khalil Gibran

must first begin by apologizing for my use of the F-word. This is not a word I regularly use in daily discourse, so I feel quite uncomfortable using it here. I generally believe it to be a vulgar word and one that's used primarily by those with little self-control, at least in that moment, or by those with limited communications skills or simply by those that just don't give a f——k! The only reason why I've stepped out of my comfort zone to use the F-word in this case is because I believe its use is absolutely necessary to convey the exact sentiment that was conveyed to me. Sure, I could have said, "not caring at all, not giving a damn," "not giving a rat's ass," or even "not giving a shit," but I don't believe any of those phrases have the punch that I need, plus none of them were what was actually said. I need you as the reader to know exactly what was said, and how serious what was said is, so you can feel the true extent of the problems we're facing as a nation.

This chapter title reflects the third part of a response I received from a young lady when I had asked her, "Why do you use drugs?" The first two parts of her response were, "because I like getting high" and "feeling numb." So, when we put all the parts together we have "I use drugs because I like getting high, feeling numb, and not giving a f——k!" When she said that, I asked her if she was kidding, and she replied, "I'm dead serious!" I then asked the other ladies in our group if they concurred, and they answered resoundingly that they did. Now, these ladies weren't high when they said this, so I suspect this is how they really felt. Therein lies the problem: we have people seeking to having no regards for the rest of us, as the reason they voluntarily use drugs. So the votes are in, and we'd better be listening; otherwise we'll never be able to say we weren't told.

When I asked this lady to kindly explain what exactly "not giving a f——k" meant, she said it means "not caring about anything; what other people think, what other people do, how other people feel, not caring about following rules, regulations, having any responsibilities, nothing!" Now, in the first chapter of this section, I talked about people using drugs because they like getting high. In the second chapter, I wrote about how people use drugs because they like feeling numb. In this third and final chapter of this section, I'm writing about people who use drugs because they like "not giving a f——k" about anything. Now, there's a major difference between these three premises. The first two intimately involve only the people taking the drugs, but the third premise involves all of us. I realize that it could easily be argued that all three involve us, and I wouldn't disagree, but for the sake of addressing the greater public liability, I've chosen to focus on number three.

In this chapter I'll discuss how the pleasure of a few, will jeopardize the safety of many. After all, how safe do you feel knowing you're driving down roads and highways with people who "don't give a f——k" about you! I'm sure you'd feel a lot safer if they just stayed home and off of the roads. Think about it, at any moment, those people could jeopardize your life and the lives of your families and never even blink! Can you imagine, people willingly wanting to enter a state in which they will feel absolutely no compunction in running you over with their cars or hitting you over the head with a bat to take your wallet. The concept becomes even more disturbing when we contemplate how we're continually working to pass new rules and regulations and fund new treatment programs to help and benefit these same people who "don't give a f——k" about us.

Let Chaos Rule?

Please allow me to further illustrate my point: As a hypnotherapist I am always using imagery to spark imagination and stir emotions and allow people to view what they say and what they do, differently. Imagine having every city and every town in every state divided into two. One side would be called the "user" side, and the other side would be called the "nonuser" side.

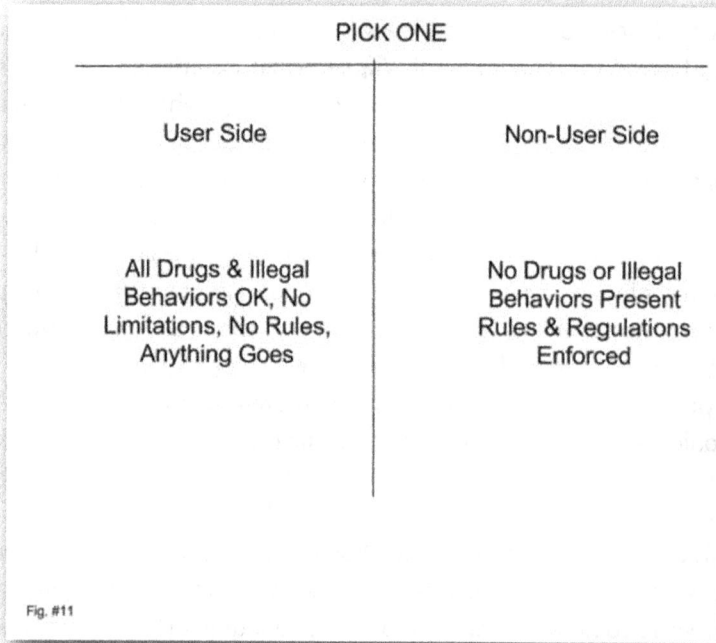

PICK ONE

User Side	Non-User Side
All Drugs & Illegal Behaviors OK, No Limitations, No Rules, Anything Goes	No Drugs or Illegal Behaviors Present Rules & Regulations Enforced

Fig. #11

On the user side, as the diagram illustrates, "anything goes." You can drink all the alcohol you want, drive drunk, drive the wrong way down the highway, and never be fined or jailed for any of it. You can shoot all the dope you want and never hear anyone say "don't" or "stop." No police will put you in jail, and no one will judge anything you do. You can eat until you explode because no one will ever mention that you should consider losing weight for your health. You can chain smoke while on oxygen without requiring the posting of any WARNING—OXYGEN IN USE signs on your front door. You can have all the indiscriminate sex you want and transmit all the communicable diseases you desire without any consideration whatsoever!

Whenever I've painted this vivid picture of how things could possibly be and then discussed it in a treatment setting, I've seen patients' eyes glaze over as their mouths water with delight. They say, "We could have anything and do anything?" I respond, "Certainly! This is the user side!" I explain how everyone there is doing what they want and as much as they want. I mention that if they have any children, of course the children will have to removed and taken to the nonuser side until they're old enough to legally make their own decision. After a few sad faces and a few seconds pass, the patients are smiling again with the notion of living in such an amazing place that allows them to do anything. Just as everyone has packed their bags and is ready for nirvana, I remind them that since everyone on their side is doing whatever they want, that includes all the people providing services for them. I say what that means specifically is that your dentists and your doctors, your gynecologists and your proctologists are all on something. Your surgeon is on dope, and your cardiologist is on crack, and everyone providing you anything is on something that drastically impairs their judgment. All of a sudden, almost in unison, all the smiling faces turn into faces of disappointment as patients reconsider living on the user side.

The takeaway is this: I want to be irresponsible, undependable, unreliable, and un-predictable, but I want everyone else who attends to me to be in complete control of their faculties. It's like having a case of Peter Pan syndrome, where we want to be children forever and never grow up, feeling footloose and fancy free and with no cares in the world. And like children, we also want to be excused for our bad behaviors because we're only children, but we still want to be surrounded by re-sponsible adults who can take care of us. So this is interesting! No one now wants to be on the user side; they all want to be on the nonuser side, but still using. And that's what we currently have in America: users who don't want to be adults taking advantage of nonusers who are being adults, and it's just getting worse!

All I've said is in an effort to demonstrate how users just don't care how they're impacting the rest of us, as long as their own desires are being met. Maybe this next example will make my point a little clearer. Have you ever been in a pub-lic restroom, standing over the sink and washing your hands, and you overhear someone on a toilet who's grunting and groaning and then flushes the toilet? I know I have, on more occasions than I'd like to remember. Anyway, just as you hear the toilet flush, you see the person in the mirror as they emerge from the stall and walk directly out the restroom door. You stand there kind of motionless because you can't believe they're leaving after using the toilet without washing their hands. We're in the year 2016, and just about everyone in America has been given the "wash your hands" speech by now. So why do you think it's still an issue? Why are some people still not following that simple rule of good hygiene? It's been scientifically proven that germs can pass from one person to another and transmit all kinds of diseases and even cause epidemics. So again, why wouldn't everyone be on board with something as simple as washing their hands? Do these people who don't wash their hands believe that germs don't exist and it's all a lie and some sort of conspiracy? Who knows? What we do know for certain is that these people create problems for the rest of us.

If you're a *Seinfeld* fan, you probably remember an episode involving Jerry and the owner of a pizza restaurant. It's the same scenario. Jerry is at the sink washing his hands as the restaurant owner and pizza maker exits the toilet rubbing his hands together. The difference is that the owner knows Jerry, so he walks up behind him and says, "Now, Jerry, with these hands, I'm gonna make you a delicious pizza pie!" The scene ends with Jerry standing there with his mouth open and a look of horror on his face. It all seems innocent enough, but is it? Who wants their food prepared by someone who has just wiped their ass and not washed their hands? Only the people who like the taste of feces, would be my guess. So, why would any person do that to another person? Is it because they don't care, or because they don't give a damn, or because they don't give a rat's ass, or don't give a shit, or is it simply because they just don't give a f——k about anyone but themselves?

SECTION VI

The Fourth Element of Addiction: Lust Unleashed

Passion is like nature's fruit that grows stronger with
every rain or dies abruptly upon sudden drought.
—A LANCEISM

n these pages, readers will discover unequivocally what addiction has unleashed
and will awaken to the fact that the lustful people among us are truly in a fight
for their lives. This section explores the fourth of the six elements of addiction.

CHAPTER 16

Where Have You Been All My Life?

Like with Pandora's box, with some
people, it's just a matter of when.
—A LANCEISM

"Where have you been all my life?" is the question we ask once we're under the trance of psychoactive drugs. Suddenly, life appears brighter and richer in all dimensions, and a life without our new friends seems totally unimaginable. This is the essence of lust.

"Love Is a Many-Splendored Thing" is a beautiful song and very true when it's really love: something that brings true joy and soul satisfaction. Lust, on the other hand, may sometimes get easily confused with love and be perceived as something that promises you nothing but the best that life has to offer. However, since the beginning of recorded time, lust has proven to be nothing more than a destructive, tawdry imposter of love, simply masquerading as the real thing, an imposter that historically promises to leave only misery and casualties in its wake and create an energy demand beyond all others.

Many definitions speak of lust only in sexual terms, but I believe lust to have much broader applications. My definition of lust is "the unhealthy desire for or preoccupation with someone or something that is best left alone. The endless chasing of something that is best left uncaught." Lust, this wanton desire to experience and possess bodily and sensory pleasures, can rule our lives, and in some cases, takes our lives. Lust exists entirely based on a flawed belief: that one's pleasures or appetites and satisfaction should come before all else and all others. Lust is truly the wellspring of all addictions. Once lust develops in a person, this self-indulgent, hedonistic view of one's life puts everyone in their path at high risk. Until the person understands what has happened, and until they become willing to accept the reality of their distorted worldview and sincerely desire to change, nothing will change within the individual.

Previously I demonstrated through the CSU model of habituation how lust develops, and now I will show you how lust is sustained through the "crossover." It's all about column A and column B.

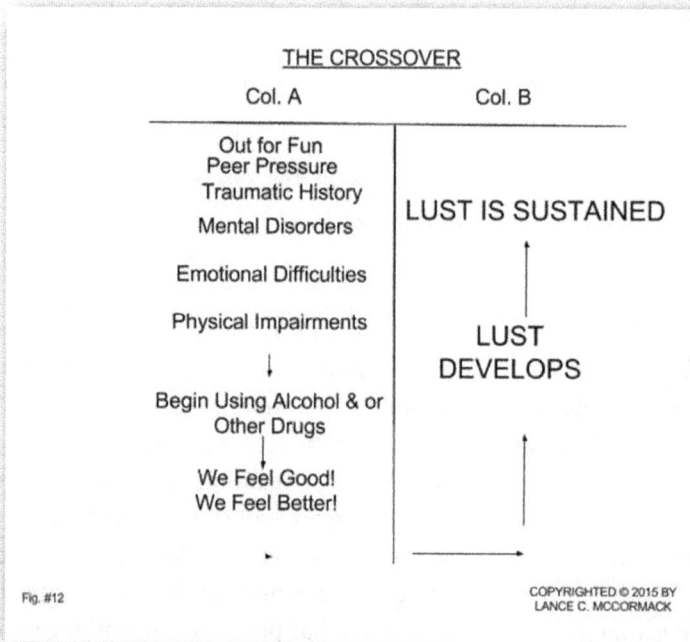

THE CROSSOVER

Col. A	Col. B
Out for Fun Peer Pressure Traumatic History Mental Disorders Emotional Difficulties Physical Impairments ↓ Begin Using Alcohol & or Other Drugs ↓ We Feel Good! We Feel Better!	LUST IS SUSTAINED ↑ LUST DEVELOPS ↑

Fig. #12

COPYRIGHTED © 2015 BY
LANCE C. MCCORMACK

As you can see, whether we begin using drugs to have fun and experience pleasure or begin using drugs to self-medicate or begin using drugs through our doctor's suggestion, it all shakes out the same in the final analysis. Lust for that drug or that activity is what results when we cross over, and at that point there is no longer any distinction. At that point, the reasons for continued use are all the same: *lust*! Why we began using drugs is no longer material. And from that point, lust is sustained by continued use or even more powerfully sustained by our continued dreaming of our initial encounters with our objects of desire.

We can all see that curious person who's willing to do or try anything at least once becoming that drug addict. We kind of expect that. They don't think much about warnings or listen to much of what others suggest not doing, and they generally discount the gravity of anything they hear. The surprise comes from that part of the population we didn't expect to become addicts. We never imagined that the hardworking, well-educated, church-going people among us would ever succumb to addiction. That's because we were told that addiction had a face. We were led to believe that we could calculate which people would become addicted based on their ethnicity and/or social class, as opposed to how people thought or what behaviors they followed. Man, were we wrong! As I've said many times before, this propensity for labeling everything and everyone in America has only caused us to misunderstand each other and how things genuinely work. Let's stop doing that!

Fig. #13

LUST

BY LANCE C. MCCORMACK

In the crossover, you can see how both the party-loving drug user and the unsuspecting, self-medicating drug user end up in the same place, with raging addictions. As my illustration depicts, once we make the crossover, it no longer matters which boat we arrived in, because now we're all in the same boat called lust, and this boat has a gaping hole in it! I hope I've made that point crystal clear. The difficulty comes when we're dealing with sixty-year-olds who try to convince us that the reason they continue to use or do whatever is because of their traumatic history, their mental disorder, their emotional difficulties, and/or their physical impairments. Now, I'm not trying to dismiss or diminish any problems a person may have, and I sincerely feel empathy for their conditions. My goal, however, is to make certain the person understands the difference between the two columns. It's extremely easy and convenient to use column A as the reason for continued use, especially since so many counselors/therapists, family members, and friends buy into it.

Now, while you may claim that the pain you feel from whatever happened to you as a five-year-old still remains like it happened yesterday, and that's why you continue to use, I'm not buying it. You shouldn't either, because you know it isn't the truth, and until you can be honest with yourself, we've got nothing! Because column A and column B are distinctly two different things, and we shouldn't get the two confused if we really want to stop the behavior. That confusion started years ago, with the theory that the two areas of concern—the personal, problematic history and the drug use—were indivisible and one and the same. They speculated that once we uncovered a person's underlying personal problems and sufficiently addressed those, the person's drug habit would instantly vanish. Some people still practice under that delusion today. However, I have never seen that to be the case. What I have seen to be the case is, you could work on a person's traumatic history for a hundred years and unravel every reason for everything that's ever happened to that person, and that person would still be hooked on their drug of choice. The reason is because it's still their drug of *choice*.

When we are taking medications as prescribed, generally our risk for addiction is lower, but not zero. But when we start taking medications, prescribed or otherwise, with no regard for their destructive value and only seek to get more relief, sedation, or pleasure from their increased use, we run the greatly increased risk of making the crossover. Once we've made the crossover, there's no turning back, because at that point, an imprint has been emblazoned on our soul. It's like jumping off of a building after deliberating for an hour; once you jump, all deliberations are over, and only consequences remain!

What makes lust for anything so challenging to overcome? The challenge exists because lust is a "thinking" problem, not a disease, and because it's a thinking problem, we are constantly confronted with deciding which thoughts to think about. Now, I know no one is actually even talking about lust as a disease per se; it's addiction that we're usually talking about as being a disease. But lust is the wellspring, the mother of all addictions, so one would infer from that connection that lust must also be a disease. As a result, we are treating lust as a disease when it is far from that. Actually, a disease would be easier to treat; our doctors would give us some helpful suggestions and a few prescriptions, and voila, we'd get better! But we all know that we're already being given suggestions now and being given even more than a few prescriptions now, but we also know in our heart of hearts that they aren't working.

So I suspect the plan is to create new drugs, stronger drugs, that will treat this "disease" more effectively. After all, sooner or later, we have to come up with the perfect pharmaceutical cure for this disease, because there's a lot of money riding on this. What if it's not a disease and we're wasting a lot of time, money, and energy traveling down the wrong road? Do you think it would have been time, money, and energy well spent? Absolutely not! We already know that what we're doing isn't working, but we keep doing it anyway. Lust is an element of addiction and is neither a disease nor part of a disease but rather is the result of *compounded thinking*, whereby one's thoughts intensify sequentially. This cyclical sequence is illustrated below:

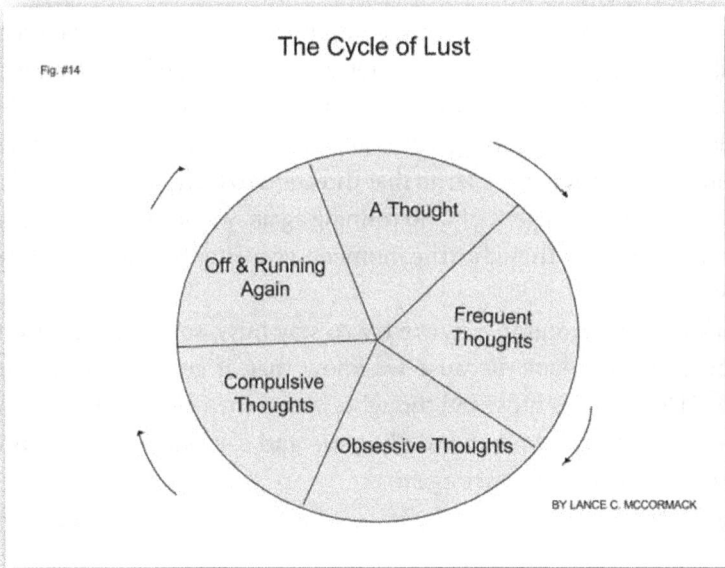

The Cycle of Lust

Fig. #14

A Thought

Off & Running Again

Frequent Thoughts

Compulsive Thoughts

Obsessive Thoughts

BY LANCE C. MCCORMACK

This is how lust is sustained, through thinking and dwelling on thoughts. Where the mind goes, the body is sure to follow. In the first stage, we begin with a thought, one conjured from our dreams, perceptions, and experiences and reinforced by our interpretations. With that thought, we begin to create vivid images in our minds, utilizing all of our senses—sight, sound, scent, taste, and touch—and we imagine the pleasures to be had in these things. These solitary thoughts alone provide a level of pleasure. An imaginary pleasure, a pleasure in considering the remote possibility of experiencing what we've conjured up in our minds. This level of satisfaction only whets our appetites for more.

With a spark of excitement, we happily agree to dedicate our free time to the self-indulgent ritual of thinking repetitive or frequent thoughts (stage 2) about our object(s) of desire. In this stage we have created a specific focus of attention that begins to take shape and create an internal heat that, albeit just an ember, is a heat that smolders nonetheless.

In stage 3, our kindling has caught fire, and our flame's intensity is clearly evident as our frequent thoughts are now obsessive thoughts that interrupt our daily lives and activities. Our desires now seem inescapable and ones that must be satisfied. Our desires are all consuming now and leave willpower little ammunition for defense. We have allowed a spell to take hold, and we are now in real danger of hurting ourselves and others.

In our penultimate stage, stage 4, compulsive thoughts, we have succumbed to our all-consuming thoughts of obsession and have compelled ourselves through our thinking to satisfy our desires through any and all means possible. Our mind is completely on board, and our body is anxious to comply. Our once-internal fire has become a raging external inferno that threatens to leave an entire family in ruin.

In our final stage, stage 5, off and running again, we need no explanation. The goal is to interrupt our thoughts the moment we invite them into our heads. Yes, I said invite!

That's the whole reason why we try to stay busy, so we don't have time to stroll down memory lane. Because we know that, if given the opportunity to dream, we'll likely invite those old thoughts in and then entertain those thoughts as they become more frequent and obsessive and compulsive, and then we'll be running down Main Street once again.

The Big "O"—and It's Not *Orgasm*

Scenario: Picture yourself living with your partner. Imagine having an addiction that has caused your relationship all kinds of problems over the years. Recall all the arguments, fights, jail terms, and personal losses that have resulted from your addiction. Recall all the finger pointing, threats, and ultimatums you've received because of your continued use. Think of how tired you are of hearing the phrases "stop drinking," "stop using those drugs," "stop gambling," and "stop watching all that porn." Feel how sick you are of being controlled by your partner and not being allowed to do what you want. Well, here's your opportunity, and you know what they say about opportunity: when it knocks, you'd better answer it.

You happen to overhear a phone conversation between your partner and her sister in California, and the gist of the conversation is that the sister is having a serious problem there in California and is asking your partner for her immediate help.

Your partner: That's terrible!
Her sister: Sis, I really need you here as soon as possible.
Your partner: Not a problem, I'll be on the next available flight out. I expect it will take a while to resolve this problem, so I expect to be with you for at least a month. Don't worry. I love you!

Man, this is like having just hit Powerball! Your ears can't believe what they've just heard, and you feel like the luckiest person in the world. Opportunity has struck and struck big! Once the phone hangs up, this is what transpires.

You: Is there a problem, honey?
Your partner: Yeah, my sister needs my help, and I have to go to California.
You: California? That's so far away! Honey, when do you have to leave, and how long will you have to be away?
Your partner: I know it's far, but I have to go. I have to make arrangements now for the next flight I can get. I expect I'll have to stay there for a least a month to help take care of things.
You: Honey, that's too bad! I know you love your sister, so I understand that you have to go, but I'll really miss you nonetheless.
Your partner: I'll miss you too.
You: Can I help you with anything?

Does this scenario sound at all familiar to you? Well, this scene is playing out every day across America where we perceive an opportunity to use whatever we use in complete peace and without any outside interferences. The moment the opportunity arises to use, free of accusations, complaints, judgment, and reprisals, lust kicks into high gear. We calculate the time we have to use and then determine when we'll have to stop using in order to be squared away in time for our partner's return. This way no one will have to know anything—no harm, no foul. The instant that thought enters our minds, it quickly catapults through the cycle to compulsion, and we tell ourselves, "Oh yeah, I'm really doing this."

Let me give you an example of how lust works and how time has little to do with our success in recovery. The key to recovery is intent.

Audrey was patient at a methadone clinic assigned to my caseload years ago. She was young single parent with several children. She was a model as far as patients go: dosing as scheduled and always appearing to be in good spirits. She dressed extremely well, always in designer clothing and sporting some new, name-brand pocketbook. She smelled of expensive perfume and drove a fancy, late-model car. From the outside, she looked the part of a person really motivated to get the job done and move on with her life without drugs. I had a concern though. The clinic had a few requirements of its patients, and one requirement was that each patient see her/his clinician a minimum of fifty minutes a month in counseling. It never seemed like an unreasonable requirement to me, but it turned out to be like pulling teeth for most patients. Many times I would wind up chasing patients through the parking lot to ask to see them. I would tell them that there were only a few days left to the month and that I hadn't seen them yet. They would always promise to see me the following day, but it never seemed to happen.

Inevitably, it would come down to the last day of the month, and I'd have a whole bunch of people still to see. So in order for me to do my job and fulfill the clinic's counseling requirement, I would have to put a hold on each patient in my computer in order to prevent them from being given their methadone until they saw me. This practice went on each and every month, like clockwork, for five years. I always wondered why the patients saw it to be so difficult to see me or whoever their counselor was for a measly fifty minutes out of thirty days.

Methadone is an interesting drug. It's an opiate-like drug, a synthetic opiate, otherwise known as an opioid, and one used to help users of other opioids reclaim their lives. The main reason it's supposed to benefit opioid users is because it's a long-acting drug that provides the patient with time to feel normal and be able to accomplish their everyday tasks of living without having feelings of withdrawal. Normally the opioid user has to use every few hours and spend every day searching for where and how they're going to get their next fix. Not with methadone; it provides the user with the confidence that they'll be withdrawal-free for twenty-four to seventy-two hours at a time on average (of course, each patient is different based on their individual metabolic rates). So methadone sounds like a wonder drug, and to some, it may appear to be so, but I'm still not convinced.

Okay, back to the measly fifty-minute-a-month counseling requirement. Honesty, think about it: How could anyone see this miniscule amount of time a month to be excessive or prohibitive if they're sincerely interested in getting off of drugs? The opportunity to sit down with an addictions specialist and discuss strategies for ending one's dependence on drugs should be something that each patient who's sincere about recovery would jump at. Wouldn't you think? Well, that's not the case—not even close. Actually, when my patients finally saw me and we were done and I said to them, "Good to see you again," they would reply, "No problem," as if they had done me a favor, because now I could keep my job since I'd fulfilled my requirement of having them fulfill their requirement. Is that sick or what? I was trying to help them with *their* drug habit, and somehow they had done me a favor.

Well, back to Audrey...she had earned our highest level of take-home status. In some methadone clinics, they allow patients to earn the privilege to not have to come in daily to get their dose of methadone. This privilege is earned over time when the patient has been compliant and has fulfilled all clinic requirements, in addition to testing negative on all of their regular urinalysis screens. Most patients are thrilled by the idea of earning take-homes because it allows them more freedom and they don't feel the pressure to get to the clinic every day before it closes. At our clinic, the highest level of take-home status a patient could earn was thirteen days, and Audrey had earned it. She would come in and pick up thirteen bottles of methadone, and then we would see her again in thirteen days when she returned those same thirteen, now empty bottles, so she was rarely at the clinic. Twice a month we saw her because she usually scheduled her counseling session for one of those days she was getting her bottles. The idea was, she had to be at the clinic anyway, so she might as well get the counseling stuff done at the same time.

I hope you're starting to get the feeling that Audrey wasn't necessarily the ideal patient after all and that she wasn't necessarily that gung ho about learning all she could about recovery. One day when Audrey was in the clinic to pick up her bottles, I had happened to be walking by and stopped to talk with her. She was the only patient in line, so we were able to speak freely. As we were talking initially, we were looking at each other eye to eye, as people normally do when having a conversation. Minutes later, I noticed Audrey was looking down intently at the floor and no longer looking at me as I spoke to her. I felt it was odd because here I was looking at her face, and there she was staring at the floor. I asked Audrey why she was looking at the floor and not at me, and she replied, "No reason. I can still hear you." I continued to talk with her but asked her again why she was looking at the floor, and she again replied, "I can hear every word you're saying, so don't worry, just keep on talking."

Finally I had had enough of this odd conversation, and I looked down at the floor, only to see a small piece of white paper. I bent down and picked the paper up and looked at Audrey's face as I did. To my amazement, Audrey's forehead was sweaty, her pupils were dilated, and the sides of her mouth were dripping saliva. It was like watching the Pavlov's dog experiment. As I held the paper in my hand, I decided to wave it from side to side, only to see Audrey follow my every movement as if she were in some kind of trance. I then said, "Audrey, it's just a bubble gum wrapper. What did you think it was?"

She replied, "A heroin wrapper."

The moment I said "bubble gum wrapper," Audrey's face returned to normal: her face dried, her pupils returned to normal size, and her mouth stopped salivating. It was a very sad thing to see. Audrey had been in treatment for eight years and had earned the top take-home status, which is supposed to indicate a high level of recovery, but had displayed all the evidence that, had that wrapper had heroin in it, she would have relapsed as soon as she could get that wrapper in her hands.

Audrey's case is crystalline proof that time in treatment is not the most important factor in recovery, but intent is. What we really want is what will make the difference between recovery and a life of relapse. Audrey had never displayed that counseling was an important part of recovery. Actually, she had displayed exactly the opposite, that counseling was just an imposition and not something that she would ever do voluntarily. She saw no value in it. She, like most of the patients I met, would have preferred that our clinic had a drive-through, where patients would drive quickly by, state their names, and the nurses would throw bottles of methadone into their cars. Audrey really didn't care if she ever saw a counselor.

I've just given you a few scenarios of how the "Big O" works, so now you'll have an opportunity to try it for yourself. Picture yourself all alone in the desert surrounded by all the alcohol and other drugs of your past choice. All the objects you've ever lusted over are there and it's just you and them. But, before we go any further, I want to preface this image with the reality of the "three to five" rule. This rule exists for all human beings and states: three to five weeks without food, we're dead; three to five days without water, we're dead; and three to five minutes without oxygen, usually we're dead. So now, back to the desert…there you are all alone with all your old favorites, but this time without anyone to see you or say anything to you. No one to say, how could you, I thought you were over that or if you do it, we're done! So, what do you do? And although I won't be able to know your response, you will, and your response will tell you where you are in this process of recovery. You have just taken a test! Feel free to retake this test as often as you like, to gauge how you're doing and how far you still have to go.

This is the problem we face as a nation. We don't understand the true motivations of drug users, so we keep on treating them incorrectly. Addiction is about lust, so we have to treat lust. Addiction cannot exist without lust! As long as the user continues to lust for his/her objects or activities of desire, he/she will continue to be living under severe torment. The severe torment exists because users know they are living a lie every day and not getting what they really want because of all of the constraints imposed upon them by the rest of society. They are following protocols and procedures that they must follow; some in order to maintain their jobs and families, some in order to qualify for medications and state and federal monies, and some just in order to stay out of jail, but all the while, they're all just looking for opportunities to get high when no one can catch them. It's that simple!

Lust is based on reverie—on memory and dreams of the past and on hopes for the future. Lust keeps alive possibilities of what we believe will make us feel more alive and what will make us feel less afraid. Lust is about thinking about ourselves when we should be thinking about others. Lust may or may not involve external drugs but will always involve the chemicals that we produce in our minds and bodies. Lust survives on not knowing if or when we will again experience that deeply satisfying feeling that we desire above all else, which we consider to be unconditional love. Lust will never end until the objects of our desire are no longer seen as desirable.

CHAPTER 17

"If There's a Cure for This, I Don't Want It!"

Make sure what you want is worth wanting,
before you devote your life to a dying cause.
—A LANCEISM

The line "If there's a cure for this, I don't want it" is from a great song entitled "Love Hangover" that was sung by Diana Ross and was very popular in the eighties. I remember many a person moving and grooving passionately to that song back then. I know I was one of them. Its lyrics evoked sensuality, while its music produced an almost hypnotic quality that enticed and virtually massaged you as each verse repeated the sultry message that once you enter the dreamlike state of love, you'll never want to leave. As the song suggests, if there was a cure for love, you wouldn't want it, and its other lyrics state, "If there's a remedy, I'll run from it." I'm suggesting that not only Diana Ross feels this way, and although what we feel with drugs is lust and not love, in this dreamlike state, it's nearly impossible at times to discern the difference.

So we've unleashed this beast called lust that has us salivating for more and disregarding everyone and everything while in its hot pursuit. It's like becoming part of a cult where we're willing to do anything for our leader. We have fallen under its spell and have willingly relinquished ourselves to this "higher power." At this point, we'll lie for our leader, we'll rob for our leader, we'll kill for our leader, and we'll die for our leader. Yes, drug taking is a cult, and we as drug users are cult members, or more accurately, we're cult followers, and drugs are our leaders! It gives a new meaning to that old phrase "Take me to your leader." Throughout history there have been memorable cults and many not so memorable cults. One cult that perhaps deserves mention was located in Guyana, a country in South America. Under the mad direction of its cult leader, Jim Jones, a reported 918 people died on November 18, 1978, in a mass murder/suicide at the Peoples Temple Agricultural Project, better known as Jonestown and the Guyana incident.

Let's contemplate how a cult member is created. Generally, cults comprise the disenfranchised among us, the people who don't feel their lives are meaningful and who don't anticipate finding a place in the world as it currently exists. They envision their world to be full of conspiracies and egregious injustices and feel blistering irritation and frustration with every breath. They possess a desire to rebel for rebellion's sake and a scorching curiosity to experience the prohibited at all costs. They revel in causing drama and delight in wreaking havoc. I know this description sounds like I'm talking about your teenager, but for the most part I'm not, although teenagers are particularly prone to the appeal of charismatic cult leaders. Teenagers are so vulnerable because cult leaders know their target audience, and they intuitively know how to spot followers wherever they are. And once cult leaders have found their prey, they court them relentlessly. Of course, the more obviously defiant the target, the easier and quicker the conversion. So the people among us who are angry and argumentative and plain old stubborn as hell quickly rise to the front of the selection list for any cult leader. These people are ripe for lust to fill their hearts, as their hearts are begging to be filled with something. These followers can't wait to get started to express all their pent-up anxieties and downright dissatisfaction with life in general. They can't wait to get out from under others' perceived control and exercise their free will. They can't wait to show the world who they are by their acts of noncompliance and to put the world on notice as to how they intend to be ruled by their desires instead of by others.

To be ruled by our desires sounds somewhat captivating but also quite scary. To be ruled by anything sounds…not good. Lust, however, does just that: it rules, and we follow. And once we become bona fide followers, we do whatever it takes to remain followers. The more we do, the more we need to do, and the more we need to do, the more we are ruled! As we discussed in the last chapter, lust is "the unhealthy desire for or preoccupation with someone or something that is best left alone. The endless chasing of something that is best left uncaught." Lust is therefore intangible and something that only exists in our minds. Lust is a "thinking" problem, and one that will only go away once it's actually perceived as a problem.

The problem is like this chapter title suggests, "If there's a cure for this, I don't want it." In this case, lust is not seen as a problem, but rather as a godsend for which we desire no cure, and that's a major problem!

Think about how successful we usually are at feeding our infants when they have no desire to eat what we're trying to feed them. Even if we attempt to force-feed them, we are usually highly unsuccessful, and our attempts are extremely messy at the very least. On the other hand, how difficult is it to feed them something they want to eat? Well, that's the predicament we're in, trying to treat people who don't want to be treated. It doesn't work, and it wastes valuable time, energy, and money.

Fantasy vs. Reality

I was talking to a man named Fred one day, and he told me a story of how he'd come to make an important decision. He recounted being in the military and meeting a girl:

> I was a gate guard on a naval base, and I had met a girl that used to come on to the base because she had base privileges as an officer's daughter. One thing led to another, and before long we were dating. She had three little children, and all under the ages of five. They were the cutest kids, and I loved them as if they were my own. My girlfriend wasn't the sweetest mom to them, although I could see she cared for them in her own special way.
>
> Their father wasn't in the picture, so she was the only one in their lives until I came along. I spent all the time I could with her whenever I wasn't on duty at the base. We had a great time together, talking and laughing and just enjoying each other's company. She smoked marijuana on occasion and thought it was funny to blow the smoke in the kids' faces and then see them run around giggling. I didn't find it to be humorous, and I would often tell her so. Nonetheless, our relationship moved forward, but not without reservations. She was a nice girl, and I was definitely infatuated with her, but there was something missing. I just didn't know where we were going in life because I didn't feel we had much in common or that she had much ambition. I know I loved her, but I was increasingly unsure as to how our relationship would fare long term. Despite my doubts,

we got married within a year, and I felt good being a father and having a ready-made family.

Within months I was called to sea and expected to be gone for at least six months. Aboard ship I had many a day and many a night to think. Many nights as I lay there in my bed, I would think of home and my wife and our kids. I would think of how I missed them, and then I would think of the doubts I had about whether I had made the right decision to get married. After all, I was young and thought I was in love, and I had little time away from her to really see our relationship objectively. I was so immersed in it while I was home with her, it was like I couldn't see the forest for the trees. But now at sea, with time away and my mind clear of any distractions, I could see our relationship clearly for what it was, and I could distinguish the fantasy from the reality.

The fantasy was based on our mutual infatuation, but the reality was that we were very different people with very different goals and expectations for the future. So as I lay there in my bed, or "rack," as they called it, I asked myself one simple question, "Can I see myself being happy with her five years from now?" My instant response to myself was "No!" First thing in the morning, I wrote her a letter explaining exactly how I felt and apologized for breaking her heart. I told her that she was a wonderful girl and one who would make some guy very happy one day, but that I unfortunately just wasn't that guy.

This is what lust is all about: being lost in an illusion. Being unable to separate the fantasy from the reality. While we're immersed in the illusion, we suppress our inner voice that's telling us anything contrary to the illusion. Time away, however, can be exactly what we need. If utilized correctly, time can provide us with the clarity to see things as they really are. I say "can" because time is interesting and can be used in different ways. The common way we use time when we're away from what we think we want is to spend our time pining for that someone or something as if a death had occurred. We're essentially heartbroken and grief stricken and displaying feelings of depression and emptiness, and we can't wait for the torture to be over. Although that's the most common way we use time away, it's not the only choice we have.

Remember the saying "Absence makes the heart grow fonder"? Well, not necessarily. Sometimes it works like the other saying: "Out of sight, out of mind." As I mentioned earlier, time away can free our objectivity and allow us the opportunity to step back and look at the whole picture clearly and unobstructed. It's like standing on the top of the Empire State Building in New York City seeing everything below like chess pieces on a chessboard. From that view, you can see which moves you must make in order to win the game. The only question at that point is do you really want to win, if it means no longer doing what you think you love?

Seeing Things as They Are

As important as it is for the addicted person to see things as they are and not remain in the world of illusions, it's even more important for us to see them clearly and as they are so we don't get caught up in their illusions. After all, their choices are just that, their choices, and we must never forget that. We can remain supportive, but never to the detriment of our own well-being. That would just be foolish!

If There's a Remedy, I'll Run from It

Think about all the treatments and all the treatment facilities around the nation, and still we're still facing an opioid epidemic. They say that addicts need more centers and more treatments and more compassion and more funding, but no one is talking about what we need. We need fewer addicts and fewer alcoholics! We need more people stepping up and doing the right things for themselves and their families. We need fewer people starting to use drugs and more people being responsible for their own lives. We need people to understand that we cannot and will not carry them for their entire lives. We need more mature people who are not only of adult age but who act like adults. For starters, that's what we need.

The remedies are everywhere! Help is everywhere! All alcoholics and addicts need to do is reach out, and there'll be someone who reaches back. There's an abundance of compassionate people out there, but they're not out there to be manipulated. They're there to help us move forward and reclaim our lives. But for the people who don't want their lives back and who want to just keep making the rest of society miserable, they have little compassion. They have little patience for the people who want to turn addiction into a game. So it's imperative for the addicted person to understand how the Game of Lust works before they sign up to be a player. Please take a look at the accompanying diagram, as it outlines the game.

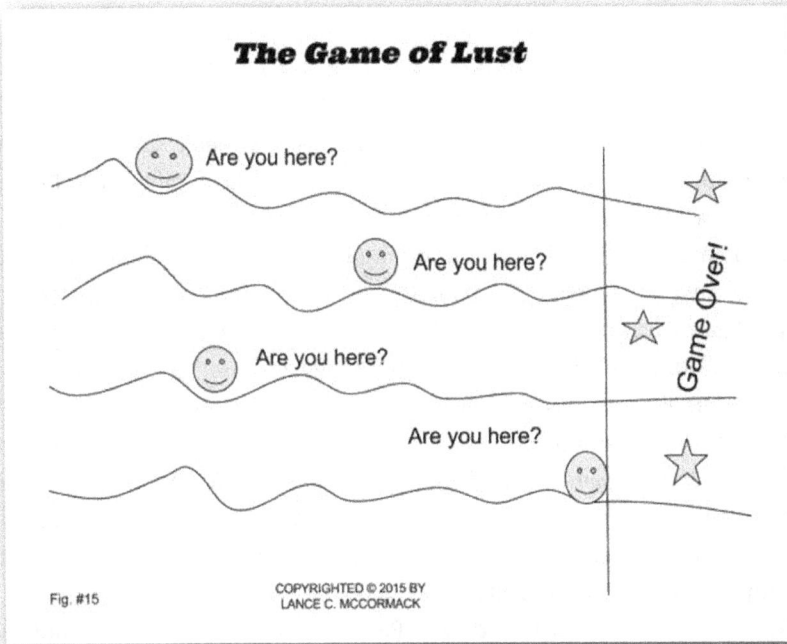

The Game of Lust

Are you here?

Are you here?

Are you here?

Are you here?

Game Over!

Fig. #15

COPYRIGHTED © 2015 BY
LANCE C. MCCORMACK

Pretend the horizontal lines you see in the diagram represent real waves in the sea.

Then imagine I drew a vertical line that's perpendicular to the waves in the sea and called it "game over." Now, what if I asked you to locate the vertical line I just drew in the sea? Would you be able to? No. The answer is no. No matter how long you looked, or whether you used the Hubble Telescope to look for that line, you'd be unable to find it, because it's the sea, but that line represents " game over." Now, the smiley faces you see in the diagram represent where you could be with your addiction. Of course you may believe that you still have many runs left in you or many boxes of wine still to drink, but are you sure? The object of this game is to calculate where you are exactly in relation to game over. However, that presents a problem because since you can't find the line that represents "game over," it would be impossible for you to know where you are in relation to that line. That just makes sense! Now, if you knew where that line was, then that would be different, but you don't and you can't, so my suggestion is to stop wherever you are, because once you reach "game over," it's game over, and I think you know what that means. Does that make sense?

We All Know There's a Cure

First of all, what is a cure? Many of us look at a cure as being something we take or something we're given to get better. I see a cure a little differently; I see it as something we become aware of that avails us of the opportunity to begin the process of internal repair. This addiction repair entails an overall energy overhaul. That means we must repair all the damage to our mind and to our body. I see the mind as a naturally harmonious body consisting of a multitrillion-cell energy network collaborative, directing and responding to stimuli to and from the internal and external world. My vision of the mind therefore has no specific location, but instead represents a field of energy that permeates and surrounds our entire physical self. So to repair the mind is a comprehensive task, and one that can only be accomplished by those who are truly serious about recovering. Repairing the physical body will be easy in comparison. So yes, we all know there's a cure, but are we ready to seize the opportunity to begin the work?

Maybe you remember the story of Pandora's box from Greek mythology. In brief, a man named Epimetheus had gone against the wishes of the God Zeus, and Zeus vowed to make Epimetheus and all humans pay for his wrongdoing. His plan was to mold this alluring woman from clay with the help of Aphrodite and then set her on the path to capture the heart of Epimetheus. Zeus named this temptress Pandora. When Epimetheus met Pandora, he fell instantly spellbound by her beauty as was planned, and the two were soon married. Upon their marriage Zeus gave Pandora a most beautiful box (or jar) but told her to never open it under any circumstances. She readily agreed, but as time went by, Pandora's curiosity grew with each passing day. She questioned why anyone would give her such a beautiful box and not want her to open it. She imagined the box to be filled with precious gems and the finest of silks and gold coins beyond belief.

Pandora felt tortured by not knowing what the box contained but didn't want to anger her husband, who had also agreed to not open it. After much deliberation and several half-hearted attempts, Pandora's lust for the contents of the box finally prevailed, and she opened the lid of the box and was shocked by what she saw. She had expected to be blinded by the brilliance of its contents but instead saw nothing, until she was surrounded by stinging moths that represented all the evils of the world. These moths had flown out of the box and promised disease, misery, pestilence, sadness, and death to the world. They stung Pandora as they flew until her husband arrived and closed the box's lid. Upon closing the lid, one little voice emanated from the box to be let free.

Prometheus decided that since all the evils were already out, there couldn't be anything worse remaining inside. Cautiously he opened the box and saw this beautiful dragonfly flutter out and go directly to heal Pandora's wounds. This dragonfly was named Hope, and despite Pandora having freed all the evils to all the world, Hope had come to capture them.

So although we don't listen nearly enough, and we do things we shouldn't and sometimes even create hell on earth, as the saying goes, "Hope springs eternal." But as eternal as hope may spring, time is still of the essence, and we don't have forever to get this right. So there's no time like the present to do what we can do now. The cure could be as simple as, from this point on, we could start listening to others who are trying to help us and keep us from opening those damn boxes.

What's This about Rock Bottom?

We always hear people saying, "I guess she'll have to hit rock bottom before she stops," or "He hasn't hit rock bottom yet," or we'll hear the user say, "I haven't hit rock bottom." Well, I have good news for all of you: you don't have to hit rock bottom in order to change! Don't let anyone convince you to the contrary. The concept of having to hit rock bottom is not only self-serving, it's downright dangerous. The reason it's self-serving is because when addicts say, "I haven't hit rock bottom," they're putting everyone on notice that they intend to continue doing whatever they do until they've lost and destroyed everything. They're clearly telling us that they are working ardently in that direction and that they expect to be there at some point. At that point, they make no promises other than they'll be at rock bottom. That's dangerous.

Why should the nonaddicted ones among us have to wait for the addicted ones to decide that their reign of terror and destruction is finally over? The idea that we must be patient as the addict continues to destroy everything they touch seems like extortion, and extortion is illegal in America. So the notion of the nonaddicts being held hostage until the addicts decide to release us is in flagrant violation of the First Amendment, and that's clearly unconstitutional. Now, addicts also have First Amendment rights, and their rights must also be upheld as long, as they haven't broken any laws in order to satisfy those rights. The bottom line is that both the addicted and the nonaddicted have rights, and neither group's rights should interfere with rights of the other. We must learn to work together as a collaborative so that neither side is dependent on the other; that way we can both get what we want.

In regards to a remedy, the need for a remedy only exists when someone believes there's a problem. If there's no perceived problem, then there's no need for a remedy. Lust distorts our perceptions and makes it virtually impossible to see when problems exist and therefore leads us to run from any remedies. Here's an example:

Scenario: Waiting to hit rock bottom is like…standing on the subway station platform waiting for the 6:00 p.m. train headed northbound, when you notice an earlier train on your platform about to leave. This train happens to be the 5:30 p.m. train, and it's also headed northbound to your destination. You see all the passengers on board with their arms outstretched to you yelling, "Get on." You yell back, "No. I'm waiting for the six p.m. train." The passengers look at you quizzically as they can't understand why you wouldn't like to take an earlier train, especially since it's also going to your destination. Suddenly, you notice them pointing to a crazed gunman in the distance running in your direction and firing a machine gun. Now, you notice he's still quite a distance away, so you don't quite see him as a threat yet, and you decide to stay where you are. The question is, at what point do you decide to get on the train, or do you just continue to wait for your train and hope that the gunman will run out of bullets by the time he gets to you?

SECTION VII

The Fifth Element of Addiction: A Traumatic Brain Distortion

To be lost and believe you are found while
floundering aimlessly in the dark is truly a loss.
—A LANCEISM

These chapters will be devoted to how thoughts bend and how thoughts can be straightened again and redirected onto a path to fulfilling life's dreams, and also to how trauma and drama can become destructively entwined and interconnected. This section explores the fifth of the six elements of addiction.

CHAPTER 18

Keeping Your Brain in the Game

The bored mind suffers by creating a world it can barely endure.
—A Lanceism

What is a traumatic brain distortion, or TBD? It's a term I coined to describe how the human mind becomes warped and perverted as it systematically relinquishes more of itself to a drug or an activity. It's like a traumatic brain injury (TBI) in that our brains change and the ways we interpret information change as a result, but it's different in that it's an inside job with a TBD. We choose to change our brains with a TBD, and it's not the result of an external injury. How much we negatively change our brains depends on many factors, but mainly on our levels of resistance and unwillingness to listen to others and on our persistence to remain unavailable and closed to helpful suggestions.

Think about It

By now we know that tampering with our chemistry can impact our cognition. We know how things we eat, drink, smoke, snort, inject, or otherwise get into our bodies can affect our mental and physical states. Sometimes the impact of chemicals on our brains and bodies can be subtle, and at other times, their impact can be deadly. Clearly chemistry changes cognition, but did you know that cognition changes chemistry? The way we think can actually determine our chemical makeup. Our thoughts can trigger certain chemicals to be released in lesser or greater amounts or to not be released at all. Our worldview can influence our stress hormones and our levels of anxiety, or it can influence internal chemical reactions that lead to calm and feelings of contentment. So we have a huge responsibility as human beings: to control which chemicals we put into our bodies and to control which chemicals we produce in our bodies. When we're producing or taking in the wrong chemicals, we can't make sensible decisions or even know where to look for answers. We wind up spending our lives looking in the wrong places and then being surprised at not finding what we're looking for there.

I once heard a very interesting story by the late Mr. Wayne Dyer. He was a pre-eminent writer in the self-help genre, and he made very good sense in his writings. It seems a gentleman arrived home one night, and as he walked in his house and turned on the lights, a circuit blew, and there he was standing in the dark. Then, as he stumbled around trying to get his bearings, he dropped his keys. Now he was groping in the dark, still trying to get his bearings and also trying to find his keys, and he couldn't feel them anywhere. After many minutes passed and he was still unsuccessful in his attempts to find his keys in the dark, he happened to notice some light filtering in between some curtains. He then realized the light was coming from a brilliant street lamp in front of his home. Quickly he darted outside to the street under the brilliance of the street lamp, got down on his knees and proceeded to look frantically for his keys.

While he was looking for his keys, his neighbor happened to be pulling up in his car and saw him in the street down on his knees and asked him if everything was okay. The man replied, "I dropped my keys, and I can't find them." His neighbor parked his car and rushed over to help him find his keys. After about ten minutes of searching, the neighbor asked the man, "In what general area did you drop your keys?" The man replied, "I dropped them in the house, but the light was much better out here." The neighbor immediately stopped looking for the keys, scratched his head, and walked silently into his house and locked his door.

The story I just recounted may sound odd or even crazy, but isn't this what we do all the time? We spend countless days, maybe years of our lives, looking outside of us for the answers to our lives, when we know full well that the answers lie inside of us. That's part of the distortion we face when we don't really want to change something. This distortion exists in people without addictions, so can you imagine how distorted things are for those with addictions. We're taking all kinds of medications: methadone, buprenorphine, Adderall, Campral, Antabuse, naltrexone, Vivitrol, the gum, the patch, Wellbutrin, Chantix, type 2 diabetes medications, and whatever else clinicians, nurses, and doctors suggest, and somehow we're expecting those things to be cures. We all know they're not! We know that the only cures that exist come from within us and that by looking outside of us, we're just wasting valuable time.

You're Not Doing Us Any Favors

Marjorie was a smoker and had just turned sixty-one. She came to me as a referral from a surgeon who had told her she needed to stop smoking before she would perform surgery on her. Marjorie had been diagnosed with COPD and throat cancer. As a result of her advanced emphysema (her form of COPD), Marjorie was always connected to an oxygen tank. She reported that she had smoked since she was thirteen and stated she had always enjoyed everything about smoking. She said she didn't even believe that her throat cancer had been caused by her smoking cigarettes, but rather by her genetic predisposition due to both her parents having been smokers. Marjorie said she was just coming to me to stop smoking to appease her surgeon. She said, "I'm not doing it for me. I'm just doing it for her." Marjorie added that she even considered contacting an attorney to see if her surgeon actually had the right to deny her a surgery that she desperately needed. Marjorie said, "I don't want to stop smoking, so I don't think it's right for my doctor to make me, and the minute I can smoke again, I will."

I then asked Marjorie, "Aren't you even afraid of blowing up your house, since oxygen is so flammable?"

Marjorie smiled and then replied, "I just have to remember to remove my oxygen tubes before I have a cigarette."

Does Marjorie's story sound even a little distorted to you?

Make Up Your Mind

After meeting many people in the substance-abuse field and at my hypnotherapy office, I've learned how easy it is for us as humans to be influenced by others. I've learned how easily our thoughts can be derailed and how easily we can lose our focus and in the process lose our way. It's so easy that it's actually scary. The great news, however, is that as easily as we can lose focus, we can regain our focus if done in a timely manner. We as human beings possess minds that are extremely powerful, yet they are as fragile as newly hatched dragonflies, and this is without the use of any drugs. So we must decide which mind we want to be dominant: our powerful mind or our fragile mind? Just imagine once drugs are introduced how vulnerable our powerful minds become. In my next diagram, I've outlined how our thoughts can bend and how we can get our thoughts back on track.

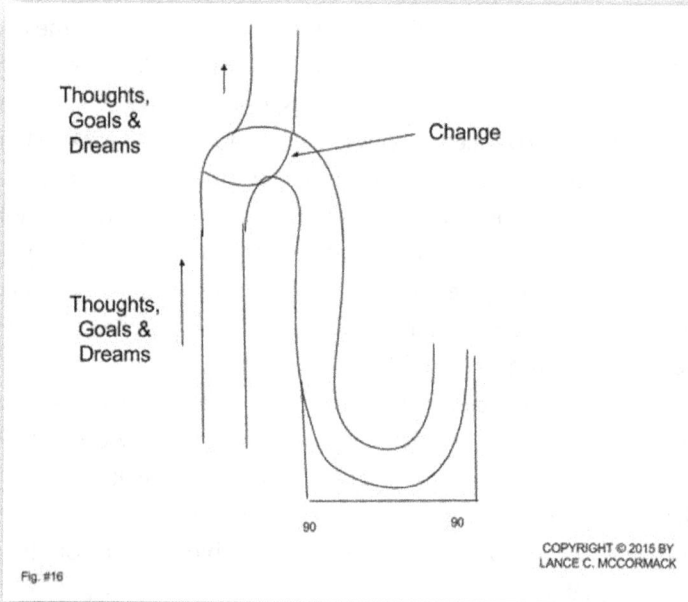

Fig. #16

Thoughts, Goals & Dreams

Change

Thoughts, Goals & Dreams

90   90

COPYRIGHT © 2015 BY
LANCE C. MCCORMACK

This diagram depicts how we begin with thoughts and dreams of the future. As our experiences grow and our minds continue to develop, the people we meet, along with their powerful influences on us, either strengthen our already established thoughts and dreams or start to undermine the attractiveness of our chosen direction. Here is where our thoughts are the most vulnerable, when we start to question whether we're on the right road to our happiness or start to doubt the likelihood of our success.

Although questioning and doubting can be beneficial, they generally are not if these introspective inquiries are the result of negativity from others who have accomplished little and who have little interest in our success. Nonetheless, if we choose to be swayed by their influence, our thoughts begin to bend or veer off our initial path and travel down another path, to a less developed, baser facsimile of ourselves. And the more our thoughts veer off, the more difficult it becomes to get them back on track.

Imagine being made of hollow steel and being nice and straight. Now, consider bending your top end slowly downward to make each of your ends parallel to the other and each side of equal length. Now, further bend either end to where it's looping back up and parallel once again. This is pretty much like my illustration, although my lines aren't necessarily parallel, but you get the point. This is to represent how steel can bend and what happens to steel when it bends. The more it bends, the longer and thinner it becomes. To be longer and thinner may sound pretty good as a weight-control strategy, but not necessarily as a plan if you want a stronger piece of steel. Because when steel is made longer and thinner, it's also made weaker, and when it's made weaker, it's made less able to withstand pressure and more vulnerable to being broken. Once we bend steel so dramatically, it's changed dynamically and can never be the same ever again. However, that doesn't mean it can't be successfully utilized again and serve a great purpose; it just means that the steel will be forever changed and different and that it will have different uses. This reminds me of a poem by William Wordsworth, "Ode: Intimations of Immortality from Recollections of Early Childhood." These lines are but a few selected from the complete poem, but beautifully emphasize my point.

> What though the radiance which was once so bright
> Be now for ever taken from my sight,
> Though nothing can bring back the hour
> Of splendour in the grass, of glory in the flower;
> We will grieve not, rather find
> Strength in what remains behind;
> In the primal sympathy
> Which having been must ever be;
> In the soothing thoughts that spring
> Out of human suffering;
> In the faith that looks through death,
> In years that bring the philosophic mind.

So I guess the answer is that we must carefully consider how our thoughts are bending and recognize that the quicker we can identify when we're off track, the quicker we can get back on track. Initially when we're only a few degrees off and make the necessary changes, it's a smooth transition back, but as the diagram illustrates, when we continue to bend further and further downward, we will need to exert at least 180 degrees of effort in order to get back in the direction of our dreams.

The Way Back

Sometimes when we can't see things clearly, we can benefit from having faith that others can. Say one day you were referred to a counselor for help, and you knew you needed help. You went to see how you could stop your addiction. During your conversation with your counselor, he made mention of your shoes. He commented that he needed a pair of nice black shoes like yours. You quickly corrected your counselor and said that your shoes weren't black, they were red. Your counselor then replied, "No, your shoes are definitely not red. They're black." You of course adamantly replied, "I know what color my own shoes are, and they are red!" Now, this not a story about color blindness; this is a story about the value of blind acceptance, a.k.a. faith.

Over the course of your continuing conversation, more counselors entered your area, and as each entered they were asked what color your shoes were. Each counselor said your shoes were clearly black. Now there were six counselors, all attesting to your shoes being black. At what point do you accept what these counselors are saying, seeing that they have no motivation to tell you anything other than what they see? Since you went to see them, why wouldn't it benefit you to accept what they're saying? Is it possible that *you* are the one who's seeing things incorrectly, or do you need more people to tell you before you can accept what you hear? How many more people will have to tell you: a hundred, a thousand, a million? What is the number that must be reached before you are convinced? Hopefully at some point, you will take a leap of faith and trust that others have no ulterior motives to be telling you anything other than was is, and you will see finally that they are sincerely trying to help you.

CHAPTER 19

Trauma Meets Drama

Our strength is not in our isolation, but in our
connection to others. The more we connect to our
world, the stronger we become in all ways: mentally,
emotionally, physically, and physiologically.
—A LANCEISM

n our field of addiction, trauma may be both a catalyst and a result. At some point, it becomes extremely difficult to determine which caused which, if that even matters any longer. It does appear, however, that trauma and drama seem to go hand in hand, of that we are certain. As unfortunate as trauma is for anyone, it only becomes worse when alcohol and other drugs are involved. The key is to recognize trauma quickly and address it quickly before self-medicating becomes the chosen first course of action. One definition of *trauma* is "a disordered psychic or behavioral state resulting from severe mental or emotional stress or physical injury" (*Merriam-Webster's Collegiate Dictionary*).

So our mind is disrupted and our behaviors deeply affected, and we are left to clean up whatever mess as best we can. As I mentioned earlier, the speed at which we address the traumatic impact is key to recovery. Each moment counts when we're drinking and drugging to numb traumatic events. Drinking and drugging only magnifies the events and makes them that much more difficult to handle. This is where trauma meets drama, and every day becomes another situation.

For people in the drug world nothing is simple, every day, all day, is filled with emotional disturbances, slights, bad blood, arguments, fights, and lots of tears, guilt, and regrets. This roller coaster of emotions rarely ends, even with the onset of sleep, because then the opportunity for drug dreams and nightmares exists. Unfortunately, this is the life of someone who has given himself/herself up to a substance or an activity. This someone is otherwise known as an addict. The stories of drama abound in this field of addiction and would easily fill libraries.

A Peek into Our World

Sam reported enduring many cases of trauma in his life, but now his life consists of mainly causing trauma and creating drama for others and himself. Sam is a middle-aged guy around forty and in pretty rough physical shape; he walks with a severe limp and constantly complains of pain from arthritis throughout his body. He attends a methadone clinic daily and purports to be stable on his daily dose. He's been a patient there for more than ten years and reports that he has no intentions of ever leaving. He states, "Why fix something if it ain't broke?" Now to me, that would mean that methadone is helping him and that he is feeling better and able to do all the things that he claimed he couldn't do when he was chasing heroin: be a responsible person, be an upstanding citizen worthy of respect, and be an overall good person. This sounds all well and good, but it doesn't support what Sam is actually doing. What he is actually doing every day is being a menace to society and quite the opposite of all the things he claimed he would be since he's no longer chasing heroin.

Sam and I were talking one day, and he had to laugh as he told me a story. He said he was up the street the day before at the intersection and really got this lady going crazy while she was stopped at the light. He said he walked in front of her Mercedes while she wasn't looking and then slammed the hood of her car real hard with his hand. Sam said she jumped so high in her car, her head almost went through the roof. He said he wanted to laugh, but he knew he had to remain serious. He screamed at her at the top of his lungs, "You just hit me! Don't you see me walking here?" He said that she looked so frightened and confused, it was hilarious. Next, Sam told her to pull over so he could get her information, but she sped away. Sam said he quickly wrote down her license plate number and called 911. Apparently, the woman was found and apprehended within the hour for having left the scene of an accident. This lady happened to be a leading surgeon at a nearby women's hospital. She mainly performed surgeries on women with breast and ovarian cancer. But instead, on this day, she was in handcuffs attempting to explain to officers that she hadn't hit anyone and that she wouldn't have driven away if she had.

Well, Sam's whole scam here was to have the lady elect to settle this newly opened case out of court with a quick cash payout. He had done this before and had been successful, but not this time. Sam happened to have forgotten an outstanding warrant he had for shoplifting a few years ago, and he was taken into custody while his new case was ultimately dropped due to his criminal history and lack of corroborating evidence. The problem is that we have thousands and thousands of Sams out there every day disrupting the lives of good, hardworking people, and we have thousands and thousands of new Sams joining their ranks every day.

That was just one story, an average story, but these stories get much more convoluted and much more dangerous.

Suzanne was the daughter of a crack- and heroin-addicted absentee mother. Her mother was only present when she couldn't get drugs; otherwise she could be found down by the underpass shooting up with her cohorts. Suzanne says,

> I was only ten when this life began for me. My mother had been smoking and shooting crack for a few years, and before I knew it, so was I. So here I was, all of thirteen, being passed around for crack—crack for me and crack for Momma. The more guys, the more crack, and we both had insatiable appetites for crack, so I got passed around a lot. My mother never seemed to care, despite her occasional half-hearted apologies. She just had one thing in mind...actually two, crack and heroin, and nothing else mattered. As weird as it sounds, I felt kind of good being able to make her feel good.
>
> I remember how our apartment became the neighborhood crack house and shooting gallery with people coming in and going out all day and all night. There I was introduced to threesomes and trains, where I felt like I was just three holes on a conveyor belt sliding from one person to the next, letting each one do their thing. I was only sixteen, but at times I already wanted to be done with my life. Around that time I began tearing off pieces of my skin, first on the backs of my hands, then on my arms, and then later down the fronts and backs of my legs. My mom always tried to stop me, but eventually I would start tearing again when she wasn't looking. It made me feel calm and in control of my life, as crazy as that sounds.

I had mixed feelings when I heard my mother was sick with AIDS and brain cancer. I loved my mother, and I still do, but I also hated her, and I still do. I loved the memories of my mom when I was five or six and how she was silly and very playful and how she'd spend all day with me just tickling me and making me laugh. I loved how I favored her, with big blue eyes and long, wavy, blond hair. I even loved how guys looked at her like she was a goddess and how they all would say how lucky my father was. Those were good times before my father left. The story was that he had caught my mom with a friend of his and he never forgave her, and one day he just never came home. That was about twelve years ago. Ever since then, my mom has been on a self-destructive death ride, and I've been a passenger in her car.

Ever since her diagnoses, she's been getting sicker and sicker and coughing all the time and pretty much bedridden. Her mind just doesn't seem to work like it used to, and she forgets a lot. Sometimes doctors come to the house, but mostly nurses come bringing her scripts for more pain meds. She'd get scripts for bottles and bottles of opiates every month, and like a dutiful daughter, I'd get them filled and then sell them for what we both really wanted: more crack and more heroin. Before long I was selling all of her meds to support my own habit and not giving her any at all. The hardest part was having to watch her go through painful withdrawals every day, knowing she was having them all because of me, but I didn't care as long as I wasn't having them. Yeah, I was a selfish bitch, but I think I was just trying to pay my mom back for what she had done to me by not having been a mom and not having taken care of me like she was supposed to.

I remember we had a shag carpet, and it was filthy from all the traffic we had in the house, and not just from people, but from dogs, cats, and mice. I remember we had such a flea problem that I always wore high socks just to block some of the biting. And bed bugs, well, they were everywhere. My mom had neuropathy in both legs from years of shooting up in her feet, calves, and thighs. Matter of fact, she had it so bad she couldn't even feel the fleas biting her legs or feel the bed bugs crawling in her hair, but I could see them jumping on and staying there for a while. Some of it felt like payback; some of it just made me feel like getting high and staying high. I found Mom dead one day on the couch from an overdose of heroin and fentanyl, and the first thing I did was search her pockets for the stuff that got her so high. I couldn't find any more. She must have taken it all. She always was a selfish bitch!

Stories like Suzanne's are sickeningly common. They begin with trauma and then are filled with drama, which leads to even more trauma. Once we allow drugs to enter the scene, we open ourselves to a new dynamic filled with horrible experiences in horrible places with horrible people. There is no shortage of trauma to be had; whenever we want it, we'll be able to find it, and drama will be there too, waiting to hold our hand and keep us company. Once we're immersed in this life, we can no longer see ourselves or things as they truly are, due to a brain distortion, so when we are ready to change, we must seek help from those who can see us clearly. Are you ready yet to rewrite your story, or will your story just be another for a self-help book?

SECTION VIII

The Sixth Element of Addiction: A Damaged Mind, Body & Spirit

We are here not because we do not know the answers;
we are here because we do not like them.
—A LANCEISM

The following chapters will detail how our minds, bodies, and spirits are corrupted through drug use and how we can restore them through nonuse. This section explores the sixth and final element of addiction.

CHAPTER 20

What More Have We to Lose?

Personal change rarely occurs until we
believe it's absolutely necessary.
—A LANCEISM

To have a damaged mind, body, and spirit is to be in dire need of surrender, but to avoid acknowledging that surrender is the only viable course of action, we many times delay the inevitable or forgo the opportunity altogether. This surrender is not to the thing that's caused us our problems, but to the fact that we can no longer exist the way things are. Our lives are always at stake, and no matter how bad things currently are, they can always get worse. There is always more to lose.

This reminds me of a funny little story I once read on the Internet, entitled "The Secret Elixir of Longevity." Gloria, while out for a walk, notices this little old man rocking in a chair on his porch, and she approaches him and says, "I can't help noticing how happy you look." Gloria smiles at him and asks, "What is your secret for a long, happy life?"

"I smoke three packs of cigarettes a day," he replied. "I drink a case of whiskey a week, eat fatty foods, and never exercise."

"That's amazing!" Gloria responds. "How old are you?"

"Twenty-six," he replies.

I see young people all the time in terrible shape, damaging their minds, their bodies, and their spirits, and all they can tell me is, "Hey, you only live once." Hey, is this really what you call living?

I envision the mind as a naturally harmonious body consisting of a multitrillion-cell energy network collaborative, directing and responding to stimuli to and from the internal and external world. Therefore, this mind has no specific location but instead represents a field of energy that permeates and surrounds our entire physical self. So to repair the mind is a comprehensive task and one that can only be accomplished by those who are truly serious about recovering.

Damaging your mind through the ravages of addiction is like volunteering to have a deadly virus infect your central nervous system, your peripheral nervous system, and your entire field of energy, just to see if it really can. Then once you're convinced that it has, you profess to love this virus and proclaim emphatically that you want it to stay forever. As I've mentioned, the mind has no specific location, because it exists everywhere throughout our physical bodies and even possesses the power to extend well beyond our physical form. Therefore, when the mind is infected, it is no minor event, but one of cataclysmic proportions. This impact cannot be overstated. Once the damage has begun, a spell has been spun. And until the spell is broken, the mind's infection will only turn to sepsis and ultimately overtake the mind's ability to defend itself. After all, what's the harm in being addicted to things that can make you feel so good? Well, here's a small list for starters:

- having a lifetime of interrupted thoughts
- losing everything on any given day
- being ruled by something that doesn't even know you exist
- loving something passionately that can never feel your love
- needing more to feel the same
- feeling like you never have enough

Imagine having a lifetime of interrupted thoughts. All your days and all your nights totally consumed with the thoughts of doing whatever it is that you're obsessed with doing. Having an endless DVD of the same old movie playing 24/7. Whether it's a drug or an activity really doesn't matter because it's all the same. It's infected your mind, and now this virus is in control and running rampant through your thoughts to ensure that you know absolutely who's in charge of you. No matter where you are, whether here on Earth or orbiting a distant star, your mind will be with you, and you will still be craving, wanting, wishing for that something, for that feeling that you claim makes you feel more alive than you can humanly express. The sad part is that you will never realize what's happening to you as long as you remain spellbound.

Imagine signing up for the privilege of losing everything you have and everything you are on any given day. Starting off any day with the idea that no matter what it takes, I will get what I want to satisfy my desires. No matter what I must give up, forfeit, exchange, or do, I will, and whatever the outcome, so be it. All things will be in jeopardy: my work, my family, my life—it's all up for grabs today and every day as I search to fill that hole in me that needs filling. Today I am willing to give up everything, and if I do, I understand that I will have no one but myself to blame.

Imagine being ruled by something that's not even alive. We've all heard and read about rulers throughout history, and they have all been people. People have either allowed themselves to be ruled by other people or have come under the rule of others forcibly or due to having little control of their own. Few of us have come to be ruled by drugs or harmful activities forcibly, although it does happen. Most of us, however, have allowed ourselves to be ruled by these things by not listening to those who love and care about us. Additionally, we have exercised little self-control of our own, despite our innermost thoughts and intuition that have attempted to deter us from perilous predicaments. We have become ruled as a result of wanting to be ruled by something, yet this something will never even know we exist.

Imagine loving something passionately that can never feel your love. This type of love is considered unrequited because it's love that cannot be reciprocated. This unilateral type of affection has no way to be returned, since this object of affection is not alive. We have chosen to fall deeply and head over heels for something that can feel neither our love for it nor the pain that it causes us. To passionately invest our time and energy in this manner appears to be an ill investment of an emotion better suited for someone than something. To feel safe in giving yourself to inanimate things, knowing they have no feelings, is to guard yourself from being hurt by the living.

Imagine always needing more of whatever in order to feel the same. It's like having a slice of pizza for lunch for the first time and really loving it and then each day after that needing an additional slice of pizza in order to feel the same level of enjoyment you had with your very first slice. That's pretty much where we're at with addictions, always needing more to feel the same. We're always talking about just trying to feel normal—not high, just normal. It's called *tolerance* in clinical terms, and it simply means we're never satisfied with what we previously had and that we're always looking for more to achieve equilibrium. Picture zombies dragging down the streets of every city, every town, and every county, all throughout the United States, searching for more of what they believe they need, and you'll have the picture. This is what our streets look like now, and zombies are what we look like now, so we don't have to imagine; all we have to do is look.

So let's say you can imagine always needing more to feel the same, but can you imagine never being able to have enough? Never being satisfied, ever. Can you truly imagine that? It's like the saying "One is too much, and a thousand is never enough." Now, that's a problem—a real problem! So what can we do to help people who will never be satisfied? Any suggestions? For an answer to that question, maybe we should ask all the people intimately involved: the addicts and their caregivers and all the people who have lost someone due to those addicts searching for that next best high. So what more do we have to lose? Everything!

CHAPTER 21

What Have I Done to My Body?

*Some things are permanent; more things are
present. One needs but now for change.*
—A LANCEISM

A body damaged through the use of alcohol and other drugs is a body confused as to what its owner wants. Our bodies are truly wondrous things
and capable of miraculous things, but they need clear direction from us.
They constantly send us messages through the way we feel, and it's up to us to
acknowledge those messages and to act on them or not. Our bodies look to us
for guidance, and when they break down, it's due to our lack of clear communications to them. After all, our bodies are comprised of at least fifty trillion cells,
and they're all ours. It's like having fifty trillion little soldiers, all at our command.
They will move mountains for us, and they will also die for us, depending on the
commands we give them. The confusion comes when we don't understand that
this biocommunication exists, and our actions continue to confuse our cells as to
what they should do.

It's like having type 2 diabetes and being on a strict low-sugar diet because
excess sugar is slowing your body's healing process. You notice that every time you
bang your leg or get a cut, an infection sets in, and the wound just seems to linger
and never quite heal. The great news is that your body has cells called leukocytes
that are specifically designed to respond to infections and initiate healing, and they
are more than able to do the job, as long as they believe you want the job to actually
be done. Now, I know this may sound kind of strange, insinuating that your cells can
know what you want, but as strange as it may sound, they can. Your cells and mine

know when we are serious about fixing something and when we are not, and they respond accordingly. So, when we go out and buy an extra-large pizza and then wash it down with a liter bottle of soda and then top it all off with some chocolate-chocolate-chip ice cream and coffee cake, our body knows. It knows we are just playing around and that we don't really want to fix anything, so our cells don't respond like it's an emergency; they take their sweet time, as if you had all day. But you don't, and before you know it, gangrene has set in, and your leg is about to be amputated. This scenario happens every day, all across our nation, and the sad part is that it's totally preventable. We're told which foods are high in sugar, and then we're told to monitor our sugar, yet we go out and buy all the things we know are high in sugar and then act surprised when our wounds won't heal. So is this because our cells have failed us, or is it because we have failed them? We haven't allowed them to help us, even though that's what they're designed to do.

During our addictions we put our bodies to the test, day in and day out, asking much more of them than we ever ask of ourselves. In this dysfunctional, unilateral relationship, we continue to play dodgeball with our bodies by throwing stones at them and expecting them to dodge every stone no matter how weak we become. But even a wondrous, miraculous thing like the human body can only endure but so much. At some point, the stones overtake our weak, defenseless bodies and put us in a place where we can no longer be a harm to ourselves or to anyone else. That is our body's last recourse. Before that point, it will do all it can to correct our course so as not to be left without viable options. Yes, we have made a mess of things, but not a mess that cannot be cleaned up if we act now, but the window of opportunity is quickly closing! Below, I have listed some major parts of the body that most likely have sustained damage throughout our descent into destruction. These areas will need to be addressed in the recovery process:

- brain
- heart
- liver
- pancreas
- kidneys
- stomach
- immune system
- reproductive organs
- nervous system

Our Brain

Some of the areas impacted by drug use include the cerebral cortex, the brain stem, and the limbic system. These areas constitute what we call the brain. Each of these areas serves specific functions even though they work closely together. Our cerebral cortex is the home of our thoughts, where we process what our senses present to us. What we see, hear, smell, taste, and touch are all interpreted by the cerebral cortex.

Then we use this input to make decisions as to what we will do with the information we've received. This whole thinking process is gravely compromised once we introduce drugs of abuse, and the more drugs we use, the more compromised our brain's functioning becomes.

Our brain stem, another integral part of the brain, carries out more rudimentary or mundane functions, albeit very critical life-sustaining functions. The routine actions of the autonomic nervous system like heart rate, breathing, and sleeping are under the domain of the brain stem. As you can imagine, alcohol and other drugs damage our brain stem's functioning and impair our heart's beating, our ability to breathe normally, and even our ability to regulate our sleep. Clearly as we impact our brain stem's ability to work properly, the very basic functions of our lives are under siege.

Lastly we have the limbic system, an extremely interesting part of our brain that's involved with the perception of feelings and emotions and how we react to pleasurable sensations. It's also known as our "pleasure center." As with many animals, once we delight in a pleasure, we want to experience that pleasurable thing again and again, until we can no longer derive pleasure from that thing or until that thing is no longer viewed as pleasurable. Once our brains become used to receiving drugs of abuse, they change inexorably and are altered in unique ways that change our personalities as well, due in large part to our new perceptions of the pleasures derived from those experiences. At this point, our emotions and our level of pleasure seeking are both grossly exaggerated and immeasurably enhanced.

Once we tamper with our pleasure centers or with the ways we expect to experience pleasure, we raise the bar or the threshold for pleasure, and we cross over into a realm of wanting that creates an ever-increasing bodily demand that wants to be constantly fulfilled. So because we have compromised our brains through drug use, severely impacted our ability to think and act responsibly, and greatly disrupted our senses and completely dysregulated our emotions, our brains can become our enemies.

Our Heart

The heart is a beautiful, vascular organ designed to pump blood efficiently throughout our bodies. Alcohol and other drugs, however, definitely impede the beautiful functioning of our heart, setting the stage for cardiovascular events such heart attacks, arrhythmias, valve irregularities, collapsed veins, stiff arteries, heart wall thickening, and a host of bacterial and viral infections. Whether the drugs are depressants like alcohol or opioids, hallucinogens like LSD, stimulants like crack or methamphetamine (the perfect heart attack drugs), anxiolytic sedative-hypnotics like Valium, Xanax, or phenobarbital, or whatever other kind of drugs that we use to alter our senses, they all interfere with our cardiovascular health. They collectively run the risk of inhibiting or exciting our heart and influencing our heartbeat, our blood pressure, and our body's core temperature. The result of these influences can trigger a multitude of reactions: seizures, heart failure or cardiomyopathy, respiratory failure, cardiac arrest, and others. The heart is essential to providing blood for our entire body, so once this pump no longer pumps, the rest of our body no longer functions.

Our Liver

A beautiful organ that rests comfortably on our right side, usually protected by our rib cage. I say usually because it is generally protected only when it's not swollen due to inflammation. When it's swollen, our liver can extend below the protection of the rib cage and become quite vulnerable to any direct trauma. Our liver is also usually soft and rubberlike, again unless it's been damaged, and then it feels more hard and less pliable. One function of our liver is to convert what we consume into energy that can later be utilized by our bodies. Another function of the liver is to rid our bodies of waste and other toxins. These key functions play a major role in the challenge to adequately process and dispose of alcohol and other drugs of abuse. The liver is known to be quite resilient, but even given its amazing resilience, it's not invincible and is prone to a myriad of infections, viruses, and diseases.

Hepatitis C (also called Hep C or HCV) is just one virus that inflames our liver and impacts its ability to process food, excrete toxins, and maintain our energy. Millions of people in the United States currently have HCV, and many millions more throughout the world have it and can potentially pass it on to countless others. Many who have HCV may also have HBV (hepatitis B virus). These viruses are mainly transmitted through direct contact with the blood of someone who has it. This contact usually comes in the form of sharing instruments that are contaminated with blood (needles used for intravenous injections, syringes, or straws used in snorting anything). They can also can be readily transmitted through sexual contact and through any other means we can possibly conceive that involves direct contact with blood, semen, or any other bodily fluids from an infected person. Some people may know they have HCV or HBV, while others may not, so if you've been involved in the risky business of sharing anything that involves blood, you should get checked.

Some forms of hepatitis are not communicable but can still cause chronic liver damage nonetheless. These can be contracted through alcohol use and through the use of pharmaceuticals, either prescription or over-the-counter products, that inflame our liver. Unfortunately many people today have chronic hepatitis from having used over-the-counter pain remedies for years. Even obesity can damage the liver's ability to work properly, and the liver becomes chronically inflamed as a result. Since our livers are used to process things we consume, anything that can potentially inflame our livers can cause hepatitis. The great news is that the earlier you get tested, the sooner you can be treated and on your way to recovery—provided, of course, you stop doing what you were doing.

Next we have cirrhosis, a liver disease that causes cell damage and hardening of the liver's tissues. Cirrhosis is mainly caused by sustained overconsumption of alcohol, which leads to a swollen liver that can no longer perform its functions properly. Untreated hepatitis C can also develop into cirrhosis, which is considered end-stage liver disease. Cirrhosis can also develop as a result of poor eating and unhealthy habits that lead to a buildup of fat in our liver. This nonalcoholic type of cirrhosis usually begins with NASH (nonalcoholic steatohepatitis), which consists of inflammation of the liver due to a buildup of fat in the liver that causes it to enlarge over time due to continued damage.

This type of cirrhosis has become increasingly common due to the increased prevalence of type 2 diabetes. The recommendation for improvement would include lifestyle changes consisting of healthier foods and drinks and exercise. Still, in some cases a liver transplant may be the considered the best long-term option for sufferers of cirrhosis.

Our Pancreas

Another mess we get ourselves into is developing chronic pancreatitis. Many times hepatitis can run concurrent with pancreatitis since the liver and pancreas are connected by the duodenum. Drinking alcohol to excess is a major cause of pancreatitis, and if left unabated, it becomes chronic pancreatitis, which can lead to pancreas cancer, and you don't want that! I hear that's very painful and not a comfortable way to die.

Our Stomach

The stomach is another beautiful organ that nature has provided. This muscular organ resides on the left side of our abdomen and is the recipient of all the things we eat and drink that are passed through the esophagus. Through the muscular actions of squeezing and churning and the aid of the secretion of powerful digestive acids, the stomach processes and digests its contents and prepares it for passage to the small intestine. Alcohol and other drugs can play a significant role in this process and present many challenges to the user.

Beginning at the top, alcohol consumption can lead to cancers of the mouth and of the esophagus. Once alcohol is in the stomach, it can cause heartburn and can damage the stomach's lining. As a result, nutrients may be challenged in their efforts to be absorbed, thereby leaving the user prone to malnutrition and unhealthy weight loss and muscle atrophy. Alcohol can also lead to chronic stomach constipation, diarrhea, and overall stomach upset, which can be associated with disorders of the bowel. As our body succumbs to malnutrition from excess alcohol consumption, so does our brain, as it needs nutrients to function properly. As for nutrition, alcohol offers little value and takes more from us than it ever gives. The more alcohol we drink, the less food we normally desire, until such time as we desire virtually no food and desire only alcohol. Anatomically, this is one reason why so many alcohol abusers have very slim, nonmuscular arms and legs and present with fullness only in their stomachs from their alcohol intake and related stomach gases.

Opioid abuse results in many of the same side effects as alcohol abuse. Opioids depress the central nervous system and all the functions of the body. So not only is our thinking slowed, our physical actions slowed, our respiration slowed, our sexual functioning slowed, but our digestion is also slowed, and that can lead to severe constipation. In some cases, constipation is so severe, and the GI tract's functioning so impaired, that the colon can literally explode due to being so impacted with feces, in which case we'll have to be connected to a colostomy bag to expel our waste. When we're using alcohol, opioids, and stimulants, we generally aren't drinking much water, and as result, our bodies are routinely dehydrated, which makes it increasingly difficult to maintain the stomach's muscular contractions that move wastes and toxins from our bodies. In addition, as our focus on opioids persists, little focus is on eating and drinking good things, and our nutrition suffers dramatically, with severe weight loss, bone loss, muscle atrophy, and mental confusion.

Like all the rest, stimulant drugs like cocaine negatively impact our stomachs. Unlike alcohol and opioids that can relax blood vessels, stimulant drugs like cocaine and methamphetamine constrict vessels. This makes pumping of blood throughout the body that much more difficult since it is now being pumped through narrower vessels. We are generally aware that this constriction of blood to the heart can lead to heart attacks, but less is widely communicated about how this constriction of blood affects the stomach and GI tract. As less blood is available to parts of the intestine, the intestine can die from a lack of blood and become gangrenous and require that the user undergo immediate surgery in order to survive. The bowel itself is also under attack with the use of cocaine, and countless tissue cells can be irreparably damaged. Blood clots, ulcers, and holes or perforations in the stomach are common in cocaine and crack users and create a constant threat to their survival.

Our Kidneys

Our kidneys filter our blood, extracting excess fluid and waste, which is then excreted in our urine. Urine is created from this waste. Therefore, all the drugs we ingest must pass through our kidneys and must be filtered by them. Alcohol damages the kidneys and challenges their ability to filter blood. While our kidneys work to regulate the amount of water in our bodies, alcohol consumption serves to do the opposite, by acting as a diuretic and forcing water out of our bodies. So it's easy to picture that as our bodies are depleted of water through dehydration caused by consuming alcohol, our kidneys are overworking and overheating. It's like a car engine that counts on its water pump to keep it cool, but its water pump is pumping too little water to cool its engine, which causes the engine to heat up and impact the operation of the entire car.

Besides alcohol, drugs like heroin and cocaine and others can also wreak havoc on our kidneys' ability to regulate our blood by either increasing or decreasing blood pressure, destabilizing electrolytes, causing buildup of fluid and wastes in our blood, contracting bacterial and fungal infections, and predisposing us to a condition called rhabdomyolysis. This dangerous condition breaks down the body's muscle and releases its proteins into our blood, which then can lead to kidney failure. These are just a few things that can happen to our kidneys from drug use. Dialysis treatment is common for those users or heroin, cocaine, and alcohol, and its annual cost can be staggering. The function of dialysis is to filter our blood when our own filtering system has failed, or when we have failed it.

Our Immune System

Our immune system is like our very own military defense system that is there to guard us continuously against foreign intruders. This complex cellular system consisting of organs, tissues, and countless millions of cells that act to prevent and combat any and all parasites, bacteria, viruses, or fungi that want to take up residence in our bodies. When this system is compromised by alcohol or other drugs, its ability to do its job is also compromised, and invading armies may prove to be stronger than ours unless reinforcements arrive.

HIV and AIDS are abbreviations for human immunodeficiency virus and acquired immune deficiency syndrome, respectively. They both are caused by the virus, but if HIV is left untreated, it can develop into the disease AIDS. HIV is a virus of the immune system that greatly lowers its ability to defend against infections and other cellular intruders.

Similar to hepatitis C, HIV is transmitted in bodily fluids like blood, semen, vaginal fluids, rectal fluids, and even breast milk, and through mucous membranes including those found in the mouth. The usual transmitters of HIV/AIDS are people with HIV/AIDS who are engaged in unprotected sexual activities with non-HIV/AIDS partners and intravenous drug users with HIV/AIDS who share their needles, syringes, straws, and so on.

Anal sex is considered the most prevalent way to transmit HIV/AIDS, and vaginal sex is considered the second most common way. Coming in at a close third is sharing needles or syringes and any other intravenous paraphernalia, including rinse water, with someone with HIV/AIDS. Unfortunately unlike the hepatitis C virus, once you contract HIV/AIDS, you can't get rid of it. Fortunately, however, there are many medications that can allow a person with HIV/AIDS to live a reasonably healthy life, providing they are willing to change their behaviors. HIV tests are offered at many locations, including hospitals, clinics, and substance-abuse centers, and even through home test kits available either online or at local pharmacies, so there's no reason why you can't confidentially find out if you need treatment.

Our Reproductive Organs

Sexually transmitted diseases (STDs) and sexually transmitted infections (STIs) are common in the world of drug abusers, since sexual activity is more indiscriminate when we're drunk and high and our inhibitions are severely reduced. Everyone looks better at closing time, and contraceptives of any kind seem totally unnecessary and downright unappealing. Everyone has a clean bill of health, and all forms of sex are up for grabs. Unfortunately, despite the magic of the moonlight, syphilis, gonorrhea, chlamydia, herpes, and HPV are all infections or diseases that can render our reproductive organs null and void. They are all generally sexually transmitted and are highly contagious and can be spread through all types of sex—vaginal, anal, and oral—and in some cases even through deep, prolonged kissing. Many of these conditions can even be passed on to our unborn babies. With all these conditions, men can experience sexual dysfunction and penile damage, and women can experience a disruption in regular menstrual cycles and other changes, including infertility. Both women and men can develop sexually related cancers, either of the penis, vagina, anus, and/or throat. Some of these sexually transmitted infections and diseases leave visible scars, represented by sores or warts, and while others may be less obvious, they all potentially share an emotional scarring that can last a lifetime.

Our Nervous System

Lastly, but certainly of no lesser importance, is our nervous system, which consists of our central nervous system and our peripheral nervous system. It's the whole package: our brain and spinal cord as well as all of the peripheral nerves that run throughout our entire body. That's a lot of nerve endings responding to the use of alcohol and other drugs. I'd be writing volumes if I attempted to list all of the ways that drugs could damage the nervous system, because our nerves feel the impact of every drug we take. So whether they are depressed by drugs or stimulated by drugs, our nerves are involved all the time and every time. Maybe our nerves are constantly overstimulated, and we develop neuropathies from too much alcohol or too much whatever else, or maybe our nerves are inhibited, and we develop chronic constipation or depressed respiration due to drugs. In either case and in all cases, the brain, the spinal cord, and/or the peripheral nervous system are involved. All of our organs are attached to nerves, and the way we feel and think dictates our actions, so it's all about our nerves!

In this chapter I have outlined nine areas of our bodies that are affected by alcohol and/or other drugs. I have not listed all areas of the body, just enough to give you an idea of how extensive drug damage can be. Once we embark on this journey of chronic drug use, we should be prepared to fasten our seat belt, because it's going to be a bumpy ride.

CHAPTER 22

How Can We Damage a Spirit?

Once we've lost our way, few can see us as we were.
—A Lanceism

What is a spirit? Many things have been written about it, and still the spirit presents a mystery to many. The idea that it's something we can't see but that we're still supposed to believe in poses a problem for some people. To accept that spirits are all around us, watching us, guiding us, loving us, or maybe even resenting us, is a difficult proposition. Research says that most of us are visual people when it comes to learning, and so we learn best by seeing things like diagrams, pictures, or photos, as opposed to listening to stories or lectures from others or even touching or doing things ourselves. However, when it comes to believing something, I think many of us believe most in what we can actually see and touch, more so than in what we hear about or read about. "Show me" seems to be the mantra of our time, and anything that we can't be shown seems to leave us quizzically wondering.

When we're asked to envision something that has no particular figure or form but is claimed to possess a presence of some sort, we feel, at the very least, a bit uncomfortable. Many of us would like to believe that spirits exist, especially when we think of loved ones who have passed away and who are physically no longer here. Somehow the notion of their essence still being here is very comforting to us. Although, I do believe that spirits exist in those dearly departed, for this discussion on how a spirit can be damaged, I've chosen to focus on the spirits of the living. I've made this decision because these are the spirits we can control. Consequently, I define the spirit, "the essence of the energy in all living things." However, I don't see the spirit as a "thing" of its own, per se, but rather as the nature or the quality of the energy of that thing. And the thing that can be seen is the radiance of that spirit that I call the aura.

I realize these definitions may sound confusing, but the concept is quite simple. We are made of energy, and our energy radiates an essence that embodies our spirit, and our spirit is made manifest in an aura that can be felt and sometimes seen by others—humans and other animals alike. We have all met people who give off certain vibrations, an essence that either warns us or welcomes us to their spirit. These people radiate anger, fear, hatred, or love, and we can feel their energy. These emotions are but a few of the manifestations of the spirit. Our spirits are expressed through our actions and behaviors and through how we interact with others. Many of us have heard the expression "mean-spirited." What exactly does that mean? It's a reference to someone or something, because animals also can qualify, that has a mean way about them; their very nature, their very essence, appears to be unkind and unwelcoming. We have all seen these people, and our tendency is to stay as far away from them as possible.

In the following diagram, I have illustrated for our visual learners how alcohol and other drugs damage our bodies, alter our minds, and damage our spirit as we consent to continual energy exchanges.

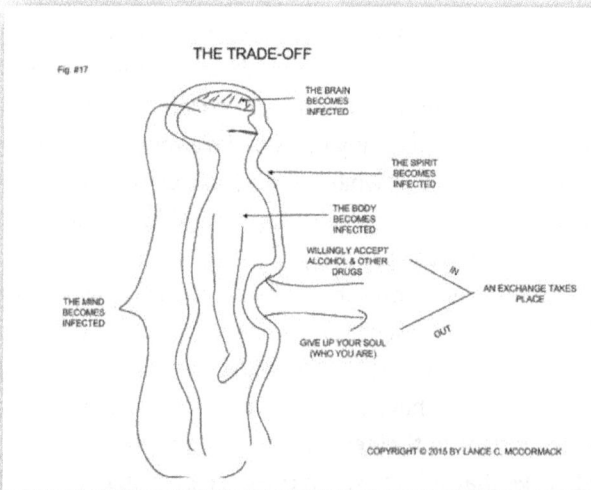

THE TRADE-OFF

Fig #17

THE BRAIN BECOMES INFECTED

THE SPIRIT BECOMES INFECTED

THE BODY BECOMES INFECTED

WILLINGLY ACCEPT ALCOHOL & OTHER DRUGS

IN

AN EXCHANGE TAKES PLACE

THE MIND BECOMES INFECTED

GIVE UP YOUR SOUL (WHO YOU ARE)

OUT

COPYRIGHT © 2016 BY LANCE C. MCCORMACK

In the trade-off, I illustrate how, once we demonstrate that we are willing to accept alcohol and other drugs into our bodies by taking them, we are also willingly making a transaction. This transaction constitutes an unequal exchange of everything we have and everything we are in exchange for a substance. As my drawing depicts, once addiction takes hold, we give up our soul as it infects our brain and all our body's parts, every bone, tissue, and muscle fiber, and then it infects our mind, which is all the energy in every cell and every molecule in our bodies, and then that infection permeates our spirit, the very essence of who we are. In the end, we are barely recognizable, even by the ones who love us, because by then addiction has even infected our aura, and at that point we represent just a distant stranger who was once someone they knew.

Freedom Comes at a Price

My definition of the term *renew* is not "to make like new" but rather "to start anew, begin again, or to start over." Things change and we change with addiction, so nothing is the same or will be the same. That's just the way it is! It doesn't mean we can't start over and still be someone great, if we're willing to put our addiction behind us and move on. The solution is simple, but the challenge requires our full participation. Throughout the world's history, change has always exacted a price, and it's no different for us. Freedom from addiction also comes at a price, and the price is our desire to be free.

In my second illustration, I show how we respond systematically once we change and stop drinking and drugging. First, our cells are no longer inundated with toxic substances, and they can return to doing what they were designed to do, instead of being constantly interrupted by drugs inducing overexcitation or deep inhibition. Next, we begin with a new daily regimen, one loaded with a diet of nutritious foods and drinks that are full of all the cell-building nutrients we need to strengthen ourselves from head to toe, and then we incorporate an exercise component designed to promote rigorous oxygen exchange and natural dopamine creation.

Once we begin this process of cellular restoration, the impact is exponential. As each layer of cells, each layer of tissue, each individual part of our brains and our bodies renews as it responds to our enhanced nutrition, the whole of our bodies, what I classify as the mind, is renewed. This is the result of breaking free from the tyranny of confusion that had once unleashed enemies to destroy it. During this process, we unquestionably take back our soul and become who we want to be. Finally, as our mind continues to strengthen and our cells become increasingly healthier, our physical energy returns, and the essence of our energy, known as our spirit, is renewed. We are feeling alive once again and feeling a new reason to be alive, and that change is evident in everything we do. Yes, there's no doubt we can damage a spirit, but we can most assuredly renew a spirit as well!

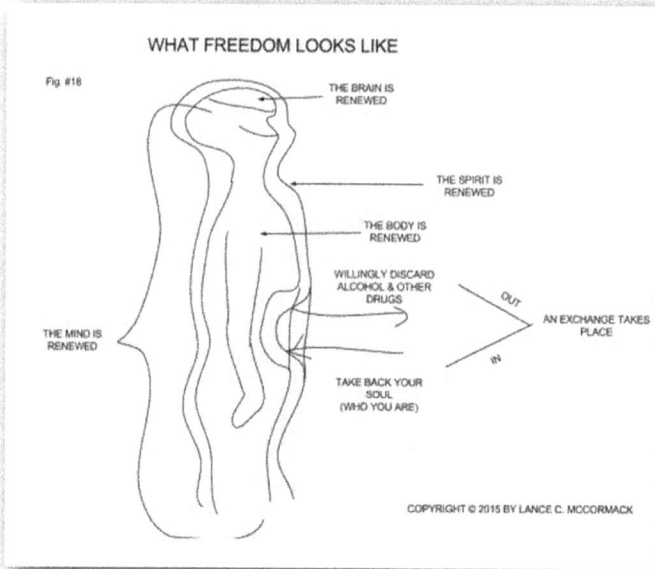

WHAT FREEDOM LOOKS LIKE

Fig. #18

THE BRAIN IS RENEWED

THE SPIRIT IS RENEWED

THE BODY IS RENEWED

WILLINGLY DISCARD ALCOHOL & OTHER DRUGS

OUT

IN

AN EXCHANGE TAKES PLACE

THE MIND IS RENEWED

TAKE BACK YOUR SOUL (WHO YOU ARE)

COPYRIGHT © 2015 BY LANCE C. MCCORMACK

Now We Know How Addictions Begin

This chapter has represented the last part of the six elements of addiction. In each part and in each chapter, I have strived to communicate the "how" of addiction and emphasize the gravity of addiction and convey through anecdotes, personal experiences, and clinical information the comprehensive damages created by addiction. In the next and final section of this book, I will detail the work required to end addiction once and for all. This section should leave you fully aware of your choices and your immeasurable power and leave you absolutely prepared to exercise whichever option you choose. The work required for recovery from addiction should not be viewed as any light undertaking whatsoever, but should be welcomed as a multilayered process of self-development and enlightenment that promises unparalleled rewards.

SECTION IX

Addiction Ends When You End It

By believing passionately in something that does
not yet exist, we create it. The nonexistent is
whatever we have not sufficiently desired.
—Nikos Kazantzakis

Have you hit rock bottom yet, or are people just tired of dealing with you? In either case, things have worsened, and life is much more complicated now because of you. It's been a fun run, but maybe now it's time to grow up. If you're ready, just say the word, and you'll see the flood of support rally around you and feel the universe safely envelop you in its palm, now that you've made the decision to reconnect. These final chapters will be devoted to how readers can unlock the most powerful, lifelong components to beating addiction once and for all.

CHAPTER 23

Enough!

See what needs to be done, do it, and be done with it.
—A LANCEISM

*B*asta. That means "enough" in Spanish, and in Italian too. Enough is enough, right?

Well, in our world of addiction, enough is never enough until it's enough. What that actually means is two things: the idea that we never get enough to satisfy our insatiable desires, but also that once we decide in our hearts and in our minds that we've had enough, we've had enough.

There's been a lot written about what gets us to that point of stopping an unhealthy behavior, and I believe what I've read to be mostly valid. We understand it's a complex issue involving not only exogenous and endogenous chemical dependencies but also many psychological, nutritional, and environmental factors. We realize that there has to be a reason or an impetus to change a behavior; otherwise it just won't happen.

One very well-known and respected model or theory of change is called the stages of change, and it talks about the psychological and cognitive processes that we must go through in order to change a behavior. It's a very well-developed model that's been utilized with great success throughout the world for decades. It began as a model in the United States designed to explain in detail the thought processes involved for a tobacco smoker to become a nonsmoker. It's a wonderful model, and I've used it countless times in individual, group, and seminar settings. Despite its many merits, however, I've found it lacking in the area of emotions. This particular model sounds and feels very logical to me, and it makes perfect sense. It's like decisional balancing, in that we're constantly weighing the benefits and the costs of our behaviors. The only problem is that addiction is neither logical nor sensible. Addiction is based on emotions, and those emotions are seldom logical or rational. So this model is fine to use as long as we realize it's just part of the recovery plan and that we'll have plenty of other work to do before we're done.

My model of change is called the emotions of change, and just as its name implies, this model focuses solely on how our feelings are behind any changes we make to our behavior. No matter the behavior, how we feel when we're involved in that behavior is the key to why that behavior persists or ceases. These feelings either pull us closer to that behavior or drive us farther away. Once our feelings toward those things of desire change, our behaviors change. So the only way to effect change is to affect the way we feel about those things. Therefore, if any change is to occur, most of our emphasis must be in this area, with our remaining focus on strengthening our mental and physical health conditions and eliminating any nutritional deficiencies.

In the following diagram, you can see the simplicity of this model. But although its design is simple, the depth of its constituents are not. The complexity of this model resides in what it represents, and that is *conflict*. The emotions of change are about the challenges of personal conflict resolution, and that extensive undertaking has proven to be the most difficult of all for the human being. In my model there are four axes, similar in design to those of the Newtonian atom, and they are enclosed in a circle and contain a center not unlike a nucleus. My idea for this model is to show how we are at the center of our individual worlds and how our emotions are at the center of the conflicts that we experience. The negative emotions we feel continue to conflict with the positive emotions we feel about what we're doing. As all these emotions whirl around us continuously, presenting mental and physical turmoil, subconsciously we continue to seek a peaceful resolution. And the more our negative emotions weigh heavy on our minds, the more we are poised for change, and the more available we become to resolve our conflicts.

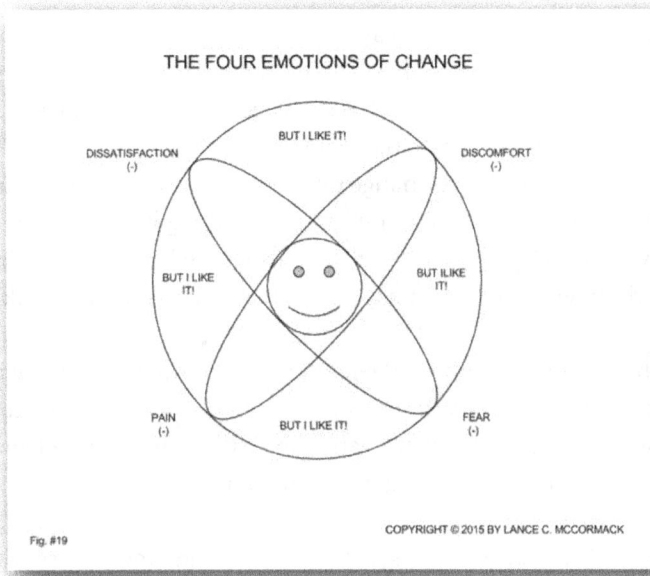

THE FOUR EMOTIONS OF CHANGE

BUT I LIKE IT!

DISSATISFACTION
(-)

DISCOMFORT
(-)

BUT I LIKE
IT!

BUT I LIKE
IT!

PAIN
(-)

BUT I LIKE IT!

FEAR
(-)

Fig. #19

COPYRIGHT © 2015 BY LANCE C. MCCORMACK

I see four main emotions that can create change: dissatisfaction, discomfort, pain, and fear. I'm certain there could be others, but I consider these to be the main contributors to change. Many people would quickly suggest that love would undoubtedly be a main contributor or catalyst for change, and I can see why they would say that. The only problem I have with love as a main catalyst for lasting change is that through my experiences, love unfortunately has rarely been enough to effect other than temporary change. For as wonderful and powerful as love is, when it comes to addictions in particular, love by itself just isn't enough, unless of course we're talking about self-love. But if we're discussing making changes based on the love we have for another, then no, it isn't enough. The reason love is not enough is because we already believe we have found unconditional love in what we're doing, so any other love is interpreted as an imposter. Even if change is to occur as the result of that love for another, the change is generally contingent upon the strength of that ongoing relationship and lasts only as long as things run smoothly in that relationship. Once any discontent, perceived discontent, or contrived discontent enters, resentment for having prematurely stopped a behavior quickly replaces the catalyst of love that caused the cessation of that behavior, and the behavior promptly resumes.

Besides all the emotions that can create change, we have one emotion that stands boldly in their way: "But I like it!" This emotion is called lust, and it serves as a constant deterrent to change. That's why you see a smiley face in the center of the diagram, because despite whatever harmful things we're doing, we believe we're having a ball doing them! Change ultimately cannot occur until lust is finally understood and at minimum diminished to something like "I used to love it but no longer even like it." It's kind of like the feelings we have for an ex who did us wrong and whom we could pass on the street today and not even look at.

Emotion 1: Dissatisfaction—a deep emotion involving an internal disturbance or conflict as to how things are going, how our lives are proceeding, and how we perceive others are perceiving us. These are just a few of the visceral insights into not feeling happy or content with who we currently are.

Emotion 2: Discomfort—feelings of embarrassment and unease with our current situation and an assessment of how problematic our lives have become because of our decisions. Noticing the inconveniences we suffer regularly and all the hardships we endure just to continue to have things our way.

Emotion 3: Pain—whether medically real or imagined, emotional or physical, our pain is very real to us, and it's something we feel intensely that makes us acutely aware that we have a problem. It's something that plagues us from the inside out and pushes us constantly toward a remedy.

Emotion 4: Fear—an all-encompassing emotion that keeps us fighting and running and emotionally paralyzed and unable to mobilize our resources genuinely.

At least one of these four emotions must be present for change to occur. If change is currently not present, then either none of these four emotions are currently present or the intensity of these emotions are not severe enough. As the intensity increases with one or more of these emotions, change becomes more possible, but still not guaranteed. Some of us will unfortunately go the distance and never tap out. Usually, however, that isn't the case, and change does occur at some point.

I remember when I was a young boy and we used to play a game called uncle. This ingenious game entailed one boy (the twister) twisting the arm of another boy (the twistee) behind his back until the twistee could no longer tolerate the pain, whereupon the twistee would finally say uncle, and the twister would release the pressure on the boy's arm. I was sometimes the twister but more times the twistee, so I speak from personal experience. Since I thought I was tough, this game always took a while, because I would hold out until the bitter end, saying all the while that I couldn't feel anything yet and asking the twister if he was going to start twisting anytime soon. This of course enraged the twister and caused him to twist my arm even harder. Finally, after my arm was almost torn from the socket, I would concede, but even then only to say that I was getting tired of standing there, so I decided to say uncle just to get the game over with.

If you know anyone like the twistee I mentioned (me), then you personally know how hard it is to convince someone to give in when they don't want to accept defeat. And that's when alcohol and other drugs aren't even involved. They will keep on doing what they want to do until they can no longer do it. So the emotions of change model comes in handy as a therapeutic model, so you as the caregiver won't waste precious time working tirelessly with someone who is purposely trying to hold out until the bitter end just to prove a point. Instead you will focus on your own well-being or on others who are ready for change now, and not continue to provide fuel for the self-destructive behaviors of those not yet ready. Because these four emotions of change also apply to how the addicted person feels about how their caregivers feel about them. Part of their addiction is tied to attracting attention and being noticed and being cared for, and the addiction is just an elaborate, dramatic means to an end that unfortunately becomes something else entirely and a lot more than they ever expected.

We as caregivers are faced with a decision, either to continue to play the game that usually ends in stalemate or to force the player's hand by upping the ante and increasing the intensity of the emotions of change. Will we communicate to them how our perceptions of them have changed dramatically, how their lives have become clearly unmanageable, how their pain is abundantly evident, and how we fear they will never return to us? Will we express with sorrow our decision to sever our ties to them until they finally make the decision to take their lives back and reconnect with us? In any case, will we be strong enough to accept the consequences of our decision, knowing the dire nature of that decision? If the answers are yes to all these questions, then the chances are better than 50 percent that we will be successful and achieve a positive outcome.

Change will occur, if it is to occur, once the level of intensity of our emotions grows to a level that is no longer tolerable. Whether our dissatisfaction with ourselves or our predicament becomes unbearable, or our discontent, pain, or fear becomes greater than our psyche can endure, we decide when it's finally time to change. In either case, the higher the intensity of our emotions, the less our disingenuous smile remains, until one day that smile is altogether replaced with a heartfelt smile that illuminates our faces like the sun and represents change. And as we say, "Enough," we also show our gratitude by saying, "Thank you."

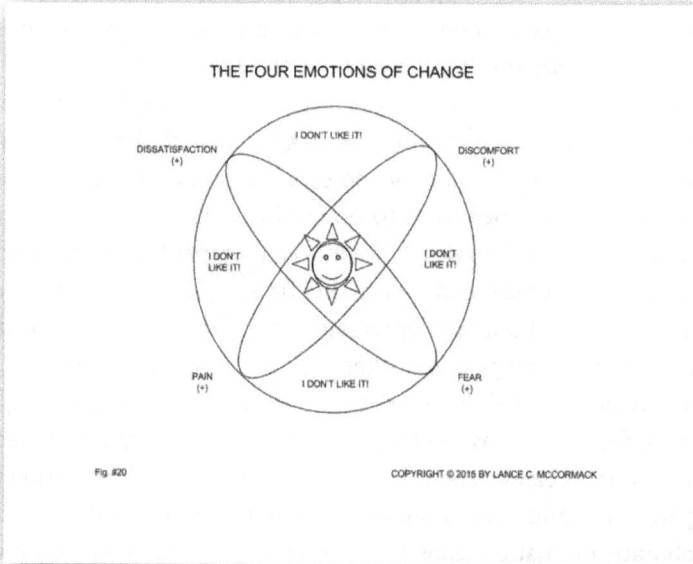

THE FOUR EMOTIONS OF CHANGE

DISSATISFACTION
(+)

I DON'T LIKE IT!

DISCOMFORT
(+)

I DON'T
LIKE IT!

I DON'T
LIKE IT!

PAIN
(+)

I DON'T LIKE IT!

FEAR
(+)

Fig. #20

COPYRIGHT © 2015 BY LANCE C. MCCORMACK

212

CHAPTER 24

Whole Again

We must force ourselves past what is careful and
comfortable to achieve what is possible.
—A LANCEISM

meet a lot of people with addictions in many different settings—large groups, small groups, seminars, workshops, individual sessions, family sessions, and in just casual settings while standing or sitting around talking. Have you ever spoken with someone and noticed that even though they're standing right there in front of you, they're not there with you? Their body is there, but their spirit is somewhere else. Kind of like when spouses just tune each other out because they think they've heard it all before. They act as if they already know what their partner's going to say, so why bother even listening?

Sometimes they're right, but not always! I notice that all the time with the people I meet struggling with addictions. It's not just because I'm boring, which sometimes I'm sure I am, but because they have become used to being present just to fulfill treatment obligations. Many people are in treatment due to family pressures, legal requirements, and so on, and not because their hearts are really in it. And we all know that's entirely different, and it's that kind of difference that makes them just "molecules in a chair." Just energy occupying a physical location but spiritually checked out.

There's no true benefit to being just molecules in a chair. Don't be just molecules in a chair. I remember one guy holding his head in his hands dramatically and looking up as he entered our group room, saying, "Not another group. I've been going to groups for thirty years, and there's nothing you can say that I haven't already heard before. No offense to you, but it's the truth!" I replied, "Perhaps, but maybe this time you'll listen."

Who Do You Want to Be?

If we're contemplating changing who we are and what we're doing, then we'll need to know who we want to be and what we want to do. And since time is always of the essence, we can make this transition even easier and quicker by finding people whom we admire and just emulating them. We can find people with all the attributes we desire and just copy them in every way. You don't even have to know these people personally; they can be people you've seen on television or even read about. All you need is to have some type of feeling about who they are that makes you want to be more like them. Why continue to hang around people who think like we used to think and act like we used to act, when we can easily transform ourselves into our ideal selves!

This is how it worked for me. As a young boy of about age seven, I was filled with anxiety each time I left my apartment in the projects in New York City. Over the years I learned that through visualization I could transcend my current predicaments by engaging my imagination. I learned that through imagery I could mentally be somewhere else more pleasing and as result feel more pleasant. This technique worked effectively until I was in my early twenties. Then my anxiety began to rear its ugly head once again, and my visualization techniques alone proved insufficient to address my discomfort. I suspect the images I had used as a young boy had become too distant in my memory at that point to bring them into focus with the crystalline intensity I needed.

Luckily, I had another sense to draw on. From when I was a young boy, I had also been an avid fan of James Bond, 007. I thought he was the coolest guy I'd ever seen! In his movies, he never appeared flustered in any situation, no matter how tense or how dangerous.

James Bond always kept his composure and was able to calmly get through anything life threw at him. I had wanted to be James Bond in the worst way! Remembering my previous experiences with anxiety and how visualization helped me get through years of fears, I decided to test how visualization coupled with auditory stimulation would work.

Each James Bond movie had a great soundtrack and a theme song, and one theme song in particular really captured my attention. This song was "Thunderball." Whenever I heard that song, I would stand a different way, sit a different way, I would adopt a certain posture that exhibited this air of confidence, and I would even speak differently. I no longer felt rushed and uneasy, tense or anxious, but instead I felt calm and in control. Once I heard that song, I became James Bond, so that song became my song! That song was to be my theme song for as long as I needed it to be.

I realized at that point that there was actually a formula to feeling better and changing my life: visualizing something pleasant in my mind + hearing inspirational music in my head = feeling something amazing in my body. Three senses: visual + auditory = kinesthetic. All I ever needed to do was visualize who I wanted to be, add motivational music, and I could become that person and feel highly motivated to accomplish whatever I desired. For years, whenever I was going out socially or getting ready for an important event and wanted some additional confidence, I just pictured myself as James Bond doing something cool in the foreground and hearing my theme song, "Thunderball," playing in the background, and instantly my whole demeanor changed, my confidence soared, and I was ready. Imagery and music are magical, and we fortunately have access to both.

Transforming ourselves is just that easy! We can become whomever we choose to become, just by studying someone and replicating what they do, what they say, and how they think. Our greatest task is to find someone worthy of replicating. In our field of addiction, we must be especially careful to select the right person. In recovery, for instance, we must understand the distinctions between having a sponsor and having a role model. A sponsor is a great person to help us stay away from whatever it is we're struggling with because she or he knows what we're going through based on personal experience. To have someone who can feel our pain because they've been there and done that can be extremely comforting and immensely helpful. The role of a sponsor cannot be overstated. A role model, on the other hand, is someone we look up to and admire, not necessarily because of their similarity to us, but because of their dissimilarity to us. This is someone who doesn't necessarily know anything about us or what we've been through, someone who provides a completely different outlook on life than we currently have, and that can be amazingly refreshing and beneficial.

Many times this difference is what we really need in order to see how others get through their challenging lives without succumbing to using alcohol or other drugs. So choose your role models wisely, and become that person you've always wanted to be!

I think Thomas Troward may have said it best: "The law of flotation was not discovered by contemplating the sinking of things, but by contemplating the floating of things and why things floated naturally." This is what I'm talking about. I believe that Mr. Troward was referring to much more than boats and ships. My interpretation of his saying in regards to recovery is that we will learn more by hanging around those who have not done what we've done (those who've floated naturally), than by hanging solely around those who have done what we've done (those who've sunk). For as comforting as it may be to commiserate with people who have been down in the gutter as we have, they may not necessarily be the people we need to surround ourselves with, simply because many of them are still struggling themselves to maintain sobriety. We can benefit more from those who have been successful at not succumbing to addictions at all. After all, life is challenging to all of us, we all will face tough times and unwelcome situations that will take us out of our comfort zones, yet not all of us will become addicts. Why?

It's Time to Get Our Energy Back!

As we continue to dig out from the wreckage of addiction, we must never forget that it's all about energy. That's where it starts and that's where it ends. We touched briefly on energy in chapter 9 and discussed some ways in which to redirect energy so that it's working for us. One method of redirection is diversion, in which we can refocus our energy by diverting it into more worthwhile areas. Recall our example of the glass in chapter 9, and how once we drilled a hole in the glass, all the energy it once contained was released and diverted elsewhere. In this chapter with my energy restoration model, you will see how our myopically focused initial energy is released, diverted, corrupted, and then ultimately restored into worthwhile entities.

THE ENERGY RESTORATION MODEL

FIG. #21

100 % YOU

COPYRIGHT © 2014 BY LANCE C. MCCORMACK

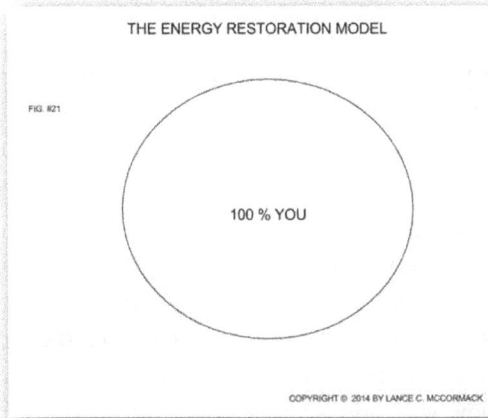

Imagine being an infant again, and think about what we must have focused on: being feed, being held, being comfortable, being attended to, and being connected. Maybe we contemplated greater things, maybe not; maybe we just focused on the basics. I'd say that our focus then was all on us. As I've depicted in figure 21, our world initially was centered 100 percent around us, and the only reason anyone else in our world even existed was to serve us. Fortunately for others, at some point early on, we recognized that there were others like us who also needed and wanted what we needed and wanted. We acknowledged Mom, we acknowledged Dad, we noticed perhaps that we had siblings. Later on we met our grandparents, aunts and uncles, cousins, and so on. We developed friendships, romantic relationships, and may have even had children. Concurrently we found jobs and maybe nurtured careers. In a short amount of time, we had diverted 50 percent of our energy away from us and onto others whom we had deemed worthy of our time and energy, and that was fine. Apparently, it was never intended that we remain focused solely on ourselves forever.

While we diverted 50 percent of our energy elsewhere, we also retained 50 percent of our energy for ourselves. We kept this energy to fuel our self-esteem, our self-worth, our mental and physical health, our faith in something greater than ourselves, our heart or compassion for others, and finally our soul, the energy that keeps us all together. Now, we still have 100 percent energy within us, but no longer 100 percent energy focused on us, and that's good, very good!

In figure 22 you'll notice that our world now is divided into twelve sectors, with each sector labeled for all the areas where we've devoted our energies. We have a full life, filled with people we love, activities we enjoy, and an overall belief in ourselves that we have value. We nurture our relationships with Mom and Dad, with our brothers and sisters, and with our grandparents. They get to really know us, and we get to really know them. We develop deeper friendships and even fall in love. Perhaps we marry and have children. We continue with our education and secure gainful employment, and we revel in our hobbies or leisure activities that make it all seem worthwhile. Meanwhile, as we continue to do the right things, we develop greater self-esteem, greater feelings of our worth, a better sense of our mental and physical strengths, a deeper belief in something greater than ourselves, and a compassionate connection to others that makes us feel complete in our soul, and that feels wonderful!

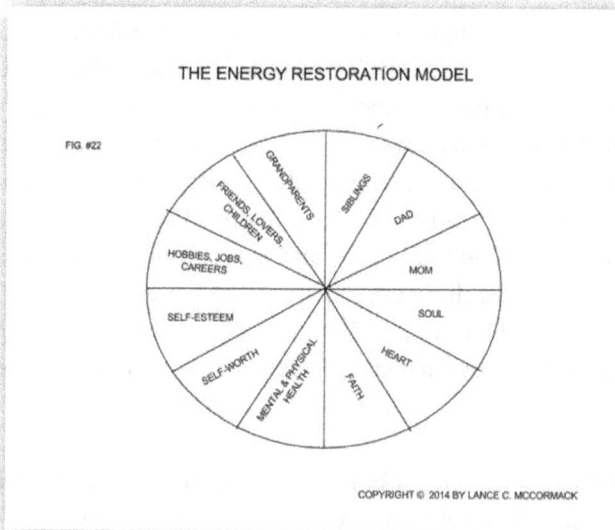

THE ENERGY RESTORATION MODEL

FIG. #22

GRANDPARENTS, SIBLINGS, DAD, MOM, SOUL, HEART, FAITH, MENTAL & PHYSICAL HEALTH, SELF-WORTH, SELF-ESTEEM, HOBBIES, JOBS, CAREERS, FRIENDS, LOVERS, CHILDREN

COPYRIGHT © 2014 BY LANCE C. MCCORMACK

Next, in figure 23, you'll notice that we have introduced drugs into our world, for whatever reason, and things have changed dramatically as a result. The drugs have gravely impacted the sectors of our lives and therefore gravely impacted us. Our relationship with our mom suffers, our relationship with our dad suffers, our brothers and our sisters all feel the pain as we pull away further and further away from them. Our grandparents become distant, and our friends, lovers, and children become like strangers to us as we become laser-focused on our new love interest. Our hobbies become nonexistent, and our jobs and careers fade quickly into obscurity.

As if severely impacting our relationships with others wasn't enough, we dig even deeper and impact the innermost parts of ourselves that make us who we are. Our self-esteem goes out the window, our self-worth right behind it, our mental and physical health takes a nose dive, and our faith, along with our heart or compassion for others, is gone like it never existed. All we have left at this point is our soul, and we barely have that. Now we have gone from having 100 percent of our energy divided among beautiful things to having just one-twelfth, or 8.333 percent, of that energy left to devote to those things, while the lion's share of our energy, 91.667 percent of it, is now devoted to drugs. At this point we are weak, vulnerable, and downright toxic. Toxic to ourselves and to everyone with whom we have any contact.

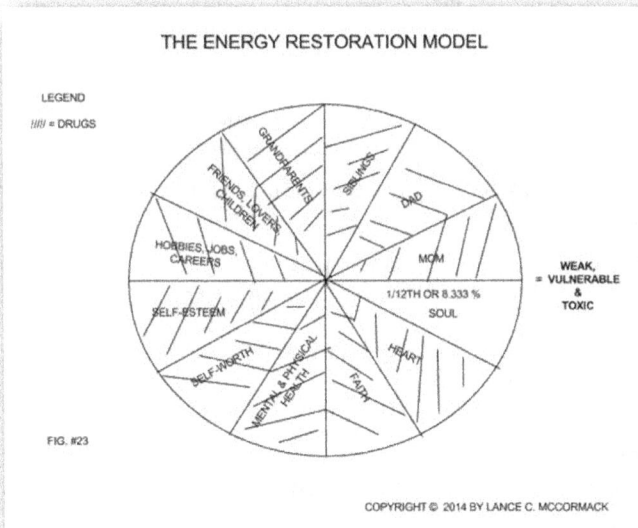

THE ENERGY RESTORATION MODEL

FIG. #23

COPYRIGHT © 2014 BY LANCE C. MCCORMACK

As we continue to drink and drug and drift into a new world of isolation, we come to understand through communications with others that they too have a life and a world with sectors similar to ours. In figure 24 I have illustrated how we are connected to others and how our toxicity spreads to them and impacts their sectors as well. Picture yourself at work when you receive an emergency call about your significant other, your SO, who has been taken to the hospital after having been found naked on Main Street, bent over and kissing the ground in a narcotic stupor. The paramedics had to use Narcan to revive your wife, and she's currently being held for medical observation. As you respond to the caller, your supervisor happens to overhear your communications. So you tell your supervisor you have to leave and your supervisor says, "Again? This is the eighth time this month that you've had to leave suddenly, and you have work that needs to get done here!"

You respond, "My wife really needs me, and she's the most important person in my life, so I have to leave regardless of the work."

Your supervisor then replies, "Well, I guess you've made your choice, and now I have made mine. You're fired!"

Once the dust settles and your wife is back home and back to doing what she does, you realize when you open a stack of bills that you no longer have a job. At that point, reality sets in, and you finally acknowledge that you are a person too and that your life matters too! That's how it generally works. Those of us who are in the lives of addicted people sooner or later come to the realization that we can no longer remain connected to them, because we will only go down the tubes with them if we do.

Self-preservation kicks in at some point, and we say, "Enough—I'm out of here!" So we cut them loose (yes, those are scissors depicted in figure 24); one by one, people cut ties, until finally the addicted person is left all alone to do whatever it is he or she desires.

Here's a letter from a young lady I met in treatment who finally realized she had to cut the cord to save herself:

Mom, Ma, Mommy—
When I think of you, I see a spirit as free as can be
I picture the world just you and me
But let's be real, some damage has been done
It's no longer just weekend fun

Who really introduces their baby girl to heroin and crack?
You fucked up, and that's a fact!
But do you realize what you've done to me?
I've been in jails and institutions and death is always a maybe
From shoplifting to robbing our dealers
The drugs became our only healers

Don't get me wrong, you always kept me safe while out on the streets
But our addiction has showed us defeat among defeat
Today I've realized a lot of things
For example, how to bring more loyalty to you than anyone or anything
else brings
Does that mean anything to you?
Or are you gonna think it's just another one of my "boo-hoos"
I'm sorry this sounds so mean
But I'm sick of being known as a heroin fiend,
All I want is the *both* of us to get better,
But I've realized that's not possible after reading your letter
You feed me bullshit day in and day out
Manipulating my mind—giving me no way out!
So, I guess I've come to a very hard conclusion.
I need to cut you out, but I love you, so don't let that be a confusion
It's not going to be forever, I hope
As long as you don't choose dope
You're my world, Mom, and don't ever forget it
I'm doing this for us, so we don't end up in a casket

Love, Me

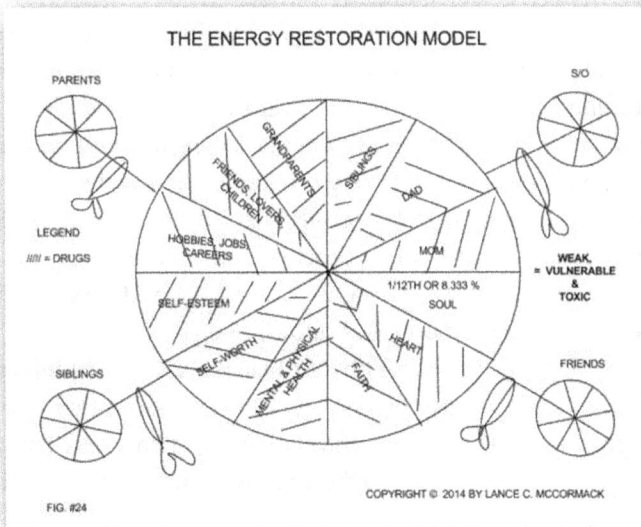

THE ENERGY RESTORATION MODEL

FIG. #24

COPYRIGHT © 2014 BY LANCE C. MCCORMACK

Now, this may appear to be the opportune time to drink or use other drugs even more, since everyone now has disconnected from you in order to save themselves. We ask ourselves, "Why stop drinking and drugging, now that I've lost everything and everyone?" That's one route we can take, or we can get to work to reclaim what we've lost. Remember that "some things are permanent, but more things are present." Many things that we lose are only lost temporarily and until we change our behaviors. So the duration and the extent of our losses are all up to us!

If we're serious and we want to get back what we've lost, we must make a decision. If we're not serious and don't care about what we've lost, we must also make a decision. Either way, we must no longer wallow in indecision; instead we must choose. Ask yourself, "What do I desire most?" Forget saying all those things that sound good like; a house in the suburbs with a white picket fence, a loving spouse and 2.5 kids and instead realize that if you really desired those things most, you would have them and you wouldn't be struggling every day to stay sober. If you say you desire alcohol or other drugs most, then so be it! You are being honest and you have made your decision. But, if you decide to reclaim what you have deservedly lost, then fight and get it back. Caution: this decision is one that will entail a great deal of work and require your true commitment to change.

In figure 25 I have illustrated arrows to indicate the direction in which to begin the work that stands between us and reclaiming what we've lost.

First, we must recapture our humanity through deeds of the heart. Maybe we volunteer our time and our energy to reading bedtime stories to children at the Shriners Hospital for Children, or maybe we volunteer our time and energy visiting veterans returning from war with disabilities at the Veteran's Administration hospital. Where we volunteer our time and energy isn't really that important, as long as we're volunteering our time and energy and giving of ourselves to someone else who is in need. Addiction is all about taking: taking drugs, taking things, taking up valuable time, taking lives, and taking peace of mind and security from others. As we work honestly to restore our energy, we stop taking, and we start giving. That's what the energy restoration model is all about, giving!

Next, we work to restore our faith, our belief in something infinitely greater than ourselves. It doesn't matter what you call it or how you conceptualize this power, as long as you have something you can call on when all else fails. Something that can help you through all the roughest of times and the darkest of hours and leave you stronger than before.

With our faith restored, we can now believe that no matter what our mental or physical condition, we are not alone and we can persevere. With this power, we tackle all the problems that we have created in our minds and in our bodies, and we commit to strengthening ourselves in every way possible. Maybe we've contracted a disease—Hep C, HPV, HIV, AIDS, heart disease, cirrhosis, type 2 diabetes, tuberculosis, or something else. Maybe we've developed a mental health disorder like ADD, ADHD, bipolar disorder, or generalized anxiety. In any case, now we take charge of our mental and physical health and no longer sweep our problems under the rug, insisting to ourselves that another drink or drug will make all our very real problems disappear. Instead, we address our mental and physical health issues, and we work to get ourselves as healthy as we can.

As we continue to proceed swiftly through the process of energy restoration, we feel better and stronger with every step, knowing we're that much closer to achieving wholeness and true happiness. The more we do, the more worthy we feel to reenter the world we've left behind. And with our reclaimed self-worth comes a magnificent resurgence of our self-esteem. We experience a new sense of awe, admiration, and appreciation for who we are and for what we're doing. Armed with this new feeling of empowerment, we are now ready to reconnect and rejoin the world of the living!

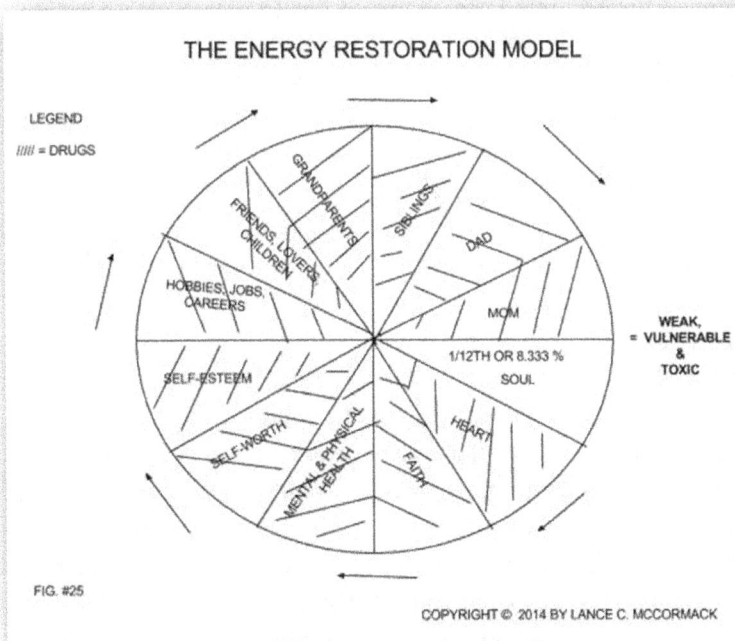

THE ENERGY RESTORATION MODEL

LEGEND

//// = DRUGS

GRANDPARENTS
SIBLINGS
FRIENDS, LOVERS, CHILDREN
DAD
HOBBIES, JOBS, CAREERS
MOM
WEAK, = VULNERABLE & TOXIC
1/12TH OR 8.333 %
SELF-ESTEEM
SOUL
SELF-WORTH
MENTAL & PHYSICAL HEALTH
FAITH
HEART

FIG. #25

We're taking delight in our hobbies again and feeling interested and excited by even the little things. We revel in seeing a sunset and gratefully look forward to every sunrise. We're revisiting old jobs and maybe venturing into new jobs. We realign with our careers and once again derive a purpose for our lives. Our friends hear our voices on the phone, our lovers feel our presence at our home, and our children know their parent has not abandoned them and is here to stay. Grandparents, siblings, and Mom and Dad all delight in seeing that we are back and ready to be responsible and take control of our lives.

We express to them all that we are sorry, and more than just sorry; we express that we take responsibility for everything we have done. Furthermore, we communicate to all parties affected that we have changed dramatically and that we will never return to our old selves, ever! Now, that's not something we're used to saying in our field of addiction. Of course, we all say we're sorry over and over again, but then we usually end our apologies with the proviso, "one day at a time." Not this time. We say, "Never again!" The difference is if we say it, then we can be held accountable for having said it. Being accountable means that if we fail to deliver, our people can justifiably get up and leave us and begin living their lives again without feeling they've let us down somehow.

Imagine being a battered woman whose partner has routinely beaten you and abused you in every way possible, and then your partner says, "I'm sorry!" Do those words really mean anything to you? Do you feel more comfortable now knowing your partner is sorry? Do those words exude confidence in you that the abuse will never happen again? The answer to all those questions is no. The words *I'm sorry* without the words *and I will never do it again* are worthless. Even with those added words, you should still run for the hills, but without an assurance that the abuse will never take place again, you have absolutely nothing but the assurance that it will.

Now, I don't want to make this energy restoration model appear to be a panacea, because it's not. Just because we are finally ready to make our amends doesn't mean that the people we've harmed are ready to hear them. All throughout our process of addiction, we have hurt many people and wreaked havoc throughout our lives and the lives of countless others, and that damage in many cases will not be easily overlooked. We will face challenges and opposition and even downright disbelief and distrust as to our genuineness, and we have to be prepared for it. Some people may just not want to be bothered with us after what we've done, and we have to respect that, no matter how painful. It would be wonderful to have everyone affected gather around the table for Thanksgiving dinner, but that could be just wishful thinking. We must recognize that life is a timed event, and that life and death continue whether we're involved in it or not.

Unfortunately, some people we've hurt will have died by the time we come to our senses, so we won't even have the opportunity to make our amends to them while they're still alive. That's how life works; time isn't promised to any of us. That's why it's critically important that we work quickly to recover and not drag this process out forever.

Now, despite what happens along the process of restoring our energy and despite who's left to forgive us, we must trudge forward with our commitment to change. At no point do we fall into despair and host a pity party for ourselves, no matter how tempting. We cannot control how others receive us or whether they perceive that what we're doing is authentic. We can only control what we're doing, so we must remain steadfast to our cause. Make no mistake, this is not the time to relapse, because if we use these challenges as an excuse to relapse, we never really wanted recovery in the first place.

Then, after all the dust has settled and we see who's left standing there beside us, we can take comfort in our efforts toward recovery and focus on our new circle of life. Now, we ardently work to maintain the energy we put into all the important sectors of our lives: compassion for others, faith in something, self-care, and into all those remaining good people who have willingly accepted us now into their lives, just as we are. Yes, life is truly beautiful!

CHAPTER 25

No Legs Left to Stand On

Putting down a drink or a drug is the easy part; what's
hard is taking a really good look at yourself.
—A Lanceism

Many addicts say they want to become free from addiction yet take very cautious steps toward that goal. They act as if taking only baby steps will succeed. They have been taught to think small, and think small they do. They say, "You must make changes slowly because nothing can be changed overnight; it's just not possible." This is what they believe, and it's this belief that keeps them trapped in the rat hole! Human beings were designed to be dynamic by nature; only time and indoctrination has trained us to be otherwise. Baby steps, my ass!

The world of an addict is like living in a self-designed, custom-made house, but with some major differences. This house is a house of addiction, and unlike regular houses that are erected from the outside, the house of addiction is built from the inside out. Also unlike regular houses, this house has no doors, no windows, and has only one way out. Its walls and ceiling are solid, and its foundation is made not of a slab but of massive cement blocks that can support this house throughout the most violent of storms. Without windows and doors, the air inside each house is limited and represents time being of the essence. This is no time for baby steps.

The number of blocks supporting each house will vary depending on each homeowner and on how large a house they've built. The size of house they've built is determined by how they've viewed the world and how they envision their place in it. Per the individual, it may be a quaint New England–style cottage or a sprawling Texas-style, ten-bedroom ranch. Each house is unique and must be handled individually.

The blocks that support these houses of addiction are known as the building blocks of addiction. These building blocks represent the feelings and emotions that we maintain that guide us through our decision-making processes. These are the feelings and emotions that create addiction, support addiction, and sustain addiction. Unless we address these feelings and emotions thoroughly, addiction will continue to flourish until we no longer exist. We can't escape our house of addiction unless we destroy its foundation. Destroying just a few blocks simply won't suffice; we must annihilate them all. Only then will the walls of the house of addiction violently twist and crack and allow the sun's illumination to enter and warm us once again as we exit victoriously.

Following is a list of building blocks. As you read through this list, please check off the blocks that apply to you, for they comprise your foundation. This list is in no way meant to be inclusive. Please feel free to add whatever blocks you find relevant to your particular foundation and omit any blocks that don't pertain to you. Each homeowner's foundation will be different, and therefore each custom house of addiction will be unique, but similar to others. Many people say they want to be free from addiction. Well, let's see. Here's your opportunity to see what you're made of, and as with time, opportunity is also of the essence. The sooner you take the opportunity to identify what you're made of, the sooner you can give yourself a make-over. After all, who knows when and if you'll have another opportunity.

Each building block has a name, and the names are as follows:

Anger: "An intense emotional state induced by displeasure." For addicts (alcoholics are always included) anger is a constant state, as displeasure is a constant in our lives. Oftentimes this emotion is displaced onto undeserving others when honestly it is our displeasure with ourselves that causes much of our anger.

Anxiety: The feeling of worry, unease or tension about things in general or about something in particular. Complaints of having anxiety are extremely common in our field, and alcohol and other drugs are readily used as a remedy. Paradoxically, however, the use of alcohol and other drugs can also create and worsen feelings of anxiety.

Argumentativeness: Combativeness. The form of expression whereby we feel compelled to present our version or understanding of something to the point of being antagonistic to others.

Arrogance: Self-importance. A characteristic of our nature that conveys our belief in being superior in some way.

Cynicism: Skepticism or suspicion regarding the motivations of others.

Defensiveness: "Intended to withstand or deter aggression or attack." This strategy is a very popular one that we use in our field of addiction. Sometimes we even preempt attacks by going on the offensive in an effort to make the other person defensive. A common strategy generally used to derail or distract others from the issues at hand.

Defiance: "Bold resistance." The act of not budging mentally and/or physically in a display of opposition. Have you ever seen a young child resist holding her parent's hand while crossing a street? This kind of opposition may appear cute at first, but not for long. Imagine this same child as a twenty-year-old. There's nothing cute about it!

Dishonesty: "Untruthfulness." A nature characterized by subterfuge. Whether we're lying about something or to someone or cheating and manipulating people or situations or downright taking things that aren't ours, dishonesty is a common trait of the addict.

Disrespect: "Discourtesy." A show of contempt or disregard for another. Now this word is huge in the world of the addicted person. At one facility where I've worked, we use an internal document called a "calming solutions form" to find out more about what things please or displease the patients. Maybe it's listening to music or reading a book that's found to be pleasurable, but what I've found to be listed most often as displeasing is "being disrespected." Of course being disrespected is something totally subjective since we're actually talking about *feeling* disrespected, and how we feel is entirely up to us. The interesting thing is that the field of addiction is filled with disrespectful, discourteous people. That's the nature of the beast!

Disobedience: "Refusal or unwillingness to obey rules of those in authority." No one is going to tell you anything because no one is in charge of you. "I'll do what I damn well please." Is this you?

Distrust/Disbelief: The belief that someone or something cannot be trusted. For whatever reason, you find reason to believe that what you see or what you hear is false and cannot be believed.

Emotional pain: Pain caused by negative feelings derived from our interpretations of past experiences.

Envy: An intense feeling that someone else possesses something you desire or deserve. Feeling dissatisfied with what you have and always wanting something else instead.

Fear: An emotion created by an interpretation that something or someone is dangerous or presents a threat to one's safety or happiness. Fear of the known or unknown. An apprehension that things aren't as they should be. In our field fear takes on many meanings, as it can represent how we feel about our growing, insatiable desire to feel pleasure or how we fear that we will never get enough to satisfy our growing demands or how we fear that we love our alcohol and other drugs more than life itself.

Greed: An intense selfish desire for more than you need of anything. The unwillingness to share the abundance of what you have with others; no one can play with your toys because they're yours.

Gluttony: An insatiable desire to consume excessive quantities of something.

Hatred: Intense loathing or hostility against someone or something.

Impatience: The tendency toward wanting one's needs addressed immediately.

Impulsiveness: Tendency to act almost without thinking, acting on reflex. Never thinking before you act and always being sorry for your actions later.

Inferiority: The feeling of being less than others in some way.

Insecurity: Lack of self-confidence. Uncertainty about your abilities to succeed.

Intolerance: Unwillingness to accept differing views, behaviors, or beliefs.

Laziness: The act of not wanting to work for anything or expend any energy to accomplish much of anything.

Lust: The all-consuming desire to experience bodily pleasures and self-satisfaction.

Negativity: Pessimism about things; the tendency to see things as "doom and gloom." The propensity to see the glass half empty. Characterized by a saying that's very popular in the addictions field, "no good deed goes unpunished."

Physical pain: Pain experienced within the body.

Pride/Ego: Inordinate self-esteem or sense of self; conceit, an ostentatious display of self. This is the meaning I wish to use for our purposes. Many times we see individuals who can obviously benefit from assistance decline that assistance because of their pride. They don't want to give anyone the impression that they are unable to handle their own affairs without the help of another. I do understand that both pride and ego can also be defined as good things and can be linked to self-respect and self-worth.

Resentment: Seething bitterness toward someone or something due to a perceived injustice.

Selfishness: The focus on oneself to the detriment of others.

Self-Loathing: Anger, disgust, or hatred toward oneself.

Stubbornness: Unreasonably set in one's ways; unwilling to bend in opinions, inflexible in one's thinking.

Superiority: The feeling of being better or higher in status than another or all others.

The preceding thirty-two acts, conditions, behaviors, feelings, and so on, constitute just a few of the building blocks that have helped form the foundations of our addictions. It's not imperative that we address these shortcomings in ourselves. Surely, we can become abstinent without addressing them, but we will not be free from the allure of addiction while these building blocks still remain in place. The more we understand about ourselves and our motivations, the stronger we will be in all areas of our lives, and the happier we can be with who we are. Recovery isn't about bringing back the person we used to be before we started with alcohol and other drugs; it's about becoming someone better. Clearly, the person we were before wasn't satisfactory to us, otherwise we wouldn't have needed to alter ourselves with psychoactive substances.

So, what do we do now that we've checked off our building blocks and identified the composition of our foundations? Now we painstakingly identify the role each block plays in our lives by mentally reviewing when we experience each thing. Next, we list examples of specific incidents when we felt that way or when we engaged in those acts or behaviors. Subsequently, we contemplate and then list why we believe those feelings, actions, behaviors, and so on, were justified. Lastly, we ask ourselves honestly, were they? For every honest response of no justification, we are one step closer to demolishing our flawed foundation and being free from the seduction of addiction. If we find only justification for all our behaviors and for all the feelings that we have, then perhaps we just need to look again!

CHAPTER 26

Reset Your Soul

*You've got to have at least an idea of what you
want before you can go looking for it.*
—A LANCEISM

So it's time to get serious. We understand that sobriety is ours for the taking, and we say we want it, but we're still not sure if we're strong enough to make it happen. In previous chapters I have baked you a delicious multilayer cake loaded with powerful ingredients, and now I'm going to give you the icing. By the end of this chapter, you will have everything you need to succeed without fail and become the person you've always dreamed of being. After this, anything you do to derail yourself, you will be doing on purpose and devoid of excuses, and that won't be nearly as much fun

Still Not Feeling a Higher Power?

Well, once again, in order to achieve recovery from addiction, we don't need to do anything other than stop using whatever we've been using and then stay stopped. It's that easy! But what if you could tap into a collective power that could ease your transition? Would you consider it? Many people I've encountered tell me they have a difficult time with the concept of a Higher Power. They say it's hard to envision something up there in the sky that is watching over them and that can help them do anything. They say that, as nice as it would be to have a Higher

Power, they'd prefer to just work with something tangible and not get involved with something that can't be proven.

Through my many encounters with people claiming to want to end an addiction, I have found a surefire way to help anyone to conceptualize a Higher Power. In three easy steps, anyone can select a Higher Power and then begin reaping its rewards:

Step 1: Take a good look around you, and observe the natural world that surrounds you. You'll see the sun, the moon, and the stars and revel in the beauty of the sea and the majestic mountains.

Step 2: Take a sheet of paper, and on the very top write the words "My Higher Power List." Next, list the numbers from one to ten, from top to bottom. To the right of number ten, write in the word "Me." Now, above the word "Me" and to the right of each of the remaining numbers, list nine things that you consider to be more powerful than yourself either physically and/or mentally, each in ascending order. These things can be people or animals, either living or dead, and can even include inanimate objects. Now, you should have a list of ten things total, starting at the bottom with yourself and ending with the most powerful person, beast, or inanimate object you can imagine at the top. This constitutes your Higher Power List.

Step 3: Now, starting at the bottom of your list, at number ten, refer back to those natural wonders we originally acknowledged—the sun, the moon, the stars, the beautiful sea, and the majestic mountains—and then ask yourself, "Did I make those?" Next, proceed through your entire list referencing those natural wonders as you go, asking yourself each time if your thing made those things. If you're like me, your answer to each of those questions will be no. The puzzling thing about that is that we created our list out of all the things we could possibly imagine, yet we agree that none of those things we imagined is powerful enough to have created all those wonders we see. And since those wonders do exist and not due to anything on our list, then it would be reasonable to conclude that something beyond our list, something more powerful than all the things we know, must be responsible for all those wonders. Then based on that conclusion, we could confidently say we acknowledge there is a Higher

Power at work. Now that we've established that, it's solely our decision whether we want to make this Higher Power our Higher Power!

This is how it looks:

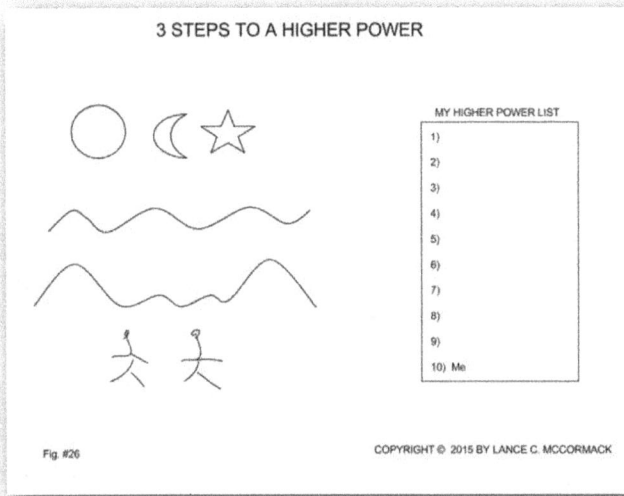

3 STEPS TO A HIGHER POWER

MY HIGHER POWER LIST
1)
2)
3)
4)
5)
6)
7)
8)
9)
10) Me

Fig. #26

COPYRIGHT © 2015 BY LANCE C. MCCORMACK

Some people say they won't believe in a Higher Power because of all the bad things that happen in life. They question how any Higher Power worth praying to could allow all these atrocities to occur and not intervene. They comment about the constant state of war, the countless heinous criminal acts, all the innocent babies born with gross abnormalities, and those unnecessarily afflicted with diseases and hunger. They ask how any Higher Power could remain idle among all this chaos and pain. So despite the idea that a Higher Power could exist, they say they wouldn't respect it anyway because it hasn't shown the mercy they would have expected from it.

My response to those people would be to please look at this next diagram and notice that we've added people to the list of things that exist but for which we have little explanation. We could take a leap and surmise that whatever entity created the sun and the moon and all those other magnificent things that exist may also be responsible for having created the first of us. Then, we could infer that from the first of us, the rest of us probably came. Those little dots in the diagram are supposed to be us. As a result, we have two sets that were created: the original set that includes the sun, the moon, the stars, the sea, the mountains, and the first of us, and then the second set or the subset that includes the first of us and also all the rest of us.

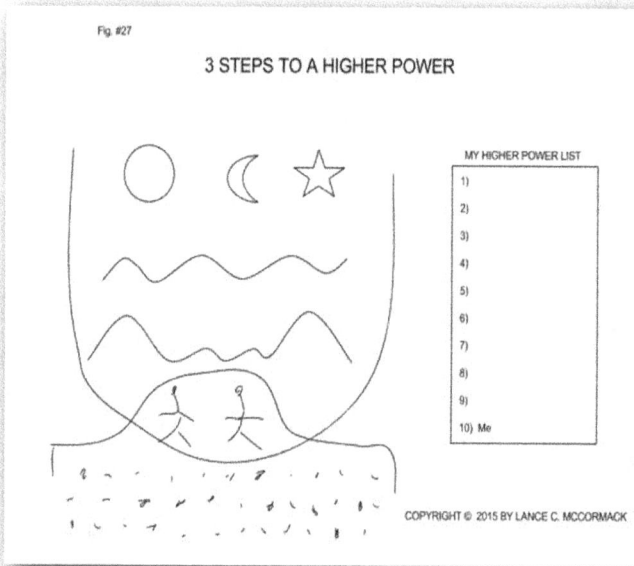

Fig. #27

3 STEPS TO A HIGHER POWER

MY HIGHER POWER LIST

1)
2)
3)
4)
5)
6)
7)
8)
9)
10) Me

COPYRIGHT © 2015 BY LANCE C. MCCORMACK

The idea is that all those bad things that we talk about have actually come from the subset and not from the original set. All the wars, all the pestilence and violence, all the disfigured and diseased among us have come as a result of our doing and that of our predecessors and not from the same entity that created the sun. That only makes sense!

I remember speaking with a pregnant young woman in a methadone program who I'd known for nearly six years, and I was very surprised when I heard her say, "I sure hope God gives me a healthy baby this time," as she stared up into the sky. She had had two children already, each of which had been taken by the state due to her polysubstance use all throughout her pregnancies. Each child had unfortunately been born with severe disabilities. I had seen this woman at the clinic through both pregnancies and always tried to intervene for her sake and for that of her unborn children, but always to no avail. She lived on the streets, despite being on Supplemental Security Income, and spent her days prostituting and shooting heroin and cocaine and popping benzos, all while being on the methadone program. So you can imagine I found her comments about God extremely distasteful. In response, I asked her to lower her gaze from the heavens as she spoke and bring it all the way down to her level and then hold a mirror up right in front of her face. I said, "You're the reason you don't have healthy children, not God."

It appears to be very easy and extremely convenient to blame God for all our misdeeds. It's a great way to take the blame off of ourselves and pin it on something we don't even understand. Generally in our society, we allow addiction to continue unabated by not holding addicts accountable for their own actions. We treat grown adults responsible for terrible acts like helpless little children who just don't know any better, and somehow we expect them to improve as a result. We are getting exactly what we deserve for undermining the power of human beings.

A Twenty-First-Century Concept

Let's take a closer look at that Higher Power that created all those miracles that we take for granted today. Consider it as an infinite energy source that's connected to every energy source. Envision this source as a mainframe computer connected to trillions of personal computers representing us. See the accompanying diagram to get a better idea of how this all works.

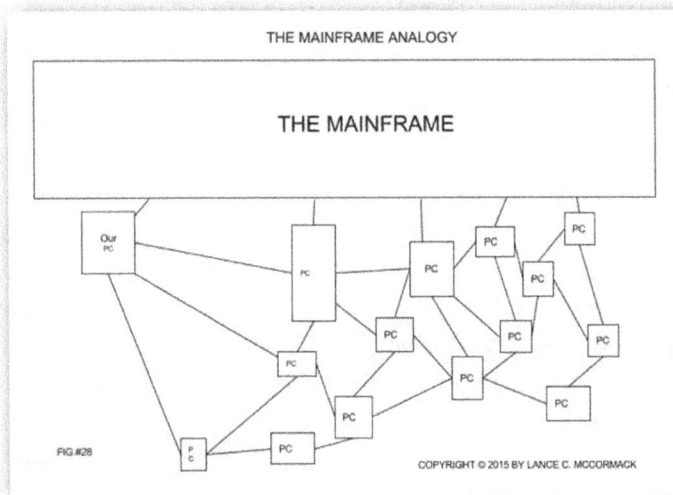

THE MAINFRAME ANALOGY

THE MAINFRAME

FIG.#28

COPYRIGHT © 2015 BY LANCE C. MCCORMACK

This mainframe computer is as vast as the cosmos and maintains as many connections as there are things that wish to be connected. Even though the mainframe, also known as the Source (God, if you like), is connected to all of us through our personal computers (our PCs), we can only feel the benefit of the Source as long as we remain connected to it. It's not as though the Source will ever leave or disconnect from us, because it never will, but we can leave or disconnect from it, if we choose. I'll give you an example. Here we are, all connected to this infinite energy source through our very own PCs, and the Source is always aware of where we go and what we do but doesn't intervene, because we've been given something very special called free will. This is the free will to make our own choices in our lives. Let's say John goes onto his PC and enters a site that reads, DO NOT ENTER. ENTER AT YOUR OWN PERIL. MALICIOUS CONTENT. EXIT NOW. Despite the ominous warnings, John proceeds because he anticipates he will like what he sees on the site, regardless of the fact that viruses have apparently begun to invade and corrupt his PC.

He notices the corruption due to his PC running slower and experiencing difficulty navigating between pages and even presenting numerous unwanted pop-ups that interfere with his viewing. Despite these inconveniences, John returns frequently to the site, only to recognize that more viruses have invaded his PC and it's become increasingly difficult to experience trouble-free viewing.

As the corruption of John's PC becomes more pervasive, John also notices that his connection to the mainframe (the Source) has also become negatively affected. He notices that his connection to the Source has become truncated and the transmission intermittent. It's kind of like that commercial that says, "Can you hear me now?" with the sound of the communications becoming more and more distant. Despite becoming disconnected from the Source, John still chooses to return to those sites that have caused all this distress, because as he puts it, "I like them. I like what I see, and I'm not going to let a little inconvenience ruin my fun." So here's the dilemma, does John continue to visit those sites clearly marked DO NOT ENTER and run the risk of entirely corrupting his PC beyond repair and disconnecting himself from the Source from which he derives all his power, or does he decide that the risks greatly outweigh the benefits and begin to reconnect?

In figure 29 we can see how John's PC has become severely corrupted due to his ongoing use of his favorite site and how his personal connections to others and ultimately to the Source have been severely impacted. How far will John go to derive pleasure, despite all the negative consequences?

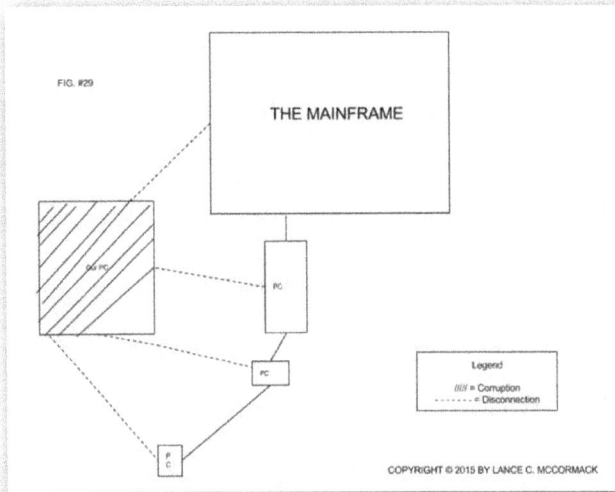

FIG. #29

THE MAINFRAME

Legend
//// = Corruption
------ = Disconnection

COPYRIGHT © 2015 BY LANCE C. MCCORMACK

The dilemma to choose between two or more opposing forces is one that we all face with the things with which we've become enamored that are tearing us apart. This is the battle in all internal conflicts. In the case of addictions, if we choose to keep doing what we're doing, then we're choosing separation and isolation over connectedness, and that will be our lot. If we choose instead to stop what we're currently doing and reconnect to the Source, then we are choosing unity and family, and that will also be our lot. Which will be your lot?

The steps to change are simple: (1) decide that we want to change, (2) stop what we're presently doing, and (3) repair the damage from what we've done. Once we begin the process of change, we will notice how our PCs (our lives) begin to improve in all ways and how our connections to others grow stronger and how our connection to the Source is reestablished and our power is restored.

CHAPTER 27

In Perpetuum Gratus—Forever Grateful!

When all else fails, we are left helpless as in the
beginning and open to all possibilities.
—A LANCEISM

So you've been doing everything by the book, exercising, eating right, getting plenty of sleep, and still you find yourself dreaming about those nasty drugs and wishing you could just use them in moderation so as to not cause a problem. Well, you can't! Actually, you can use those drugs again and go spiraling back to that rathole you've just crawled out of, or you can finally get the message. It's not all about you! It's all about connecting. Connecting to the same energy that created the cosmos, the same energy that created everything you've ever known and that created you. Who really knows how the world began? Whether it began with Adam and Eve or with a big bang roughly fifteen billion years ago will remain theories highly contested throughout time to come. What we have learned, however, is that until you connect to the source of the energy that surges through your veins, you are doomed to repeat history. Do not allow your ongoing questioning of why so many bad things happen to good people direct you to disbelief of a Higher Power. Do not allow your frustrations and conundrums to cloud the obvious.

You are here in a wondrous place, and you were created somehow. Find your somehow and connect!

When we hear about worldwide strife, hunger, disenfranchisement, and overall disenchantment with the status quo, we respond with frustration, anger, drug seeking, violence, wars, and senseless murder. We then surmise that with all this chaos a Higher Power could not possibly exist. So, it's understandable that the big bang theory could resonate comfortably with some people, not only due to its scientific explanation, but because it makes all those bad things that happen to us feel impersonal. Nevertheless, in my field as in probably few others, it is abundantly apparent that we as human beings need to feel connected on a personal level. Connected to something that can help us make it through this confusing world without falling apart. So I have decided to weigh in personally on this subject and share with you how I plan to make it through. Blessed with the ability to sleep deeply and dream vividly and, while dreaming, imagine things in such remarkable detail so as to make sense of things I could only question in my waking state, I have seen a different view of what it is to be human.

Imagine an entity—let's call it the Source—an all-powerful, omnipresent, molecular energy also known as the Ultimate Deliverer, bringing you to a place so incredible that dreams could only pale by comparison. Imagine the Source transporting you here to Earth safely through time, through billions of years, and then allowing you to begin an unforgettable journey. Imagine that on the way here to your new home, you were given, as a souvenir, the most precious gift of all, a piece of the Source. This was no tangible gift, like a watch or a flat-screen television, but energy that was breathed into the core of your very being. Your body contains the magical energy of the Source, as a gift. Picture this gift inside of you. Maybe you picture a little golden box with a beautiful bow, maybe not. However you picture your gift is just fine.

What's important is that you realize what you have inside of you. You have been given the greatest gift of all, the essence of the Source. How could you ever repay the Source for such an extravagant gift? Surely you will never, ever have enough money, nor would the Source ever ask for money. Instead of any gift that we can see, hear, smell, taste, or touch, you were given the essence of the Source. What exactly does that mean? Before you were fully developed, you were given this gift, far greater than any gift imaginable, but in a dormant state, to be brought to life over time. Imagine there being only one condition to be satisfied in order to open this gift: the belief in the giver of the gift, the Source. This gift is accessed and activated each and every time you show your belief through gratitude to the Source by saying "thank you." Isn't that what you usually say when someone gives you a gift? The more you show gratitude for the world around you, the more the power of the gift is revealed. You are not made invincible by the gift, but made unwavering in your ability to rise against any and all of life's challenges. This gift from the Source was designed to be opened early and often and treasured always. In time, as you believe more undeniably in the Source, you will believe more undeniably in yourself, for you become one and the same. The gift of the Source is one of wholeness and the ability to understand and love yourself as the Source understands and loves you. Only those who have opened their gifts and continue to open their gifts can revel in the miracles of those gifts.

We have but one job to accomplish in our lives in order to achieve true happiness. Open your gift from the Source, and you too will feel its magnificence and display the aura of the Source. Know that when the Ultimate Deliverer returns one day to accompany us home, we will undoubtedly be asked, "Did you open my gift?"

By virtue of having completed this book, consider yourself Lanceified!

Lance McCormack
1845 Post Rd., Second Floor, Suite #10N
Warwick, RI 02886

lance@lifeforcehypnosis.com

Available for:
Speaking engagements
Seminars & corporate events
School & university events
Individual coaching